Curriculum and Instruction

Curriculum and Instruction

Editors

Sarita Kumari

D.S. Srivastava

ISHA BOOKS

DELHI-110 033

Curriculum and Instruction

ISBN : 978-81-820-5164-5

Published, 2016

Published in India by

Isha Books
B-69, New Gupta Colony
Near DDA Market
Delhi-110009
E-mail: ishabooks@hotmail.com

Printed at: G. Print Process, Delhi.

PREFACE

Teaching is an art-with scientific basis. There are no "best" teaching skills useful to any and all classrooms. Teaching is complex—even complicated—and it requires many decisions every hour. It is like an iceberg in the sense that much of the work occurs before the lesson begins; it is hidden to the observer, but it must occur as planning. Planning for the next lesson begins as part of the present lesson. It also requires teacher to reflect continually upon their efforts and goals .A teacher's primary assets are his or her knowledge of the subject and his or her concern for the students. Teachers must be dedicated to the academic growth and personal well-being of students.

Teaching has been examined from many perspectives by many individuals. An enormous amount of information and advice exists about the various facets of teaching. But there is a problem: no single teaching profile works for all teachers and students in all classroom situations in all subjects. Each teacher has to develop a unique, individual style, lest he or she was seen as a utility infielder who doesn't mind being placed wherever needed at the moment. Each teacher must also learn to match teaching strategies with learner and classroom conditions.

Teaching then, requires to make many decisions about the arrangement of content (curriculum) and the type of delivery system used (instruction) to teach the content. These decisions are necessary because there are so many aspects to consider, and so many alternative theories and practices demand consideration. Making useful decisions about teaching requires knowledge and understanding of the various curricular and instructional factors that operate in the classroom, alternative conceptions of curriculum and instruction and their operational consequences, their own philosophical and pedagogical assumptions and preferences, and means of developing their own unique profile from the alternative theories and practice. This book is about these matters; the content included are address them directly and indirectly. The concepts of curriculum and instruction, process of curriculum planning and development, curriculum effectiveness, instructional design and objectives etc., are described in detail. The book will help teachers to better identify their profile and to develop instructional materials to reflect that profile.

Editor

Contents

1

Concept and Nature of Curriculum

DEFINITION OF CURRICULUM

Curriculum is a written plan that drives instruction. It delineates the skills and concepts taught and evaluated to enhance student achievement. Cave Creek Unified School District curriculum is composed of:

— content area philosophy

— strands

— program goals

— aligned scope and sequence

— learner outcomes

— assessment tools

It is intentionally designed to meet district, state, and national standards.

The term "curriculum" is generally understood as the courses or programmes of study offered by an educational institution. The concept of "curriculum" is best understood, however, from the Latin root of the word which is "currere", or "to run" as in to run a race course. To use an analogy, curriculum means the course (or path) that students have to run to finish the "race" — or put another way, all the activities which students need do if they are to finish a programme of study and achieve the intended learning goals. Curriculum is more than just a body of knowledge, a list of subjects to be studied, or a syllabus — it is all the planned experiences which learners may be exposed to in order to achieve the learning goals.

A major influence on a curriculum is the philosophical framework, or educational ideology, which is adopted during the curriculum development process itself. Two contrasting frameworks, or models, of curriculum development are the "classical" model and the "participatory" model. The classical model has also been referred to as the "rational" approach while the participatory model has been described as the "interactive" approach.

CONCEPTS OF CURRICULUM

The idea of curriculum is hardly new - but the way we understand and theorize it has altered over the years - and there remains considerable dispute as to meaning. It has its origins in the running/chariot tracks of Greece. It was, literally, a course. In Latin curriculum was a racing chariot; *currere* was to run. John Kerr defines curriculum as, 'All the learning which is planned and guided by the school, whether it is carried on in groups or individually, inside or outside the school. This gives us some basis to move on - and for the moment all we need to do is highlight two of the key features:

— *Learning is planned and guided*: We have to specify in advance what we are seeking to achieve and how we are to go about it.

— *The definition refers to schooling*: We should recognize that our current appreciation of curriculum theory and practice emerged in the school and in relation to other schooling ideas such as subject and lesson.

In what follows we are going to look at four ways of approaching curriculum theory and practice:

— Curriculum as a body of knowledge to be transmitted.

— Curriculum as an attempt to achieve certain ends in students - product.

— Curriculum as process.

— Curriculum as praxis.

It is helpful to consider these ways of approaching curriculum theory and practice in the light of Aristotle's influential categorization of knowledge into three disciplines: the theoretical, the productive and the practical.

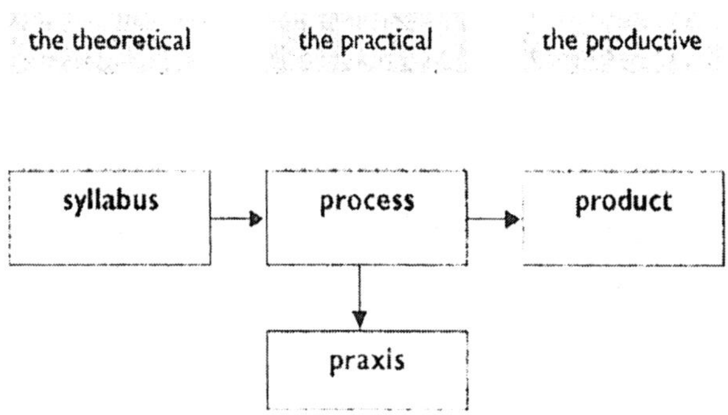

Here we can see some clear links - the body of knowledge to be transmitted in the first is that classically valued as 'the canon'; the process and praxis models come close to practical deliberation; and the technical concerns of the outcome or product model mirror elements of Aristotle's characterization of the productive.

Curriculum as a syllabus to be transmitted Many people still equate a curriculum with a syllabus. Syllabus, naturally, originates from the Greek (although there was some confusion in its usage due to early misprints). Basically it means a concise statement or table of the heads of a discourse, the contents of a treatise, the subjects of a series of lectures. In the form that many of us will have been familiar with it is connected with courses leading to examinations - teachers talk of the syllabus associated with, say, the Cambridge Board French GSCE exam. What we can see in such documents is a series of headings with some additional notes which set out the areas that may be examined.

A syllabus will not generally indicate the relative importance of its topics or the order in which they are to be studied. In some cases as Curzon points out, those who compile a syllabus tend to follow the traditional textbook approach of an 'order of contents', or a pattern prescribed by a 'logical' approach to the subject, or - consciously or unconsciously - a the shape of a university course in which they may have participated. Thus, an approach to curriculum theory and practice which focuses on syllabus is only really concerned with content. Curriculum is a body of knowledge-content and/or subjects. Education in this sense, is the process by which these are transmitted or 'delivered' to students by the most effective methods that can be devised.

Where people still equate curriculum with a syllabus they are likely to limit their planning to a consideration of the content or the body of knowledge that they wish to transmit. 'It is also because this view of curriculum has been adopted that many teachers in primary schools', Kellyclaims, 'have regarded issues of curriculum as of no concern to them, since they have not regarded their task as being to transmit bodies of knowledge in this manner'.

Curriculum as product

The dominant modes of describing and managing education are today couched in the productive form. Education is most often seen as a technical exercise. Objectives are set, a plan drawn up, then applied, and the outcomes (products) measured. It is a way of thinking about education that has grown in influence in the United Kingdom since the late 1970s with the rise of vocationalism and the concern with competencies. Thus, in the late 1980s and the 1990s many of the debates about the National Curriculum for schools did not so much concern how the curriculum was thought about as to what its objectives and content might be.

It is the work of two American writers Franklin Bobbitt and Ralph W. Tyler that dominate theory and practice within this tradition. In *The Curriculum* Bobbitt writes as follows:

> The central theory [of curriculum] is simple. Human life, however varied, consists in the performance of specific activities. Education that prepares for life is one that prepares definitely and adequately for these specific activities. However numerous and diverse they may be for any social class they can be discovered. This requires only that one go out into the world of affairs and discover the particulars of which their affairs consist. These will show the abilities, attitudes, habits, appreciations and forms of knowledge that men need. These will be the objectives of the curriculum. They will be numerous, definite and particularized. The curriculum will then be that series of experiences which children and youth must have by way of obtaining those objectives.

This way of thinking about curriculum theory and practice was heavily influenced by the development of management thinking and practice. The rise of 'scientific management' is often associated with the name of its main advocate F. W. Taylor. Basically what he proposed was greater division of labour with jobs being simplified; an extension of managerial control over all elements of the workplace; and cost accounting based on systematic time-and-motion study.

All three elements were involved in this conception of curriculum theory and practice. For example, one of the attractions of this approach to curriculum theory was that it involved detailed attention to what people needed to know in order to work, live their lives and so on. A familiar, and more restricted, example of this approach can be found in many training programmes, where particular tasks or jobs have been analyzed - broken down into their component elements - and lists of competencies drawn up. In other words, the curriculum was not to be the result of 'armchair speculation' but the product of systematic study. Bobbitt's work and theory met with mixed responses. One telling criticism that was made, and can continue to be made, of such approaches is that there is no social vision or programme to guide the process of curriculum construction.

As it stands it is a technical exercise. However, it wasn't criticisms such as this which initially limited the impact of such curriculum theory in the late 1920s and 1930s Rather, the growing influence of 'progressive', child-centred approaches shifted the ground to more romantic notions of education. Bobbitt's long lists of objectives and his emphasis on order and structure hardly sat comfortably with such forms.

The Progressive movement lost much of its momentum in the late 1940s in the United States and from that period the work of Ralph W. Tyler, in particular, has made a lasting impression on curriculum theory and practice. He shared Bobbitt's emphasis on rationality and relative simplicity. His theory was based on four fundamental questions:

1. What educational purposes should the school seek to attain?
2. What educational experiences can be provided that are likely to attain these purposes?
3. How can these educational experiences be effectively organized?
4. How can we determine whether these purposes are being attained?

Like Bobbitt he also placed an emphasis on the formulation of behavioural objectives.

> Since the real purpose of education is not to have the instructor perform certain activities but to bring about

> significant changes in the students' pattern of behaviour, it becomes important to recognize that any statements of objectives of the school should be a statement of changes to take place in the students.

We can see how these concerns translate into a nicely-ordered procedure: one that is very similar to the technical or productive thinking set out below.

- Step 1: Diagnosis of need
- Step 2: Formulation of objectives
- Step 3: Selection of content
- Step 4: Organization of content
- Step 5: Selection of learning experiences
- Step 6: Organization of learning experiences
- Step 7: Determination of what to evaluate and of the ways and means of doing it.

The attraction of this way of approaching curriculum theory and practice is that it is systematic and has considerable organizing power. Central to the approach is the formulation of behavioural objectives - providing a clear notion of outcome so that content and method may be organized and the results evaluated.

There are a number of issues with this approach to curriculum theory and practice. The first is that the plan or programme assumes great importance. For example, we might look at a more recent definition of curriculum as: 'A programme of activities designed so that pupils will attain so far as possible certain educational and other schooling ends or objectives. The problem here is that such programmes inevitably exist prior to and outside the learning experiences. This takes much away from learners. They can end up with little or no voice. They are told what they must learn and how they will do it. The success or failure of both the programme and the individual learners is judged on the basis of whether pre-specified changes occur in the behaviour and person of the learner.

If the plan is tightly adhered to, there can only be limited opportunity for educators to make use of the interactions that occur. It also can deskill educators in another way. For example, a number of curriculum programmes, particularly in the USA, have attempted to make the student experience 'teacher proof'. The logic of this approach is for the curriculum to be designed outside of the classroom or school, as is the case with the National Curriculum in the UK. Educators then apply programmes and are judged by the products of their actions. It turns educators into technicians.

Second, there are questions around the nature of objectives. This model is hot on measurability. It implies that behaviour can be objectively, mechanistically measured. There are obvious dangers here - there always has to be some uncertainty about what is being measured. In order to measure, things have to be broken down into smaller and smaller units. The result, as many of you will have experienced, can be long lists of often trivial skills or competencies. This can lead to a focus in this approach to curriculum theory and practice on the parts rather than the whole; on the trivial, rather than the significant. It can lead to an approach to education and assessment which resembles a shopping list. When all the items are ticked, the person has passed the course or has learnt something. The role of overall judgment is somehow sidelined.

Third, there is a real problem when we come to examine what educators actually do in the classroom, for example. Much of the research concerning teacher thinking and classroom interaction, and curriculum innovation has pointed to the lack of impact on actual pedagogic practice of objectives. One way of viewing this is that teachers simply get it wrong - they ought to work with objectives. The difficulties that educators experience with objectives in the classroom may point to something inherently wrong with the approach - that it is not grounded in the study of educational exchanges. It is a model of curriculum theory and practice largely imported from technological and industrial settings.

Fourth, there is the problem of unanticipated results. The focus on pre-specified goals may lead both educators and learners to overlook learning that is occurring as a result of their interactions, but which is not listed as an objective. The apparent simplicity and rationality of this approach to curriculum theory and practice, and the way in which it mimics industrial management have been powerful factors in its success.

Curriculum as process

We have seen that the curriculum as product model is heavily dependent on the setting of behavioural objectives. The curriculum, essentially, is a set of documents for implementation. Another way of looking at curriculum theory and practice is via process. In this sense curriculum is not a physical thing, but rather the interaction of teachers, students and knowledge. In other words, curriculum is what actually happens in the classroom and what people do to prepare and evaluate.

Box 1. Curriculum as process
Teachers enter particular schooling and situations with
an ability to think critically, -in-action
an understanding of their role and the expectations others have of them, and
a proposal for action which sets out essential principles and features of the educational encounter.
Guided by these, they encourage
conversations between, and with, people in the situation
out of which may come
thinking and action.
They
continually evaluate the process and what they can see of outcomes.

Perhaps the two major things that set this apart from the model for informal education are first, the context in which the process occurs ('particular schooling situations'); and second, the fact that teachers enter the classroom or any other formal educational setting with a more fully worked-through idea of what is about to happen. Lawrence Stenhouse who produced one of the best-known explorations of a process model of curriculum theory and practice. He defined curriculum tentatively: 'A curriculum is an attempt to communicate the essential principles and features of an educational proposal in such a form that it is open to critical scrutiny and capable of effective translation into practice'. He suggests that a curriculum is rather like a recipe in cookery.

> It can be criticized on nutritional or gastronomic grounds - does it nourish the students and does it taste good? - and it can be criticized on the grounds of practicality - we can't get hold of six dozen larks' tongues and the grocer can't find any ground unicorn horn! A curriculum, like the recipe for a dish, is first imagined as a possibility, then the subject of experiment. The recipe offered publicly is in a sense a report on the experiment. Similarly, a curriculum should be grounded in practice. It is an attempt to describe the work observed in classrooms that it is adequately communicated to teachers and others. Finally, within limits, a recipe can varied according to taste. So can a curriculum.

Stenhouse shifted the ground a little bit here. He was not saying that curriculum is the process, but rather the means by which the experience of attempting to put an educational proposal into practice is made available. For example, in a discussion of the so-called 'youth work curriculum', the following definition was taken as a starting point: 'those processes which enhance or, if they go wrong, inhibit a person's learning'. This was then developed and a curriculum became: 'an organic process by which learning is offered, accepted and internalized'. The problem with this sort of definition, as Robin Barrow points out, is that what this does is to widen the meaning of the term to such an extent that it just about becomes interchangeable with 'education' itself.

Box 2. Stenhouse on curriculum

As a minimum, a curriculum should provide a basis for planning a course, studying it empirically and considering the grounds of its justification. It should offer:

A. In planning:

1. Principle for the selection of content - what is to be learned and taught
2. Principles for the development of a teaching strategy - how it is to be learned and taught.
3. Principles for the making of decisions about sequence.
4. Principles on which to diagnose the strengths and weaknesses of individual students and differentiate the general principles 1, 2 and 3 above, to meet individual cases.

B. In empirical study:

1. Principles on which to study and evaluate the progress of students.
2. Principles on which to study and evaluate the progress of teachers.
3. Guidance as to the feasibility of implementing the curriculum in varying school contexts, pupil contexts, environments and peer-group situations.
4. Information about the variability of effects in differing contexts and on different pupils and an understanding of the causes of the variation.

C. In relation to justification:

A formulation of the intention or aim of the curriculum which is accessible to critical scrutiny.

More specifically, if curriculum is process then the word curriculum is redundant because process would do very nicely!

The simple equation of curriculum with process is a very slap-happy basis on which to proceed.

We also need to reflect on why curriculum theory and practice came into use by educators. It was essentially as a way of helping them to think about their work before, during and after interventions; as a means of enabling educators to make judgments about the direction their work was taking. This is what Stenhouse was picking up on.

There are a number of contrasts in this model of curriculum theory and practice as compared with the product model. First, where the product model appeals to the workshop for a model, this process model looks to the world of experimentation.

> The idea is that of an educational science in which each classroom is a laboratory, each teacher a member of the scientific community... The crucial point is that the proposal is not to be regarded as an unqualified recommendation but rather as a provisional specification claiming no more than to be worth putting to the test of practice, Such proposals claim to be intelligent rather than correct.

Thus, in this sense, a curriculum is a particular form of specification about the practice of teaching. It is not a package of materials or a syllabus of ground to be covered. 'It is a way of translating any educational idea into a hypothesis testable in practice. It invites critical testing rather than acceptance'.

Second, and associated with the above, given the uniqueness of each classroom setting, it means that any proposal, even at school level, needs to be tested, and verified by each teacher in his/her classroom. It is not like a curriculum package which is designed to be delivered almost anywhere.

Third, outcomes are no longer the central and defining feature. Rather than tightly specifying behavioural objectives and methods in advance, what happens in this model of curriculum theory and practice is that content and means develop as teachers and students work together.

Fourth, the learners in this model are not objects to be acted upon. They have a clear voice in the way that the sessions evolve. The focus is on interactions. This can mean that attention shifts from teaching to learning. The product model, by having a pre-specified plan or programme, tends to direct attention to teaching. For example, how can this information be got over? A process approach to curriculum theory and practice, it is argued by writers like Grundy, tends towards making the process of learning the central concern of the teacher. This is because this way of thinking emphasizes interpretation and meaning-making. As we have seen each classroom and each exchange is different and has to be made sense of.

However, when we come to think about this way of approaching curriculum in practice, a number of possible problems do arise. The first is a problem for those who want some greater degree of uniformity in what is taught. This approach to the theory of curriculum, because it places meaning-making and thinking at its core and treats learners as subjects rather than objects, can lead to very different means being employed in classrooms and a high degree of variety in content. As Stenhouse comments, the process model is essentially a critical model, not a marking model.

> It can never be directed towards an examination as an objective without loss of quality, since the standards of the examination then override the standards immanent in the subject. This does not mean that students taught on the process model cannot be examined, but it does mean that the examinations must be taken in their stride as they pursue other aspirations. And if the examination is a by-product there is an implication that the quality the student shows in it must be an underestimate of his real quality. It is hence rather difficult to get the weak student through an examination using a process model. Crammers cannot use it, since it depends upon a commitment to educational aims.

To some extent variation is limited by factors such as public examinations. The exchange between students and teachers does not float free of the context in which it arises. At the end of the day many students and their families place a high premium on exam or subject success and this inevitably enters into the classroom. This highlights a second problem with the model we have just outlined - that it may not pay enough attention to the context in which learning takes place.

Third, there is the 'problem' of teachers. The major weakness and, indeed, strength of the process model is that it rests upon the quality of teachers. If they are not up to much then there is no safety net in the form of prescribed curriculum materials. The approach is dependent upon the cultivation of wisdom and meaning-making in the classroom. If the teacher is not up to this, then there will be severe limitations on what can happen educationally. There have been some attempts to overcome this problem by developing materials and curriculum packages which focus more closely on the 'process of discovery' or 'problem-solving', for example in science.

But there is a danger in this approach. Processes become reduced to sets of skills - for example, how to light a bunsen burner. When students are able to demonstrate certain skills, they are deemed to have completed the process. As Grundy comments, the actions have become the ends; the processes have become the product. Whether or not students are able to apply the skills to make sense of the world around them is somehow overlooked.

Curriculum as praxis

Curriculum as praxis is, in many respects, a development of the process model. While the process model is driven by general principles and places an emphasis on judgment and meaning making, it does not make explicit statements about the interests it serves. It may, for example, be used in such a way that does not make continual reference to collective human well-being and to the emancipation of the human spirit. The praxis model of curriculum theory and practice brings these to the centre of the process and makes an explicit commitment to emancipation.

Thus action is not simply informed, it is also committed. It is praxis.

> Critical pedagogy goes beyond situating the learning experience within the experience of the learner: it is a process which takes the experiences of both the learner and the teacher and, through dialogue and negotiation, recognizes them both as problematic... [It] allows, indeed encourages, students and teachers together to confront the real problems of their existence and relationships... When students confront the real problems of their existence they will soon also be faced with their own oppression.

We can amend our 'curriculum as process' model to take account of these concerns. In this approach the curriculum itself develops through the dynamic interaction of action and reflection. 'That is, the curriculum is not simply a set of plans to be implemented, but rather is constituted through an active process in which planning, acting and evaluating are all reciprocally related and integrated into the process'.

Box 3. Curriculum as praxis

Teachers enter particular schooling and situations with

> a personal, but shared idea of the good and a commitment to human emancipation,
>
> an ability to think critically, -in-action
>
> an understanding of their role and the expectations others have of them, and
>
> a proposal for action which sets out essential principles and features of the educational encounter.

Guided by these, they encourage

> conversations between, and with, people in the situation
>
> out of which may come
>
> informed and committed action.

They

> continually evaluate the process and what they can see of outcomes.

Curriculum as the boundary between formal and informal education

Jeffs and Smith have argued that the notion of curriculum provides a central dividing line between formal and informal education. They contend that curriculum theory and practice was formed within the schooling context and that there are major problems when it is introduced into informal forms of pedagogy.

The adoption of curriculum theory and practice by some informal educators appears to have arisen from a desire to be clear about content.

> At any one time, outcomes may not be marked by a high degree of specificity. In a similar way, the nature of the activities used often cannot be predicted. It may be that we can say something about how the informal educator will work. However, knowing in advance about broad processes and ethos isn't the same as having a knowledge of the programme. We must, thus, conclude that approaches to the curriculum which focus on objectives and detailed programmes appear to be incompatible with informal education.

In other words, they are arguing that a product model of curriculum is not compatible with the emphasis on process and praxis within informal education.

However, process and praxis models of curriculum also present problems in the context of informal education. Informal educators do not have, and do not need, this element. They do not enter with a clear proposal for action. Rather, they have an idea of what makes for human well-being, and an appreciation of their overall role and strategy (strategy here being some idea about target group and broad method e.g. detached work). They then develop their aims and interventions in interaction. And what is this element we have been discussing? It is nothing more nor less than what Stenhouse considers to be a curriculum!

The other key difference is context. Even if we were to go the whole hog and define curriculum as process there remain substantive problems. As Cornbleth, and Jeffs and Smith have argued, curriculum cannot be taken out of context, and the context in which it was formed was the school. Curriculum theory and practice only makes sense when considered alongside notions like class, teacher, course, lesson and so on. One of the main outcome of curriculum experiments within youth work has been work, for example in the field of health promotion, which involve pre-specified activities, visiting workers, regular meetings and so on. Within the language of youth work these are most often called programmes or projects. Within a school they would be called a course.

What is being suggested here is that when informal educators take on the language of curriculum they are crossing the boundary between their chosen specialism and the domain of formal education. This they need to do from time to time. There will be formal interludes in their work, appropriate times for them to mount courses and to discuss content and method in curriculum terms. But we should not fall into the trap of thinking that to be educators we have to adopt curriculum theory and practice. The fact that so many have been misled into believing this demonstrates just how powerful the ideas of schooling are. Education is something more than schooling.

NATURE OF CURRICULUM

The original Latin meaning of *curriculum* was a course, but of the kind that one runs around (it came from *currere*, to run), or perhaps traverses in a racing chariot, a transferred sense. The first borrowing of the Latin word into English—in the late seventeenth century—was for a light, two-wheeled, twin-horsed carriage, the *curricle*, the sports car of carriage days. A very Jane-Austen word is curricle, as in *Northanger Abbey*:

> A very short trial convinced her that a curricle was the prettiest equipage in the world; the chaise and four wheeled

> off with some grandeur, to be sure, but it was a heavy and troublesome business, and she could not easily forget its having stopped two hours at Petty France. Half the time would have been enough for the curricle, and so nimbly were the light horses disposed to move, that, had not the general chosen to have his own carriage lead the way, they could have passed it with ease in half a minute.

By then, the Latin word curriculum had already been in use for half a century in Latin texts in at least one of our ancient universities in the figurative sense of a course of study. However, it doesn't appear as an English word until 1824, again at Glasgow University. Even more recent—dating from 1902—is curriculum vitae, literally "the course of one's life".

We have now thoroughly accepted curriculum into the language and have created the adjective curricular to go with it (and by extension, extracurricular). At first, though, curricular meant "pertaining to driving or to carriages", the only sense given in the First Edition of the Oxford English Dictionary—its educational associations are twentieth century.

Our only surviving problem with curriculum is whether the plural is to be curricula, as Latinists would prefer, or whether we should English it into curriculums. Even more problematic is what to call more than one CV: if you're tempted on the basis of a little Latin to refer to curricula vitarum, scholars will immediately correct you—this refers to a set of documents, each of which describes more than one life. The correct term is curricula vitae.

EDUCATIONAL CURRICULUM: KEY CHARACTERISTICS

1. Delivery

Delivery must acknowledge and address a diversity of learning styles while challenging dynamics of power and privilege in the classroom.

— Vary instructional techniques.

— Lecture

— Cooperative Learning

— Dialogue

— Individual Work

— Student Teaching

— Understand the dynamics of power in the room so you do not perpetuate privilege and oppression.

— Who do you call on?

— Who do you encourage to work through a problem and to whom do you provide the answer?

— Challenge the notion of Teaching as Mastery.

— Ask students what they already know about a topic.

— Ask students what they want to learn about a topic.

— Ask students to participate in the teaching of a topic

2. Content

Content must be complete and accurate, acknowledging the contributions and perspectives of ALL groups.

— Ensure that the content is as complete and accurate as possible.

— "Christopher Columbus discovered America" is neither complete nor accurate.

— Avoid tokenism—weave content about under-represented groups (People of Colour, Women, Lesbian, Gay, and Bisexual People, People with Disabilities, etc.) seamlessly with that about traditionally over-represented groups.

— Do you present under-represented groups as "the other"?

— Do you address these groups only through special units and lesson plans ("African American Scientists"; "Poetry by Women") or within the context of the larger curriculum?

— Do you "celebrate" difference or study, explore, and acknowledge it as part of the overall curriculum?

— Study the history of discrimination in curriculum and ensure that you are not replicating it.

— Are supporting stereotypes (learning about Native Americans by making headdresses and tomahawks) or challenging them (learning about Native Americans through resources by Native Americans)?

— Are you supporting or challenging the assumption that our society is inherently Eurocentric, male-centric, Christian-centric, heterosexual-centric, and upper-middle-class centric?

3. Teaching and Learning Materials

Teaching and learning materials must be diverse and critically examined for bias.

— Vary instructional materials.

— Texts

— Newspapers

— Videos/Movies

— Games

— Workbooks

— Examine all materials for bias and oppressive content.

— Does your history book show stereotypical or inaccurate images of people from certain groups or eras (ex. railroad workers)?

— Do your science materials use male-centric language?

— Do your reading or literature materials have racist language or stereotypical images?

— Does the language you use and the language your materials use assume heterosexuality, a 2-biological-parent household, American citizenship..?

— Diversify images and content in bulletin boards, posters, and other constantly-visible materials.

— Do you ALWAYS diversify, or only during special months or celebrations?

4. Perspective

Content must be presented from a variety of perspectives and angles in order to be accurate and complete.

— Present content from a variety of perspectives, not only that of majority groups.

— How do we define "classic literature" or "great books" or "the classics" and from whose perspective?

— From whose perspective do we tell history? When is "westward expansion" the same as "genocide"? When are champions of "liberty" the same as slave owners?

— Present content through a variety of lenses, not just those of a few heroic characters.

— Slave narratives to teach about slavery.

— Slave narratives to teach about colonial Virginia.

— Native American texts to teach about westward expansion.

5. Critical Inclusivity

Students must be engaged in the teaching and learning process—transcend the banking method and facilitate experiences in which students learn from each other's experiences and perspectives.

— Bring the perspectives and experiences of the students themselves to the fore in the learning experience.

— Encourage students to ask critical questions about all information they receive from you and curricular materials, and model this type of critical thinking for them.

— Who wrote or edited that textbook?

— Who created that Web site?

— Whose voice am I hearing and whose voice am I not hearing?

— Make content and delivery relevant for the students—facilitate experiences in which they connect it with their everyday lives.

— Recognize your students as your most important multicultural resources.

6. Social and Civic Responsibility

If we hope to prepare students to be active participants in an equitable democracy, we must educate them about social justice issues and model a sense of civic responsibility within the curriculum.

— Starting with the youngest students, incorporate discussions about difference and inequality into your lessons—this can be done across all subject areas.

— How has misapplied science been used to justify racism and anti-Semitism?

— Look for ways in which recognized names in various disciplines used their work and stature to fight social injustices. (It can be particularly powerful to find people from majority groups who fought certain types of oppression.)

— Mark Twain

— Albert Einstein

— Eleanor Roosevelt

— When an opportunity arises to address racism, sexism, homophobia, classism, or other forms of oppression, facilitate it.

— Have honest discussion with your students about the history of privilege and oppression in your subject area, school, education, and society at large.

— Connect teaching and learning to local community and larger global issues.

— Encourage students to think critically about the United States, capitalism, the two-party system, and other traditionally untouchable subjects of critique.

7. Assessment

Curriculum must be constantly assessed for completeness, accuracy and bias.

— Work with a cohort of teachers to examine and critique each other's curricular units, lesson plans, and entire frameworks.

— Request and openly accept feedback from your students.

— Return to this model from time to time to make sure you haven't reverted to former practices.

INTELLECTUAL COMPETENCIES IN CORE CURRICULUM

The core curriculum guidelines described here are predicated on the judgment that a series of basic intellectual competencies - reading, writing, speaking, listening, critical thinking, and computer literacy - are essential to the learning process in any discipline and thus should inform any core curriculum. Although students can be expected to come to the educational institution with some experience in exercising these competencies, they often need further instruction and practice to meet the standards of the educational institution and, later, to succeed in both their major field of academic study and their chosen career or profession.

— *Reading*: Reading means the ability to analyze and interpret a variety of printed materials - books, articles, and documents. A core curriculum should offer students the opportunity to master both general methods of analyzing printed materials and specific methods for analyzing the subject matter of individual disciplines.

— *Writing*: Competency in writing is the ability to produce clear, correct, and coherent prose adapted to purpose, occasion, and audience. Although correct grammar, spelling, and punctuation are each a sine qua non in any composition, they do not automatically ensure that the composition itself makes sense or that the writer has much of anything to say. Students need to be familiar with the writing process including how to discover a topic and how to develop and organize it, how to phrase it effectively for their audience. These abilities can be acquired only through practice and reflection.

— *Speaking*: Competence in speaking is the ability to communicate orally in clear, coherent, and persuasive language appropriate to purpose, occasion, and audience. Developing this competency includes acquiring poise and developing control of the language through experience in making presentations to small groups, to large groups, and through the media.

— *Listening*: Listening means the ability to analyze and interpret various forms of spoken communication.

— *Critical Thinking*: Critical thinking embraces methods for applying both qualitative and quantitative skills analytically and creatively to subject matter in order to evaluate arguments and to construct alternative strategies. Problem solving is one of the applications of critical thinking, used to address an identified task.

— *Computer Literacy*: Computer literacy means the ability to use computer-based technology in communicating, solving problems, and acquiring information. Core-educated students should have an understanding of the limits, problems, and possibilities associated with the use of technology, and should have the tools necessary to evaluate and learn new technologies as they become available.

Some of these intellectual competencies have traditionally been tied to specific courses required of all students during their years. For example, courses in school composition, together with mathematics, have long been the cornerstone experience of the freshman year. But a single course or two-course sequence in school composition can do little more than introduce students to the principles and practices of good writing.

Within the boundary of three to six semester credit hours of course work, neither of these sequences can guarantee proficiency. Moreover, in most curricula there are no required courses specifically dedicated to reading or to critical thinking. Thus, if a core curriculum is to prepare students effectively, it is imperative that, insofar as possible, these intellectual competencies be included among the objectives of many individual core courses and reflected in their course content.

Colleges and universities across the state have specific missions and different roles and scope. The way in which colleges and universities achieve these outcomes will thus vary. These outlines are not intended in any way to impose restrictions on the creativity of the classroom instructor or to dictate pedagogical methods.

The emergent profile of the students, however, will presumably have common characteristics insofar as they achieve the specified outcomes. A core curriculum experience will prepare them to learn effectively through the rest of their college years so that they carry these aptitudes for learning into their life careers.

Communication (composition, speech, modern language)

The objective of a communication component of a core curriculum is to enable the student to communicate effectively in clear and correct prose in a style appropriate to the subject, occasion, and audience.

Exemplary Educational Objectives

— To understand and demonstrate writing and speaking processes through invention, organization, drafting, revision, editing, and presentation.

— To understand the importance of specifying audience and purpose and to select appropriate communication choices.

— To understand and appropriately apply modes of expression, i.e., descriptive, expositive, narrative, scientific, and self-expressive, in written, visual, and oral communication.

— To participate effectively in groups with emphasis on listening, critical and reflective thinking, and responding.

— To understand and apply basic principles of critical thinking, problem solving, and technical proficiency in the development of exposition and argument.

— To develop the ability to research and write a documented paper and/or to give an oral presentation.

Mathematics

The objective of the mathematics component of the core curriculum is to develop a quantitatively literate college graduate. Every college graduate should be able to apply basic mathematical tools in the solution of real-world problems.

Exemplary Educational Objectives

— To apply arithmetic, algebraic, geometric, higher-order thinking, and statistical methods to modeling and solving real-world situations.

— To represent and evaluate basic mathematical information verbally, numerically, graphically, and symbolically.

— To expand mathematical reasoning skills and formal logic to develop convincing mathematical arguments.

— To use appropriate technology to enhance mathematical thinking and understanding and to solve mathematical problems and judge the reasonableness of the results.

— To interpret mathematical models such as formulas, graphs, tables and schematics, and draw inferences from them.

— To recognize the limitations of mathematical and statistical models.

— To develop the view that mathematics is an evolving discipline, interrelated with human culture, and understand its connections to other disciplines.

Natural Sciences

The objective of the study of a natural sciences component of a core curriculum is to enable the student to understand, construct, and evaluate relationships in the natural sciences, and to enable the student to understand the bases for building and testing theories.

Exemplary Educational Objectives

— To understand and apply method and appropriate technology to the study of natural sciences.

— To recognize scientific and quantitative methods and the differences between these approaches and other methods of inquiry and to communicate findings, analyses, and interpretation both orally and in writing.

— To identify and recognize the differences among competing scientific theories.

— To demonstrate knowledge of the major issues and problems facing modern science, including issues that touch upon ethics, values, and public policies.

— To demonstrate knowledge of the interdependence of science and technology and their influence on, and contribution to, modern culture.

Humanities And Visual And Performing Arts

The objective of the humanities and visual and performing arts in a core curriculum is to expand students' knowledge of the human condition and human cultures, especially in relation to behaviours, ideas, and values expressed in works of human imagination and thought. Through study in disciplines such as literature, philosophy, and the visual and performing arts, students will engage in critical analysis, form aesthetic judgments, and develop an appreciation of the arts and humanities as fundamental to the health and survival of any society. Students should have experiences in both the arts and humanities.

Exemplary Educational Objectives

— To demonstrate awareness of the scope and variety of works in the arts and humanities.

— To understand those works as expressions of individual and human values within an historical and social context.

— To respond critically to works in the arts and humanities.

— To engage in the creative process or interpretive performance and comprehend the physical and intellectual demands required of the author or visual or performing artist.

— To articulate an informed personal reaction to works in the arts and humanities.

— To develop an appreciation for the aesthetic principles that guide or govern the humanities and arts.

— To demonstrate knowledge of the influence of literature, philosophy, and/or the arts on intercultural experiences.

Social And Behavioural Sciences

The objective of a social and behavioural science component of a core curriculum is to increase students' knowledge of how social and behavioural scientists discover, describe, and explain the behaviours and interactions among individuals, groups, institutions, events, and ideas. Such knowledge will better equip students to understand themselves and the roles they play in addressing the issues facing humanity.

Exemplary Educational Objectives

— To employ the appropriate methods, technologies, and data that social and behavioural scientists use to investigate the human condition.

— To examine social institutions and processes across a range of historical periods, social structures, and cultures.

— To use and critique alternative explanatory systems or theories.

— To develop and communicate alternative explanations or solutions for contemporary social issues.

— To analyze the effects of historical, social, political, economic, cultural, and global forces on the area under study.

— To comprehend the origins and evolution of U.S. and Texas political systems, with a focus on the growth of political institutions, the constitutions of the U.S. and Texas, federalism, civil liberties, and civil and human rights.

— To understand the evolution and current role of the U.S. in the world.

— To differentiate and analyze historical evidence (documentary and statistical) and differing points of view.

— To recognize and apply reasonable criteria for the acceptability of historical evidence and social research.

— To analyze, critically assess, and develop creative solutions to public policy problems.

— To recognize and assume one's responsibility as a citizen in a democratic society by learning to think for oneself, by engaging in public discourse, and by obtaining information through the news media and other appropriate information sources about politics and public policy.

— To identify and understand differences and commonalities within diverse cultures.

Perspectives In The Core Curriculum

Another imperative of a core curriculum is that it contain courses that help students attain the following:

— Establish broad and multiple perspectives on the individual in relationship to the larger society and world in which he or she lives, and to understand the responsibilities of living in a culturally and ethnically diversified world;

— Stimulate a capacity to discuss and reflect upon individual, political, economic, and social aspects of life in order to understand ways in which to be a responsible member of society;

— Recognize the importance of maintaining health and wellness;

— Develop a capacity to use knowledge of how technology and science affect their lives;

— Develop personal values for ethical behaviour;

— Develop the ability to make aesthetic judgments;

— Use logical reasoning in problem solving; and

— Integrate knowledge and understand the interrelationships of the scholarly disciplines.

DIFFERENT TYPES OF CURRICULUM

Different Types of Curriculum are exsisting today. They are:

1. Overt, explicit, or written curriculum

Overt, explicit, or written curriculum is simply that which is written as part of formal instruction of the schooling experience. It may refer to a curriculum document, texts, films, and supportive teaching materials that are overtly chosen to support the intentional instructional agenda of a school. Thus, the overt curriculum is usually confined to those written understandings and directions formally designated and reviewed by administrators, curriculum directors and teachers, often collectively.

2. Societal curriculum

Societal curriculum is defined by Cortes. Cortes defines this curriculum as:

> ...[the] massive, ongoing, informal curriculum of family, peer groups, neighbourhoods, churches organizations, occupations, mass, media and other socializing forces that "educate" all of us throughout our lives.

3. The hidden or covert curriculum

The hidden or covert curriculum is implied by the very structure and nature of schools, much of what revolves around daily or established routines.

Longstreet and Shane offer a commonly accepted definition for this term.

> ... the "hidden curriculum," which refers to the kinds of learnings children derive from the very nature and organizational design of the public school, as well as from the behaviours and attitudes of teachers and administrators.... "

Examples of the hidden curriculum might include the messages and lessons derived from the mere organization of schools — the emphasis on: sequential room arrangements; the cellular, timed segments of formal instruction; an annual schedule that is still arranged to accommodate an agrarian age; disciplined messages where concentration equates to student behaviours were they are sitting up straight and are continually quiet; students getting in and standing in line silently; students quietly raising their hands to be called on; the endless competition for grades, and so on. The hidden curriculum may include both positive or negative messages, depending on the models provided and the perspectives of the learner or the observer.

4. The null curriculum

The null curriculum is that which we do not teach, thus giving students the message that these elements are not important in their educational experiences or in our society. Eisner offers some major points as he concludes his discussion of the null curriculum. Eisner first described and defined aspects of this curriculum. He states:

> There is something of a paradox involved in writing about a curriculum that does not exist. Yet, if we are concerned with the consequences of school programs and the role of curriculum in shaping those consequences, then it seems to me that we are well advised to consider not only the explicit and implicit curricula of schools but also what schools do not teach. It is my thesis that what schools do not teach may be as important as what they do teach. I argue this position because ignorance is not simply a neutral void; it has important effects on the kinds of options one is able to consider, the alternatives that one can examine, and the perspectives from which one can view a situation or problems....

From Eisner's perspective the null curriculum is simply that which is not taught in schools. Somehow, somewhere, some people are empowered to make conscious decisions as to what is to be included and what is to be excluded from the overt (written) curriculum.

Since it is physically impossible to teach everything in schools, many topics and subject areas must be intentionally excluded from the written curriculum. But Eisner's position on the "null curriculum" is that when certain subjects or topics are left out of the overt curriculum, school personnel are sending messages to students that certain content and processes are not important enough to study. Unfortunately, without some level of awareness that there is also a well-defined implicit agenda in schools, school personnel send this same type of message via the hidden curriculum.

5. Phantom curriculum

The messages prevalent in and through exposure to any type of media. These components and messages play a major part in enculturating students into the meta-culture.

6. Concomitant curriculum

What is taught, or emphasized at home, or those experiences are part of a family's experiences, or related experiences sanctioned by the family. This type of curriculum may be received at church, in the context of religious expression, lessons on values, ethics or morals, molded behaviours, or social experiences based on the family's preferences.

7. Rhetorical curriculum

Elements from the rhetorical curriculum are comprised from ideas offered by policymakers , school officials, administrators, or politicians. This curriculum may also come from those professionals involved in concept formation and content changes; or from those educational initiatives resulting from decisions based on national and state reports, public speeches, or from texts critiquing outdated educational practices. The rhetorical curriculum may also come from the publicized works offering updates in pedagogical knowledge.

8. Curriculum-in-use

The formal curriculum (written or overt) comprises those things in textbooks, and content and concepts in the district curriculum guides. However, those "formal" elements are frequently not taught. The curriculum-in-use is the actual curriculum that is delivered and presented by each teacher.

9. Received curriculum

Those things that students actually take out of classroom; those concepts and content that are truly learned and remembered.

10. The internal curriculum

Processes, content, knowledge combined with the experiences and realities of the learner to create new knowledge. While educators should be aware of this curriculum, they have little control over the internal curriculum since it is unique to each student.

11. The electronic curriculum

Those lesson learned through searching the Internet for information, or through using e-forms of communication.

> This type of curriculum may be either formal or informal, and inherent lessons may be overt or covert, good or bad, correct or incorrect depending on ones views. Students who use the Internet on a regular basis, both for recreational purposes (as in chatrooms, listserves, through instant messenger on-line conversations, or through personal e-mails) and for research and information, are bombarded

with all types of media and messages. Much of this information may be factually correct, informative, or even entertaining or inspirational, but other information may be very incorrect, dated, passé, biased, perverse, or even manipulative. The ramifications for educational practices are that part of the regular school curriculum needs to include lessons on how to be wise consumers of information, how to critically appraise the accuracy and correctness of e-information. as well as the reliability of electronic sources. Also, students need to learn how to be artfully discerning about the usefulness and appropriateness of certain types of information. And, like other forms of social interaction, students need to know that there are inherent lessons to be learned about appropriate and acceptable "netiquette" and online behaviour, to include the differences between "fair usage" and plagiarism.

VALIDITY OF AN IDEAL CORE-CURRICULUM

What is the validity of an ideal core-curriculum? Kelly suggests three arguments for it:

— philosophical/epistomological arguments based on particular views about the nature of knowledge

— social/sociological arguments of what society and its culture are or ought to be

— political/economic arguments about meeting the demands of a technological society.

With regard to the first of these arguments, 'since certain kinds of knowledge have a status and value superior to others they have a prior claim for inclusion in any curriculum that is to be regarded as educational in the full sense.' But which kinds of knowledge, and who is to decide? As Kelly says, it is very difficult to claim any objective status for knowledge and even more difficult 'to demonstrate the superiority of certain kinds of knowledge and human activity over others.'

Proponents of the second argument would see the job of a schools as being 'to transmit the culture of the society to all pupils.' The problem here again is, who decides on this selection from the culture? The Secretary of State? Further, 'to impose one culture, one set of values on all pupils regardless of their origins, their social class, race or creed is to risk at best offering them a curriculum that is irrelevant, meaningless and alienating and at worst using the education system as a means of effecting an inhibiting form of social control.'

Finally, the political/economic argument. To decree that all pupils shall have a larger scientific and/or technological curriculum component than at present is to go down the road followed by the USSR where 'prime consideration in establishing a central core to the curriculum is the economic needs of the society.' This argument has nothing to do with values or superiority, it is entirely utilitarian. Kelly is particularly opposed to it: 'an opportunity to develop an educational provision for each pupil that might be meaningful to him in his own terms will be lost and at the same time his freedom to choose for himself will be infringed beyond any point that can be justified on educational grounds... it is one thing to attempt to justify requiring pupils to engage in certain kinds of activity on the grounds that we believe this will be good for them, it is quite another to justify it as being good for society.'

Skilbeck, on the other hand, suggests that the core-curriculum ideal is valid because, to a certain extent, it already exists. Even Kelly agrees with this, suggesting that the 'hidden constraints and influences' mean that the curricula of most schools in the UK demonstrate 'their similarities rather than their differences.' Skilbeck further suggests that even the 'deschoolers' have a core-curriculum of a sort - even if it is only some vague notion of 'life-skills'. Other arguments put forward for a core-curriculum are

— continuity for pupils moving from one school to another

— the need for all pupils to study a 'balanced' curriculum.

However, as Kelly points out, 'a balanced curriculum, like a balanced diet, must be suited to the needs of the individual...

we would rightly look with suspicion on a doctor who prescribed the same diet or medicines for all of his patients.' And again, if balance means balance of 'subjects', we should remember that 'education consists of learning *through* subjects rather than the learning *of* subjects.

The questions to be addressed, then, are, what kind of core-curriculum and who is to decide? Will there be a list of subjects, central syllabuses, laid-down methods, hours per week, times of day, permitted text-books? 'To achieve a common curriculum... it is not enough to specify which subjects it must contain.'

Kelly argues that a national curriculum should be no more than a framework of principles: 'broad procedural principles, then, are the only basis for curriculum planning.' There are already great pressures on schools to conform - the organisational structure of secondary schools and universities, the public exam system, the traditional views of parents and pupils, the nature of teacher training courses. Do we need more constraints?

FEASIBILITY OF AN IDEAL CORE-CURRICULUM

What of the feasibility of a core-curriculum? Skilbeck suggests that decisions could be made in one of three ways: by central diktat, by individual schools autonomously, or by a participatory agreement. He rightly dismisses the first as being inconsistent with an open, pluralist society. Central diktat would be 'likely to fail... because of both the ideological resistance it generates and the severe difficulties of diffusion and implementation.' Kelly is even firmer about the consequences of any real attempt to impose a common curriculum: 'the teacher's role would be reduced to that of a puppet, operated by remote control and able to exercise professional judgement only in the very limited sphere of immediate methodology, if it is possible even there... if we do not accept that this is a proper role for teachers, we cannot accept the idea of a common curriculum.'

Skilbeck also dismisses the second idea (that schools should autonomously decide on a common curriculum). There would be too much variation between individual schools where lack of particular expertise or resources would limit the range of subjects or themes offered. It would lead to parochialism in an ever-shrinking world. It would exacerbate the problems encountered by pupils moving from school to school. It would make the transition from primary to secondary school more difficult. In essence, it would diminish equality of opportunity. 'While it is necessary that schools play a major part in curriculum planning, design and development, their role is not sufficient to meet all the requirements... the nature and limits of curriculum decisions as between the community and its representative agencies (central and local government, voluntary bodies) and the teachers and schools [needs] to be determined. This is precisely what is at issue in Britain in the 1980s.'

He goes on to argue that 'what the teachers have constructed - accepting that their constructions are constrained in many ways - are curricula which have met with well-merited criticism.'

So, having dismissed central diktat and school autonomy, Skilbeck is left with participatory agreement as the only viable way to arrive at a core-curriculum. 'Core-curriculum is that part of the whole curriculum which, in broad outline, is common to all schools and students, is defined by partnership by both central and local bodies, and is interpreted by schools.'

It is a pity that the Tory government, having abolished the Schools Council and abandoned the Central Advisory Councils, is now left with no obvious body to coordinate the necessary discussions by the partners in education and has therefore 'moved in to fill a vacuum.'

There is no doubt that something must be done - if only because central government has created a climate in which the public expects something to be done. It is a measure of the manipulation of public opinion which has been going on for ten years now, that something which was once regarded with great suspicion is now accepted by all the major political parties.

The big question then, is, 'are we to leave everything in the hands of the teachers and risk the occasional disaster when they abuse the freedom this gives them? Or are we to remove this freedom and risk not only inefficiency of teaching and inadequacies of educational provision but also the charge of attempting either to indoctrinate children with a particular system of values or of using them to serve the ends of the state?' Somewhere between these two extremes lies a happy medium and only if it can be found will a core-curriculum prove valid and feasible.

2

Process of Curriculum Development

Much of the curriculum found in today's schools is based on teachers' past experience in schools, input from textbook manufacturers, discipline frameworks, standards, and information from peers. Often a curriculum is only loosely joined together, with students far better acquainted with its scope and sequence than the educators who teach it.

With teachers facing growing pressure to teach more, while also being held to higher standards, this approach to curriculum is no longer acceptable. Teachers must be empowered to more effectively design their own curriculum, and to move from the position of curriculum conveyer to that of curriculum designer. School/college curricula are undergoing significant changes to ensure relevant educational content in all subject areas. The goal of the curriculum development process is to develop curricula that compare favourably with those of other leading countries.

Revisions to curricula, based on grade- and subject-specific student learning outcomes, and where applicable, standards, are complete or under development. Student learning outcomes and standards incorporate the four foundation skill areas of literacy and communication, problem solving, human relations, and technology. The focused participation of educators, scholars, industry representatives, and other community members with relevant expertise is being called upon in a consistent curriculum development process.

UNDERSTANDING CURRICULUM

The first step in this process requires getting teachers to share their curriculum with other teachers in the school. During a schoolwide meeting, teachers from each grade level summarize their curriculum on chart paper for science, social studies, language arts, and mathematics. Special area teachers write their curriculum on chart paper as well, so their colleagues can understanding the development of skills and concepts across grade levels. To ensure the integrity of the curriculum, teachers are encouraged to return to their curriculum documents. Frequently, they discover parts of the curriculum they had forgotten or had given only cursory attention.

After all charts have been completed, grade level and special area teachers share their curriculum with the entire faculty, and describe some of the teaching lessons/units they use to teach that curriculum. Many veteran teachers comment that this step provides the first opportunity they've ever had to understand the entire curriculum in their school. This schoolwide sharing process invariably highlights repetitions in content and teaching activities.

During the sharing process, teachers take notes and discuss apparent gaps and repetitions. They also discuss grade-level responsibilities. Curricular terms and content that appear on several grade levels are defined. Clear definitions help teachers articulate grade-level expectations, and move teachers closer to being able to "guarantee" learning standards for their students.

Developing curriculum maps

Curriculum mapping is the next step in the process. Teachers use large pieces of chart paper with the school months on the top, and colored sticky notes – different colours for each core area. Teachers write the different goals, objectives, and topics of the curriculum on the notes and arrange them across the school year. During this step, teachers re-examine the sequence and emphases of the curriculum.

One 4th-grade teacher, for example, realized she was devoting five months of the school year to the Civil War, while World War II and Vietnam received only a couple of days each. When asked why, she replied that "the kids really love the Civil War." Then she acknowledged that she really liked it as well, and that "I have lots of material on it." When she looked, for the first time, at her whole year's curriculum, she recognized the imbalance and cut her Civil War coverage back to a few weeks.

When all the curriculum areas have been mapped, the information can be placed on a preprinted file folder that lists all required subject areas on the side and the months across the top. The file folder provides a detailed look at all subject areas and provides clear articulation between special areas and classroom teachers. It's also an excellent resource for new teachers or teachers who are changing grade levels.

Webbing the curriculum

As the curriculum takes shape, teachers are encouraged to look at the different disciplines for common ideas, complementary skills/strategies, or other links that might be used to create a meaningful integrated study. Sticky notes are arranged and rearranged as teachers look for logical connections between and among the different disciplines. In this way, a "curriculum web," which spells out the connections, can be created.

For example, a social studies teacher who wants to explore the relationships between humans and their environment could focus on human interactions between humans and oceans. A science teacher could complement this with curriculum that examines the physical properties of water, sand, and other parts of the ocean ecosystem. And a language arts teacher could use oceans as a basis for student writing and storytelling. This in turn leads to the development of a second web, which identfies activities for delivering the curriculum. It shows specific methods, techniques, and materials teachers will use.

It's imperative that the teachers keep this curriculum webbing process focused on student interests and needs. Ask yourselves the kind of questions students are likely to ask: Why should I bother learning this? What difference does it make?. Also, be careful not to "superglue" curriculum together for the sake of saying you have created a web. There is little to be gained, for students or teachers, by trying to force connections, such as having students count seashells to provide an ocean-related math activity!

During the webbing process, many more objectives/ standards will be identified than will be used. The brainstorming provides a valuable source of ideas and may be revisited again and again to refine the curricular links.

Role of Assessment

As the school year unfolds and teachers deliver their curriculum to students, assessments should ensure that students participate in a range of activities, so they can demonstrate learning in a variety of formats. Teachers should continually discuss what students should know and be able to do, and must identify or create assessment instruments to evaluate student progress. These can include traditional tests, or alternatives such as student portfolios or performances.

Taking maps to another level

— Many schools use the maps developed during the curriculum-writing process to prepare a parent handbook, which spells out the curriculum learned on each grade level.

— Some schools post the chart papers created by teachers in the hallways, to share the progress being made and to invite all students in the school to see the "big" picture.

— Others have used the maps to generate newsletters to the parents. Curriculum topics may be shared by the week, month, grading period, or year.

— Clearly designed maps provide a roadmap for the teachers, students, administrators, and parents and provide opportunities for effective communication.

— They also help teachers and administrators analyze how they are spending their instructional time, a critical step in the era of accountability.

DEVELOPMENT TEAMS

In developing curricula, educational instistuitions generally follows a consistent process that involves

— curriculum development teams

— review panels

— field validation

— authorized provincial use

— continual updating

a. A curriculum development team is a working group comprising

— a departmental project leader/specialist who has expertise in the subject area/course under development, in curriculum planning and design, in pedagogy, in assessment and evaluation, and in leadership skills. In addition to managing all facets and stages of a curriculum development project, the project leader may act also as liaison with groups such as subject area steering committees, the curriculum advisory committee and with unit coordinators and directors in Program Development Branch. The project leader also accesses advice and feedback, as required, from key advisors such as scholars, industry representatives, parents, and

— educational organizations and associations

— a qualified writer(s) who has excellent oral and written communication skills, computer skills, and a background in the subject area/course under development; a development team may use two different writers, a curriculum writer, and a distance delivery course writer

— exemplary classroom teachers and scholars who work extensively in the subject area/course under development.

Curriculum development team members are selected through a nomination process. At the outset of a new curriculum project, the Program Development Branch sends letters to Superintendents of Education of provincial school divisions/ districts, to Principals of Independent schools, and to Directors of Education and Principals of schools, requesting nominations of teachers to serve on the development team. The nomination forms identify criteria on which selection is based, including knowledge of curriculum planning and design, knowledge of the discipline, exemplary classroom practice, ability to work collaboratively, and team diversity (e.g., geographical representation, gender balance, multicultural and Aboriginal representation).

A curriculum development team is responsible for

— gathering and coordinating all relevant research (e.g., curricula in other jurisdictions, subject area/course content, learning theory, and evaluation tools)

— receiving and assessing information from educational partners such as scholars, industry representatives, parents, and

— educational organizations and associations

— developing and writing documents, taking into consideration all relevant research, expertise, and departmental requirements

— revising/evergreening curricula

Review Panels

Review panels comprise educational partners who are invited by the department to provide feedback to drafts of a document at various stages in its development. Educational partner representation is coordinated by the project leader and may include

— representatives from various governmental departments/ branches

— representatives from educational partners such as business, industry, labour, manufacturing, and communications

— representatives from professional organizations

— representatives from postsecondary education and training institutions

— representatives from Advisory Councils for School Leadership

Feedback from review panels is used to improve the document under development.

Field Validation

Field validation of curriculum documents is undertaken in those instances in which the content focus and instructional and assessment approaches in the new curriculum for a subject area differ significantly from the content and approaches in former documents. Field validation with designated pilot teachers occurs once a pilot curriculum document is completed and mandated for field testing throughout the province. The purpose of field validation is to field test a curriculum document in classrooms so that necessary improvements can be made based on input from classroom teachers.

Pilot teachers may also be called upon to provide feedback related to learning resources, the curriculum implementation process, for use by the Western and Northern Canadian Protocol for Collaboration in Basic Education, to develop curriculum upgrades, and to strengthen the curriculum renewal process.

Pilot teachers are selected based on departmental selection criteria (e.g., subject area knowledge and expertise, gender, geography, and semestered and non-semestered schools) designed to ensure balanced representation. They receive inservice training from the department as they field test a new or revised curriculum.

Authorized Provincial

Authorized provincial use occurs once a curriculum has been field tested and revised as necessary; it is then mandated and released for authorized provincial use.

Continual Updating

Continual updating will ensure that curricula are dynamic and continuously improved. Project leaders/specialists will be responsible for working with various educational partners to identify and develop required upgrades. These will be distributed to the field as replacement pages or new insert pages upon departmental approval. This curriculum renewal process is designed to reflect the changing demands of society and to ensure that the knowledge and skills students acquire remain relevant.

CURRICULUM DOCUMENTS

Within the various subject areas, the following types of curriculum documents are being developed, as required

— curriculum frameworks of outcomes and standards

— a foundation for implementation documents

— teacher support documents

Although the majority of curricula are published in print form, the Department is moving increasingly toward electronic publication of documents. As well, policy documents and independent study and teacher mediated courses for distance delivery are being developed, as required. Each of the above three types of curriculum documents is described below.

Curriculum Frameworks of Outcomes

A curriculum framework is a subject-specific document which identifies student learning outcomes for what students are expected to know and be able to do as they relate to the knowledge and skills of a particular subject area. Standards of achievement for mathematics and language arts are also included in curriculum frameworks for Grades 3, 6, Senior 1 and Senior 4. Curriculum frameworks provide the basis for teaching, learning, and assessing in a particular subject area or course.

They also provide a foundation for further development and implementation in areas such as student assessment, staff development, learning resources. Each subject-specific curriculum framework includes the overview, student learning outcomes for each grade from kindergarten to tertiary level.

Student Learning Outcomes

Student learning outcomes are concise descriptions of the knowledge and skills that students are expected to learn in a course or grade in a subject area. Student learning outcomes are expressed as general outcomes and specific outcomes, and include illustrative examples. Student learning outcomes should not be confused with standards of student performance.

— *General Student Learning Outcomes*: Identify the knowledge and skills that students are expected to learn in a subject area or course on completion of a grade or series of grades.

— *Specific Student Learning Outcomes*: Identify the component knowledge and skills that contribute to a general student learning outcome. Specific student learning outcomes identify a range of contexts and the variety of dimensions of learning within the general outcomes. They are stated grade by grade.

Student learning contexts include

— projects

— exhibitions

— demonstrations

— exercises

— simulations

— case studies

— experiments

Illustrative Examples — Are sample student learning contexts which demonstrate or clarify specific outcomes. They are essential in showing the richness, the breadth, and the depth contained in the learning outcomes, particularly as this relates to high-order thinking, applied learning, real-life applications, and problem solving.

Each student learning outcome stated in a curriculum framework should be:

— understandable by students, parents, educators, and community members

— appropriate to the intended grade or series of grades and to the subject area

— capable of capturing the knowledge and skills expected of students

— supportive of the use of a range of teaching, learning, and assessment strategies and approaches as well as the use of a variety of learning resources

— observable, measurable, and reportable to enable the appropriate connections to be made between and among teaching, learning, and assessing. It should be stated in such a way that it will be apparent when a student has met the student learning outcome. Demonstrations of student learning can occur within contexts which range from the classroom to large-scale assessments. They can include projects, performance assessments, paper-and-pencil tests, and case studies.

ELEMENTS INTEGRATED INTO CURRICULUM

In addition to providing the requisite curriculum components (nature of the discipline, rationale, philosophy, aim, structure, student learning outcomes and standards), curriculum documents incorporate the following elements

— foundation skill areas

— resource-based learning

— differentiated instruction

— curriculum integration

— Aboriginal perspectives

— gender fairness

— appropriate age portrayals

— human diversity

— anti-racist/anti-bias education

— sustainable development

These elements are being integrated into all curricula.

Foundation Skill Areas

The four foundation skill areas are

— literacy and communication

— problem solving

— human relations

— technology

The foundation skill areas are required from Kindergarten to Higher level. They are fundamental in both teaching and learning and should be part of instruction in every subject area. Each foundation skill area represents a set of skills that will enable students to transfer and apply knowledge and allow teachers to design instruction for these purposes. They encompass both the "what" and "how" of teaching and learning across all subject areas. Therefore, every teacher will be a teacher of literacy and communication, of problem solving, human relations, and technology.

Resource-Based Learning

Resource-based learning involves the meaningful use of a wide range of appropriate print, non-print, and human resources in ways that reflect the principles of teaching, learning, and assessing. Differentiated Instruction Teachers must differentiate instruction to support learning for all students.

Differentiated instruction is one of the ways educators establish a supportive learning environment for all students. Differentiated instruction refers to the wide range of strategies, techniques, and approaches that teachers use to support student learning and to help each student, whether less able or highly able, to achieve high expectations and to realize his or her potential.

Differentiated instruction acknowledges that students learn at different rates and in different ways. Integral to understanding and applying differentiated instruction is acceptance of the premise that every teacher must work toward continuous improvement to develop and maintain a rich repertoire of strategies, techniques, and approaches and to know when, with whom, and how to employ a particular strategy, technique, or approach. The notion that all students can learn also underpins understanding differentiated instruction.

Differentiated instruction is not about individualized instruction. It is about personalized instruction, using a balanced range of strategies, techniques, and approaches so that each student's learning requirements can be met and so that all students can grow in a variety of ways.

Differentiated instruction alone will not meet the learning requirements of all students; it will, however, enable all students to achieve relative to high expectations and to realize their full potential. It is crucial to the success of all students, but it is particularly important for those students who require particular kinds of support to achieve relative to the full range of student learning outcomes and standards (for example, students with physical or learning disabilities, deaf or hard of hearing students, and blind or visually impaired students).

Even when differentiated instruction is employed effectively, a limited number of students with specific cognitive disabilities will require the student learning outcomes in provincial curricula to be modified. Other students with particularly severe cognitive disabilities will require developmentally and age appropriate, highly individualized outcomes. As well, some students for whom English is a second language may require adaptations related specifically to their language needs in order to make a gradual transition to the full range of student learning outcomes and standards.

Therefore, regardless of whether a student is achieving relative to the full range of provincial outcomes and standards or to modified, adapted, or individualized learning outcomes, differentiated instruction must play a role in all teaching, learning, and assessing so that each student's learning requirements are met.

Curriculum Integration

Student learning outcomes may elaborate on connections with other areas of learning such as other subject areas or community/home experiences. Curriculum documents may also include specific suggestions for connections.

Aboriginal Perspectives

Aboriginal perspectives are being integrated into curricula to enable students to learn the history of the nation before European settlement and to give the perspective of Aboriginal people since that time. Each subject area will address the perspectives and accomplishments of Aboriginal people, as appropriate. The goal in integrating Aboriginal perspectives into curricula is to ensure that all students have opportunities to understand and respect themselves, their cultural heritage, and the cultural heritage of others.

Aboriginal perspectives apply to learning experiences for all students. However, there may be unique and particular learning experiences that apply specifically to Aboriginal students. Aboriginal students are learners and participants in Aboriginal cultures, not necessarily experts in the culture. Their knowledge about their culture may be the same as that of other students in the class but if they do have extensive knowledge about their culture, it can benefit the entire class.

All students learn in a variety of ways and this should be taken into consideration to maximize learning for Aboriginal students as well. The intent is to ensure that high expectations in supported learning environments apply to Aboriginal students just as they do to non-Aboriginal students.

Goals of aboriginal perspectives for aboriginal students:

— to develop a positive self-identity through learning their own histories, cultures, and contemporary lifestyles

— to participate in a learning environment that will equip them with the knowledge and skills needed to participate more fully in the unique civic and cultural realities of their communities

Goals of aboriginal perspectives for non-aboriginal students:

— to develop an understanding and respect for the histories, cultures, and contemporary lifestyles of Aboriginal people

— to develop informed opinions on matters relating to Aboriginal people

Gender Fairness

To address the challenges of gender fairness and to develop student understanding in all subject areas in a balanced way, teaching, learning, and assessing must be equally accessible, relevant, interesting, appropriate, and challenging to male and female students. This will ensure that all students have opportunities to succeed regardless of gender.

Curriculum documents, learning resources, and classroom practice should reflect a commitment to gender fairness and inclusion. All students, regardless of gender, should be encouraged and supported to develop to their full potential.

Appropriate Age Portrayals

There is a growing recognition in society of the existence of stereotypes and discriminatory practices and attitudes related to aging. The contributions of all age groups, including the aging population, should be supported in teaching, learning, and assessing. Stereotyping related to age should be avoided.

Human Diversity

India is a land of rich mosaic of people with a diversity of cultures, languages, religions, and other characteristics. These aspects of human diversity should be recognized, accepted, and celebrated to create learning environments that

- — prepare all students for full participation in society
- — provide students with opportunities for cultural and linguistic development
- — encourage intercultural understanding and harmony

Anti-Racism/Anti-Bias Education

Effective schools strive to create and maintain inclusive school programs and environments that welcome diversity and challenge bias and discrimination. An anti-bias and anti-racism educational approach is a critical element in the development of curriculum documents and school environments so that students can experience learning in a safe environment and can develop the required knowledge and skills.

Sustainable Development

The concept of sustainable development is the process of integrating and balancing the economy, environment, and the overall health and well-being of society, through a consensus-based decision-making process, so that each of these areas — the economy, the environment, and society — can be sustained for future generations. This concept will be integrated into subject area curricula as appropriate.

DECENTRALIZING CURRICULUM DEVELOPMENT

At the end of the twentieth century, it is more or less universally recognized that curricula should be "open, active, flexible and intercultural", but the translation of this ideal into meaningful reality in schools and classrooms is an enormous challenge in all countries. For curriculum development to adequately respond to regional differences, as well as to socio-cultural and ethnic diversity, provision has to be made for localized and regionalized adaptations of a core national curriculum. Thus, decentralization of the curriculum development process should be integral to meaningful curricular change.

A participatory approach to curriculum development will permit the involvement of various stakeholders other than top-level policy-makers and specialized education personnel: parents, employers, religious and community leaders, and the students themselves. Systematic approaches to curriculum development can facilitate participation by various stakeholders at different stages and levels of involvement.

The Systematic Versus the Panic Approach

However, curriculum development may often be based on a "panic approach", where local or international political pressures cause rapid decisions to be made to change the curriculum without prior careful planning. The impact of international debate on major global concerns, such as environmental and population issues or women's education, is an example of such pressures. Not only is the "panic approach" not likely to be successful, but it may lead to an overload of the curriculum, increasing the difficulty of teachers' tasks. It is advisable, when faced with such issues, to examine what is already of relevance in the existing curriculum, and how new issues may be effectively incorporated on this basis. Curriculum development involving too many innovations is unlikely to succeed.

It is thus vital to examine the learning opportunities and teaching resources already available when designing new curricula or introducing specific changes, so as to avoid disparity between expectation and reality. The ways of translating stated goals into practice have to be carefully thought through from the outset.

Role of Teachers

Teachers play a pivotal role in successful curriculum change. In reality, however, changes to curricula are frequently designed almost exclusively within Ministries of Education or in specialized institutions. The is little direct involvement at primary and secondary school levels, altlhough teachers are sometimes assigned to curriculum development institutions or form part of curriculum development commissions or teams. Teachers generally tend to be regarded more as "conveyors" than designers of curriculum, although as implementers of the curriculum their contribution to the success of change is vital.

However, as decentralization spreads to schools, school-based curriculum development is a concept gaining in popularity in some countries. The closer that curriculum development gets to the school level, the more teachers are concerned. At the classroom level, teachers are involved in decision-making about the curriculum when they select textbooks and other learning materials, and design their own lesson plans and teaching approaches in translating theories and instructions into practise. They can be even more deeply involved by being given the chance to participate in the writing and design of textbooks and other teaching materials.

For teachers to be real actors in the change process or effective and motivated implementers of change, adequate teacher education is essential, both in terms of preservice and in-service training programmes. The latter should be an integral part of curriculum development processes, and should also include training in both teaching methods and assessment. One way for teachers to be actively involved in curriculum development, while improving their professional skills, is in the design and trialling of lesson units suitable for implementing changes within specific socio-cultural contexts. In order for this to be effective, they need to be adequately prepared. Curriculum conferences are proposed as settings in which teachers and other local actors could be involved.

Leaving teachers out of the design and development of curricular change is likely to result in little, if any, real change. Teacher involvement in curriculum development is advocated particularly because it can be a motivating factor for the teachers themselves in exercising their profession, raising their morale and giving them a sense of "ownership" of the curriculum.

VARIOUS APPROACHES TO CURRICULUM DEVELOPMENT

Action research approach

Action research has been used in many areas where an understanding of complex social situations has been sought in order to improve the quality of life. Among these are industrial, health and community work settings. Kurt Lewin, often cited as the originator of action research, used the methodology in his work with people affected by post-war social problems. Action research approaches to educational research were adopted in the late 60s and early 70s by the 'teacher- researcher' movement in the secondary education sector. This sought to bring the practising classroom teacher into the research process as the most effective person to identify problems and to find solutions.

An action research approach can contribute very positively to activity within the tertiary sector concerned with teaching quality issues, and with national Teaching Quality Assessment initiatives. As "reflective practitioners", we can achieve greater ownership of the evaluative process by becoming systematically self-assessing, alongside, and feeding into, external assessment processes:

> "Through systematic, controlled action research, higher education teachers can become more professional, more interested in pedagogical aspects of higher education and more motivated to integrate their research and teaching interests in a holistic way. This, in turn, can lead to greater job satisfaction, better academic programmes, improvement of student learning and practitioner's insights and

contributions to the advancement of knowledge in higher education."

Despite progress in understanding of the way in which people learn and the design of learning environments, teaching practice in higher education often remains unaffected. Traditionally, lecturers have not been encouraged to draw upon theoretical developments as a means of improving curriculum design and delivery. However, more recently, a number of initiatives at national and local levels have been established to create the conditions for innovation in these activities, and teaching/learning is becoming recognised as a more valid area of enquiry for academics across all disciplines, rather than as the unique preserve of specialists.

Action research methodology offers a systematic approach to introducing innovations in teaching and learning. It seeks to do this by putting the teacher in the dual role of producer of educational theory, and user of that theory. This is both a way of producing knowledge about higher education learning and teaching, and a powerful way of improving learning and teaching practice. No separation need be made between the design and delivery of teaching, and the process of researching these activities, thereby bringing theory and practice closer together

A variety of forms of action research have evolved. All adopt a methodical, iterative approach embracing problem identification, action planning, implementation, evaluation, and reflection.

Action research has a number of further distinctive features, as described by Zuber-Skerritt. For her, action research is:

— Critical collaborative enquiry by

— Reflective practitioners who are

— Accountable in making the results of their enquiry public,

— Self-evaluative in their practice, and engaged in

— Participative problem-solving and continuing professional development.

According to this view, action research is critical in the sense that practitioners not only look for ways to improve their practice within the various constraints of the situation in which they are working, but are also critical change agents of those constraints, and of themselves. It is reflective in that participants analyse and develop concepts and theories about their experiences.

Action researchers are accountable in that they aim to make their learning process and its results public, both to each other and to other interested practitioners, using accessible terminology. Their practice is self-evaluated in that the reflective and analytical insights of the researcher- practitioners themselves form the basis of the developmental process. Action research is participative in that those involved contribute equally to the inquiry, and collaborative in that the researcher is not an expert doing research from an external perspective, but a partner working with and for those affected by the problem and the way in which it is tackled.

Professional artistry approach

A 'professional artistry' approach stresses understanding, rather than technical skills; and it stresses moral, rather than purely technical, accountability. It focuses upon individual insight, staff development and gradualism and it expects management to provide a framework in which professional enterprise can flourish'. In other words this approach provides professionals with a certain autonomy in recognition of their specialist knowledge and moral responsibility. As Fish explained:

> The model stresses investigation and reflection on practice... [and]... it sees the practitioner as continually investigating his/her own practice.... Thus, the aim of research is improved insight into practice and the refinement of it. Theory is 'grounded' (arises from practice), what is sought is data (rather than evidence), what is collected is a range

> of interpretations from a range of perspectives and an attempt to understand better the complex human arena (rather than setting out to prove some aspect of it).... The differences in (approach to) quality assurance... between these two models of professionalism are crystallised in... the difference between appraisal (a term used in the technical rational model) and reflection (a term from the professional artistry model).

Question for Reflection

Would you prefer to build a technical rational or a professional artistry approach to early childhood curriculum development? Those contrasting approaches tell 'two stories' about how early childhood education and care might build quality curriculum and how this might be evaluated and assured:

> In one there is a vocabulary of means, efficiency, universals, law-like generalizations and bureaucracy; in the other, one of autonomy, emancipation, uniqueness, democracy, ends and values.... The former's stars include the detached academic researcher, the manager, the scientist, the bureaucrat, the inspector and the therapist; the latter's champion is the autonomous, reflective teacher-researcher who is committed to the improvement and emancipation of her work-context.

The stories of curriculum development which have captured the title of excellence in the international community arise from a strong commitment to 'professional artistry'. Reggio Emilia pre-primary schools have built through this commitment and through the preparedness to risk diversity in the name of seeking excellence for young children.

Principles for building early childhood curriculum

The following recommendations on how a 'process/professional artistry approach' to early childhood curriculum development could be built, draw on the research and thinking explored in this document to date. In particular, they acknowledge:

— the complex and changing nature of early childhood curriculum theory and practice evidenced in the research literature

— that reflection on curriculum issues, values and beliefs is helped by reflection with others

— that excellence and innovation in curriculum arises when staff are actively involved in contributing to the theory and the practice of early childhood curriculum.

With these points in mind it is recommended that the following principles be used to build a process/professional artistry approach to curriculum.

— *Principle 1*: Early childhood curriculum is based on moral and intellectual partnerships between key stakeholders.

— *Principle 2*: Stakeholders should produce broad curriculum guidance for early childhood staff.

— *Principle 3*: Early childhood curriculum workers are reflective 'professional artists'.

— *Principle 4*: Early childhood curriculum excellence and innovation are guaranteed by professional enterprise.

— *Principle 5*: Investment builds professional enterprise.

— *Principle 6*: Evaluation occurs through research and documentation.

— *Principle 7*: System-wide change builds through supporting and celebrating local partnerships and enterprise.

1. *Early childhood curriculum is based on moral and intellectual partnerships between key stakeholders*: The future development of early childhood curriculum should be built through forging strong central and local 'curriculum partnerships' between key stakeholders. The key stakeholders in early childhood education and care that would need to be involved in such a process are:

— Children aged birth to eight years of age

— Parents of those children

— Individual early childhood staff

— Schools

— Childcare services

— Early childhood professional associations

— Tertiary training providers

— State government.

The curriculum is negotiated between these partners through ongoing discussion of their values and beliefs about:

— who the young child is as a learner

— what early childhood education and care should aim to achieve

— how those aims might be achieved

— how those aims might be assessed.

2. *Stakeholders should produce broad curriculum guidance for early childhood staff*: Discussion between curriculum partners should lead to a set of statements of belief and intent that can guide early childhood staff in building their curriculum. These statements should include:

— A statement of beliefs about appropriate teaching and learning for children from birth to eight years of age.

— A statement of beliefs about how best practice can be created and maintained.

— A statement of appropriate learning outcomes for children from birth to eight years of age.

The responsibility of the central partnership could be to build a set of broad principles to guide local curriculum development based on the feedback from this curriculum consultation process. In the future the role of the central partnership would be to raise current issues and concerns that might need to addressed at a local level.

The responsibility of local partnerships could be to negotiate curriculum appropriate to their local needs, interests and concerns and their understandings of who the children are at the local level, drawing on the central statements.

3. *Early childhood curriculum workers are reflective 'professional artists'*: That the detailed principles and practices of early childhood curriculum be based on a professional artistry approach to curriculum development in which the professional insights of early childhood staff are given a privileged position when they can be shown to be well-informed and well-researched.

4. *Early childhood curriculum excellence and innovation are guaranteed by professional enterprise*: That excellence and innovation in early childhood curriculum should be built through investing in the professional artistry of early childhood staff. Professional artistry can produce excellence when staff are enterprising in how they do their curriculum work. Professional enterprise involves staff reflecting on and investigating their curriculum, their teaching and the children's learning, using the best available research knowledge in this process.

5. *Investment builds professional enterprise*: That key stakeholders are each given a clear role and responsibility in building the professional enterprise of early childhood staff. Local government, tertiary training providers, professional associations and service managers need to be given clearly defined responsibility to guarantee that staff are given the financial, intellectual and material resources needed to ensure their professional enterprise.

6. *Evaluation occurs through research and documentation*: That resources be provided to enable local curriculum 'partners' to document and investigate:

— their curriculum beliefs and values

— the decisions and actions that flow from these beliefs

— teaching and learning practices and outcomes.

Documentation of local investigations into teaching and learning can be used to build system-wide principles to guide early childhood curriculum and to evaluate children's learning outcomes.

7. *System-wide change builds through supporting and celebrating local partnerships and enterprise*: That state government make resources available to support local curriculum enterprise and encourage local curriculum partnerships. This would ensure that change is encouraged at the local level and helped to grow beyond those local boundaries.

Participatory approach

The classical/rational approach to curriculum development follows an "objectivist", product-oriented paradigm. The aims and objectives of the curriculum are set by professionals and experts who believe that they have sufficient technical knowledge to produce the desired product. It assumes that there is agreement by all interested groups (teachers, students, communities, employers) on common educational goals and, therefore, dialogue and consensus building among groups are not required.

The participatory/interactive approach follows a "subjectivist", process-oriented paradigm. It puts emphasis on participation and interaction among the various interested groups or educational stakeholders. This includes the learners themselves who are seen as having an important role to play in curriculum formulation. The goal is to stimulate different actors to participate in a dynamic, interactive process that allows their perceptions of the "ideal curriculum" to be made explicit and then made compatible and/or modified as necessary to produce the curriculum. Although there are distinct philosophical differences between the two curriculum models or approaches, they are not complete opposites and curriculum planning may include elements of both.

A complex combination of both internal, or institutional, demands and external, or societal, demands can influence the curriculum development process. Internal demands relate to the educational community itself — management, teaching staff, students, governing boards or ministries. The claims they make have to do with teaching, learning, research and outreach tasks, and specifically with finances, materials, rewards, qualifications and professionalism. External demands relate to the manpower needs, for example, and the claims on education articulated by various interest groups such as employers, families and communities.

The mission, goals, objectives and curriculum of an education institution will be influenced by external and internal demands. These demands are ongoing, often in flux and may be in conflict with each other and with the educational mission or responsibility the institution perceives for itself.

Recently, two trends, which appear to be polar opposites, have had an influence on the curriculum development process — globalization, or internationalization, of the curriculum and localization of the curriculum. The internationalization of education (and thus the curriculum) reflects the current processes of economic and political integration (the "global economy"). Increasingly, teachers, researchers and students work and communicate in an international context, a trend facilitated by various types of linkage arrangements among educational institutions and by telecommunication networks such as the Internet.

At the same time, there is a trend towards localization, or decentralization, of education and curricula. Institutions, staff and local communities, rather than national educational boards, are assuming more responsibility for developing curricula. This is the result of wider acceptance of the participatory/interactive approach to curriculum development, and of recognition that institutions, staff and communities which feel they have an active role in the curriculum development process are more committed to achieving its success.

ROLES AND RESPONSIBILITIES OF COMMITTEE/PEOPLE RELATED TO CURRICULUM DEVELOPMENT

The roles of individuals, councils, and committees in the curriculum development process appear in alphabetical order. Their responsibilities in the curriculum development process may include, but are not limited to those listed below.

Curriculum committee

— evaluates the curriculum proposal initiated at their institution.

— evaluates a proposal when a response has not been received from the Instructional Council

— assures that a curriculum proposal is well-developed and that its supporting materials adequately supplement the proposal

— Evaluates the impact of a curriculum proposal on the resources and other curricula of the college

— considers the recommendations of the Instructional Councils and Advisory Committees on the proposed curriculum

Curriculum technician

— provides appropriate forms and sections of the curriculum procedures as requested

— reviews the curriculum form for accuracy

— assembles all required forms and supporting materials to complete curriculum proposals

— attaches a Curriculum Transmittal Memorandum to a completed curriculum proposal and sends copies to the Occupational Deans, Curriculum Developers and all members of the appropriate Instructional Council(s)

— receives the evaluation of the curriculum proposal from the appropriate Instructional Council(s) and submits the Council's evaluation to the Curriculum Committee for its evaluation

— forwards completed curriculum proposal that has been approved by the College Curriculum Committee and signed by the College President to the District Director of Curriculum at the District Curriculum Office for evaluation by the District Curriculum Committee

Instructional design facilitator

— is involved in the curriculum process from its inception to its conclusion

— works with the initiator and other involved persons to produce written curriculum proposal

— coordinates activities of all involved persons at the institution to insure that the curriculum criteria are met

— is responsible for the accuracy and completeness of all required curriculum materials

— serves as liaison between institution and content expert(s) from business/industry

— serves as liaison between college and District Curriculum Coordinator

Department/division chair

— consults with appropriate dean regarding merits and feasibility of the curriculum proposal for the department/ division

— provides immediate feedback to the initiator

— provides support and guidance to initiator throughout the consultation and development stage

— refers initiator to the college Curriculum Developer for guidance in developing a curriculum proposal

District curriculum committee (DCC)

The roles and responsibilities of the District Curriculum Committee members have evolved over the years but consistently the Committee plays a major role in the following general areas:

— Casting visions with regard to the larger scope of the curriculum and pursuit of curricular goals through Committee planning, development and implementation efforts

— Facilitating curricular processes

— Providing guidance and support to the subcommittees and groups that report to the DCC.

— Broadening the curricular role – large systemic role at multiple levels: local, state, national

— Strengthening the relationship of the work of the DCC to curriculum and assessment

— Communicating DCC meeting outcomes to member's constituents.

More specific roles currently include

— Evaluating the District-wide impact of a curriculum proposal, assuring that the proposal is in accordance with the educational policies, educationally sound and in the best interest prior to recommending approval of the proposal to the Governing Board

— Serving as arbiter of conflicting recommendations concerning a curriculum proposal from different recommending bodies

District director of curriculum

— plans for the work of the DCC

— organizes the flow of information from multiple parties to Committee

— development and maintenance of curriculum system supports and resources

— formation and distribution of policies and processes in support of curriculum

— reporting on outcomes

— archiving of historical curriculum record

— collaboration with multiple external and internal parties in support of curriculum

— facilitates the work of the DCC

Director of university and college relations

— serves as a representative to the Transfer Articulation Task Force (TATF)

— interfaces with all three universities regarding transfer and substitutes for the Vice Chancellor for Academic Affairs and Student Development

District governing board

— approves any credit course and/or credit-based certificates and/or degrees before they can be offered by the institution

— approves occupational curriculum items that must be sent for approval to the Education Board.

Initiator

— consults with a department/division chair, faculty or appropriate deans concerning the development of a curriculum proposal

— works in conjunction with the college Curriculum Developer in developing the curriculum proposal

Instructional council

All involved Instructional Councils shall be given an opportunity to make a recommendation on cross-referenced courses.

— evaluates course and new occupational program proposals received from an Instructional Dean

— receives from the initiating college, occupational program modification proposals as informational items

— evaluates the quality and appropriateness of the content of a curriculum proposal and the impact of a proposal on the disciplines which have been assigned to it

— (Chair) receives evaluations of a curriculum proposal from other Council members and submits to the initiating college the written recommendation of the Council based upon these evaluations

— submits recommendation within ten instructional days of the date of the Curriculum Transmittal Memorandum. If no recommendation is received from the Instructional Council Chair by the due date, the Instructional Dean may proceed with the proposed curriculum

Instructional dean

The Instructional Dean needs to be included in the consultation and development stage of the curriculum process, he/she should be consulted before a proposal is developed at his/her college. The Instructional Dean:

— provides feedback concerning the merits and feasibility of the curriculum proposal for the college

— consults, if necessary, with the Insitution's President, faculty and appropriate deans district-wide concerning the impact of the curriculum proposal on other instructional units within the District

— provides support services and guidance to the initiator to develop support materials for the curriculum proposal. This process is facilitated the College Curriculum Developer/ Instruction Design Facilitator

— may channel feedback from a variety of sources in the consultation and development stages of the curriculum development process

— initiates the formal recommendation and approval stage of the curriculum development process by sending a Curriculum Transmittal Memorandum and the curriculum proposal to members of the appropriate Instructional Council(s).

— submits the curriculum proposal with the recommendation of the Instructional Council to the College Curriculum Committee.

— recommends approval of a curriculum proposal initiated at his/her college in order for it to be submitted to the District Curriculum Committee

Occupational dean

Serves as liaison for the Instructional Dean and the initiator, occupational department/division chairs, Curriculum Developer or equivalent, and the program advisory committee concerning the development of an occupational curriculum proposal.

Occupational program advisory committee

This committee is a group of citizens who are experts in a specific occupational field. The Committee is formally organized for a specified period of time (1-3 years) and includes at least one college representative. The Committee:

— meets at least once a year

— serves in an advisory capacity

— reviews new and modified occupational programs

— advises educators regarding occupational education programs

— provides information about the preparation of program graduates

Vice chancellor for student and educational development

— serves as chair of the District Curriculum Committee

— provides support service to the District Curriculum Committee and to the colleges in coordination with the Instructional Deans

— plans and coordinates curriculum for the District

— assigns course prefixes/disciplines to the Instructional Councils

3

Curriculum Planning

Curriculum planning is both a divergent and convergent process. It is divergent in that from a single idea many related ideas can be generated. The divergent thinking processes as used in curriculum planning is a form of brainstorming. Taking a central theme or idea you begin to diverge and think of related content, skills and processes that are reflective of the initial theme. The classic divergent part of the curriculum development process is to think of as many related or interrelated connections as possible.

The convergent part of curriculum planning comes when each newly generated smaller concept is tracked back and tested against the original theme. Thus, in order for related ideas to be pertinent to the final development of a unit, each new idea must have a direct relationship back to the central theme. When you test and verify how smaller pieces of a unit fit into a larger conceptual package, you are using convergent thinking. Curriculum planning is also convergent if you continue to take larger ideas or concepts and break them down into smaller, more discreet pieces. And, some people prefer to use convergent thinking first in the planning process by creating or taking smaller related pieces and then fitting them into a larger conceptual framework.

No matter which way one prefers to organize and create instructional plans, in order for the process to be completely effective, it is always necessary to use both types of thinking continuously. The whole planning process is dynamic and much like weaving a fine cloth or a living tapestry. Some people decide on the picture first and then choose the colors, threads and textures. Others decide on the textures, colors and threads first and then weave them into a random pattern. Either method is acceptable and still requires that you use a combination of divergent and convergent thinking.

AIMS, GOALS AND OBJECTIVES

In everyday English we tend to use the terms aims, goals, or objectives interchangeably. Within the educational lexicon, for the past twenty years curriculum scholars, planners and administrators have been trying to standardize terms so that they refer to very specific curricular components. The following definitions are broadly accepted by groups trying to standardize curricular terms so that they are not confusing to readers and users

Aims

Aims are general statements that provide direction or intent to educational action. Aims are usually written in amorphous terms using words like: learn, know, understand, appreciate, and these are not directly measurable. Aims may serve as organizing principles of educational direction for more than one grade. Indeed these organizing principles may encompass the continuum of educational direction for entire programs, subject areas or the district. Students will understand and become proficient at identifying the different types of spoken English.

Goals

Goals are statements of educational intention which are more specific than aims. Goals too may encompass an entire program, subject area, or multiple grade levels. They may be in either amorphous language or in more specific behavioral terms. Students will be able to identify and use American slang terms and phrases.

Objectives

Objectives are usually specific statements of educational intention which delineate either general or specific outcomes.

Behavioral Objectives

Indicate the specific behaviors students must demonstrate to indicate that learning has occurred.

Advantages:

— They are easy to write.

— They are easier to categorize by domain (Cognitive, affective, physical/kinesthetic/tactile).

— They are more easily evaluated. (usually by objective methods.)

— May easily be designated for horizontal enrichment or vertical acceleration into categories of:

  — must know

  — need to know

  — nice to know

  — or categories like: introduced, developed, mastered.

Using the aforementioned district aim and goal concerning the understanding and development of spoken English proficiency, here are three examples of behavioral objectives in all three domains: (and yes, the examples are meant to be a bit bizarre.)

Examples:

Aim: Students will understand and become proficient at identifying the different types of spoken English.

Goal: Students will be able to identify and use American slang terms and phrases.

— Cognitive: Students will identify and list 5 slang terms they have heard from their peers.

— Affective: Student will choose 3 of the most offensive slang terms from a list developed by the entire class.

— Physical: Students will create expressive gestures to go with their favorite slang terms.

Please note that in two of the objectives, specific evaluation criteria have been built in. This is one of the strengths of behavioral objectives.

The advantage to creating more holistic objectives (ones that fall into more than one domain) is that this process creates additional neural pathways. This allows learners to more easily remember material and processes. In the past there has been an over dependence on writing just cognitive objectives. It will be easier to develop holistic objectives in some areas of study over others. For instance, some educators find it hard to form affective objectives in the area of math. While this may be true, it is imperative for educators not to intentionally ignore instances where an array of domains can be included in lessons.

Holistic Objectives

Teachers can design holistic teaching practices by creating lessons which incorporate learning experiences from all three domains: the cognitive (thinking), the affective (feeling), and the psychomotor or physical (kinesthetic, tactile, and/or physical). Material in the psychomotor taxonomy is very narrowly defined and should be reserved to specific skilled or interpretive movements. If you are supporting one of the other domains with physical movement or physical activity, merely label that objective as physical and avoid the term psychomotor to avoid confusion.

While educational objectives are currently written in the most common form as behavioral objectives (those using explicit verbs), at more artistic and sophisticated levels objectives may be written also as problem-solving objectives, or as expressive activities that lead to expressive outcomes. All three types of objectives should be valued parts of comprehensive curricula.

The advantage to creating more holistic objectives (ones that fall into more than one domain) is that this process creates additional neural pathways. This allows learners to more easily remember material and processes. In the past there has been an over-dependence on writing just cognitive objectives. It will be easier to develop holistic objectives in some areas of study over others. For instance, some educators find it hard to form affective objectives in the area of math. While this may be true, it is imperative for educators not to intentionally ignore instances where an array of domains can be included in lessons.

Nonbehavioral Objectives

These may use more general, amorphous words to note the desired learning, such as to know, to understand, to learn, or to appreciate. Two kinds of nonbehavioral objectives are:

— Problem solving objectives

— Expressive activities that lead to expressive outcomes.

These types of objectives have the following advantages:

— They can be more artistic — not as rigid.

— They can be more reflective of real life problems.

— Several domains may be combined within one objective.

— The teacher can easily solicit input from students. (often evaluation of these objectives is more subjective, or authentic.)

— When you are integrating material, the nonbehavioral format facilitates integration more easily. Therefore, several subject areas or different content may be easily incorporated into one objective.

— These types of objectives are more open-ended and allow teachers to create related experiences based on students' interests and motivational levels.

Problem Solving Objectives

Advantages: Problem solving objectives have several distinct advantages and can be used in a number of ways.

— They are more artistic.

— They may be long term — covering a number of lessons or an entire unit.

— They can be designed to be integrative — they may combine or cut across subject areas, or they may involve a number of different processes.

— They can be used to combine a number of intelligences or cognitive functions.

— Students may become involved in the criteria statement and the development of parameters, thus giving them ownership in the process and pushing toward more intrinsic levels of learning and evaluation.

— They may allow ownership in that students can help devise parts of problems or their own problems. If students are allowed to create and construct their own problems, again, this would allow them ownership in the process and may help them go beyond problem-solving to problem finding.

— Grading is more subjective. However, this can be done in an objective manner. Remember the conditions of a problem and/or the problem parameters provide the framework for judging both the problem solution and/or the product. These parameters and/or conditions become the contract between the teacher and the students. Students may be required to judge their own work through some sort of self-evaluation process. Peers can evaluate peers. Members of the community may also become involved in the evaluation processes. These may be combined with teacher evaluations, thus creating multidimensional forms of evaluation.

— Students and/or teachers become learning partners and should decide if they are going to use problem solving objectives as culminating experiences, or as a catalyst for and method of learning new skills. Problems may be used in either way or by combining both ways.

Example

The Harrison Ford Elementary School received a $50,000 grant to create a nature trail on school grounds. The money is to be used for a trail that is both aesthetic and also one that can be used for environmental study. Create a design for the trail. Problem from, L. Wilson Every child, whole child. Tucson: Zephyr Press,

Problem conditions:

Conditions often refer to the actual appearance of finished products or are ways in which products are standardized.

— Products must be neat

— Presented on graph or grid paper

— Drawn to scale

— Students will include a key and color code drawings so that they are easily understandable.

Problem parameters:

Parameters usually deal with restrictions placed on solving the problem.

— All costs cannot exceed $50,000.

— Total area of trail and the areas surrounding the trail cannot go outside of the current property boundaries of the school's grounds.

— The trail cannot interfere with existing facilities.

— The total area of the trail must not exceed 1 acre.

— The trail must be both aesthetically pleasing and must have areas for environmental study.

— The trail must comply with general safety standards governing parks and playgrounds and be generally accessible to person with disabilities.

The problem above requires a myriad of skills and knowledge in varied content areas . Skills needed to solve this problem successfully might be — research skills; artistic skills; interpersonal skills; knowledge of ratio; botany; budgeting; mathematical calculations; graphics; and knowledge of state and federal regulations governing handicap accessibility.

A comprehensive problem solving objective may be used as an entry into a unit of study, thus providing students with a rationale for having to learn certain material and skills. Or, a problem solving objective may be used as a culminating event. In this case it provides a comprehensive way to evaluate students skills.

Problem solving lesson plans

Problem solving lesson plans may be designed in any number of ways, but they should include components from the starred items below as a minimum. Remember that even though these are designed as lesson plans, the course of each problem may vary greatly depending on the components, solutions and skills needed in solving it. Some problems are simple and can be solved in one class period, a day, or over several periods. Other problems are complex and will need days or weeks, or the problem solution and product may comprise an entire unit of study. Remember to plan accordingly, allocating enough time for students to complete the problem successfully. In writing a problem, steps should be arranged clearly and sequentially so that anyone reading the problem could easily follow its progression.

Problem-solving writing tips

— Statement of the problem.

— Conditions - include product specifications. These usually refer to how the problem looks or desired standardized components within a final product. Conditions can be used as portions of the assessment procedure. Some problems may be so open that they don't require conditions.

— Parameters - are detailed restrictions on solving the problem. These may be either very general or very specific and, again, can be used to help determine assessment.

— A partial or complete list of process skills and/or subject areas needed to solve problems.

— A listing of district aims and goals met by completing the problem. This may be done before the statement of the problem or after the problem statement, or in a the context of a grading rubric or checklist.

— Methods of evaluation and/or evaluation forms.

A rationale statement - this shouid include a brief statement as to why you are having students do the problem. This may include a restatement or be part of the aims and goals statement.

Materials' list

— A listing of teacher's responsibilities within the problem.

— A listing of students' responsibilities within the problem.

— Any extraneous support needed to solve the problem — as in community cooperation.

— Expanded lessons related to the problem or possible follow-up activities.

— Remember the rules of thumb — the more conditions and parameters you include, the more conforming, restrictive, and narrow students' products will be. The fewer conditions or parameters, the more diversity and creativity in the products. Some students may require more structure and help in solving problems, others may need less help. Make allowances for both types of students.

Expressive activities which lead to expressive outcomes

— This is the most artistic form of teaching - teachers literally orchestrate lessons by preparing a field, developing an immersion experience or investigation, and then allowing students to actively explore and discover ideas and connections. Learning takes place within the context of students' investigations, as they engage in activities and conversations, or within the context of their own active experimentation. It is a cause and effect relationship.

— Although initial or immersion experiences may be planned or structured, these merely serve as triggers, or contextual entry points. It is students' curiosity and intrinsic motivation that are the forces which carry learners toward undetermined or unplanned ends. Flexibility, adaptability and preparedness are key to the success of this type of teaching. When teachers take advantage of a teachable moment, this is the most common form of this type of teaching. Yet, very few teachers add credibility to these types of learning experiences by reflectively or actively evaluating them as formal learning.

— Due to the open-ended nature of this form of teaching, learning and actual achievement must be evaluated for achieved objectives after the activity is completed or portions of the activity are completed.

— The teacher has the obligation to the students to inform them of their accomplishments and achievements at the end of each activity or session. This can be done through discussion or through openly charting progress.

— Formal assessment may be achieved through annotated records, checklists, observations, projects, portfolios, or presentations.

The logistics are simple

— The teacher plans an introductory or exploratory lesson knowing and projecting what types of skills may be needed, or which skills might arise during the course of the lesson.

— The teacher then watches the children's reactions, and waits for questions or related interests to appear. At this point he/she may expand the original lesson based on children's questions and evidence of their curiosity. (this type of planning is highlighted in constuctivist teaching, and is closely akin to what teachers do in taking advantage of a "teachable moment.")

— The actual formal writing process notes in detail the initial exploratory or investigative experiences, and includes a projection of possible skills which might be needed, and a projection as to where the lesson might diverge.

— In the event that students don't respond as predicted, the teacher might note possible prompts.

— The teacher also should include sample types of assessments that might prove helpful in evaluating the lesson. These samples may be included in the initial plan.

Example

Drawing in a sand tray — knowing students and their developmental stages. In this exercise the primary teacher plans a simple letter recognition exercise as a trigger activity. Students are given their names printed on a piece of cardboard and asked to duplicate them in the sandtray. In the context of justifiable instructional objectives, the purposes of this exercise are to have students:

— recognize and replicate individual letters,

— recognize and replicate their names,

— exercise left to right visual progressions needed for beginning reading, and

— to exercise eye-hand coordination and both small and large muscle coordination.

Being a veteran in obseving children, this primary teacher knows that many of her students are highly inquisitive. Off the sandtray she hangs magnifying glasses so that the children can look at the sand in more detail when they have finished writing their names. If they do not do this on their own, she will ask them to do it. She also has a mircoscope set up and has collected a number of books about the sea, beaches, tides, oceans and marine life, and glass, and so forth. The trick here is for the teacher to either provide an educational environment that is so rich in stimuli that students are propelled by their own senses of inquisitiveness to ask many questions, or to offer gentle prompts so that the students respond with questions.

One child goes to the table and gets sand on his hands. Being curious he picks up a magnifier and begins to examine the sand particles more closely. His friends begin to do the same and they start to notice that the particles are different shapes, sizes and colors. These observations initiate a series of questions about the source and nature of sand. The teacher charts the children's questions and these form the basis for a two week long investigation into sand formation, beaches, types of ocean life, tides, weather conditions, vacations and even the formation of glass. The culmination of the unit is a trip to a glass blower. The unit has been extremely interesting for the students because it was initiated by their own curiosity and questions. Unfortunately, like many such spontaneous experiences, the teacher fails to communicate to the students what exactly they have learned.

Closure

Although this lesson was a great success, and anyone observing these students could not fail to notice their educational growth, this teacher devalued the credibity of this experience by never providing her students with some sort of closure or summation. In this instance, the children leave the classroom thinking that they had fun playing in the sandtray and observing the glass blower.

This form of teaching is higly artistic and very valuable in mantaining children's levels of intrinsic motivation, but as seen in the example, the fault of the teacher was that she failed to appropriately evaluate the experience. Indeed, many teachers using this form of teaching fail to communicate to students exactly what they have learned. Sometimes they also fail to annotate students' specific achievements, thus causing this form of teaching to be greatly devalued. Teachers committed to this very student-centered, constructivist form of teaching should always create evaluative experiences as part of the expressive activity. Students have a right to know what they have achieved and what they have gained from the experience.

What is involved in creating expressive activities?

The expertise and jobs of the teacher in planning expressive activities that will lead to expressive outcomes are multi-leveled. In this form of teaching the teacher acts as a master orchestrator, devising and planning trigger activities that have the potential to lead in many directions and to many different or unique learning processes and experiences. This method of teaching and curriculum development is the most artistic and complex form of teaching.

Knowledge of Developmental Stages: First, the teacher must have knowledge and expertise in students' developmental stages and with the process expectations that govern the general curriculum.

In the example of the sand tray, the teacher knows that letter recognition and reproduction are baseline essential skills for her students. She also knows that in order to achieve the cognitive and physical functions related to her trigger exercise students must be physically and developmental ready. Her knowledge of their readiness extends to the fact that in order to be successful in this emersion activity students must have some eye-hand control and some fine and gross muscle coordination. They must be able and willing to see something and then to attempt to reproduce it. Also, students must have the cognitive maturity to realize that the basis for understanding written language requires knowing that text travels from left to right and that letters are merely abstract representations of concrete spoken sounds.

Knowledge of Curricular Expectations: In planning this activity the teacher's general knowledge of the curriculum includes knowing that in addition to letter and name recognition and rudimentary writing skills, there is a general district expectation that students will be able to ask and answer their own questions. In the context of her knowledge about students at her grade level, she knows that the pathway of questioning can lead to the emergence of general research interests and skills.

Knowledge of Students' Skills and Talents: From these perspectives the teacher has noted that several of her students are naturally very inquisitive about things in their environment. In devising possible extensions of the baseline activity of letter tracing, she uses all of this knowledge to create an environment that supports students' questions about the nature and sources of sand, thus encouraging students' naturally occurring questions and innate inquisitiveness.

In preparation and anticipation, this teacher has collected both literary and reference materials that relate to sand or to its formation. And she had positioned magnifying glasses near the sand tray, as well as a microscope in order to invite questions and chart paper for scribing students' possible questions. If students don't literally "take the bait," the teacher is prepared to ask leading questions in order to get students interested in researching the formation of sand.

Ability to Relinquish Control to Students' Intrinsic Learning: Thus, the fourth skill needed to be successful at teaching through expressive activities is that of actively encouraging students to take command of their own learning. Teachers adept at this form of teaching must be able, not only to organize general immersion activities that are age-level appropriate, but they must be willing to relinquish control to students' educational agendas and natural senses of curiosity.

Predictive Talent: The next talent needed by teachers adept at expressive forms of teaching are those of being able to envision, imagine, anticipate and predict possibilities and possible outcomes. They must be prepared that students questions and initiatives might take them in many different directions.

Ability to Evaluate in Different Ways: The last component that makes this form of teaching legitimate is that the teacher must be prepared to annotate and evaluate the results of the emergent activities. Results must also be communicated to participating students so that they can begin to make the connections between their questions and their abilities to complete and be engaged in research.

The Cognitive objectives

Cognitive behavioral objectives are divided into subsets according to Bloom's Taxonomy. This area is concerned with knowledge or thought. The following taxonomies are arranged so that they proceed from the simplest to more complex levels.

1. *Knowledge:* Remembering previously learned material.

know	define	record
identify	recall	name
relate	memorize	recognize
list	repeat	acquire

2. *Comprehension*: The ability to grasp the meaning of material.

restate	identify	illustrate
locate	discuss	interpret

report	describe	draw
recognize	discuss	represent
explain	review	differentiate
express	infer	conclude

3. *Application*: The ability to use learned material in new and concrete situations.

apply	organize	
relate	employ	practice
develop	restructure	calculate
translate	interpret	show
use	demonstrate	exhibit
operate	illustrate	dramatize

4. *Analysis*: The ability to break down material into its component parts so that its organizational structure may be understood.

analyze	differentiate	experiment
compare	contrast	scrutinize
probe	investigate	discover
inquire	detect	inspect
examine	survey	dissect
contrast	classify	discriminate
categorize	deduce	separate

5. *Synthesis:* The ability to put parts together to form a new whole.

compose	plan	propose
produce	invent	develop
design	formulate	arrange

assemble	collect	construct
create	set up	organize
prepare	generalize	originate
predict	document	derive
modify	combine	write
tell	relate	propose

6. *Evaluation*: The ability to judge the value of material for a given purpose.

judge

assess	argue	validate
compare	decide	consider
evaluate	choose	appraise
conclude	rate	value
measure	select	criticize
deduce	estimate	infer

The affective domain

Affective objectives can also be divided into a hierarchy (according to Krathwohl). This area is concerned with feelings or emotions.

1. *Receiving*: This refers to the learner's sensitivity to the existence of stimuli - awareness, willingness to receive, or selected attention.

feel

sense	pursue
capture	attend
experience	perceive

2. *Responding:* This refers to the learners' active attention to stimuli - acquiescence, willing responses, or feelings of satisfaction.

conform	
allow	contribute
cooperate	enjoy
satisfy	

3. *Valuing:* This refers to the learner's beliefs and attitudes of worth - acceptance, preference, or commitment.

believe	respect
seek	search
justify	persuade

4. *Organization:* This refers to the learner's internalization of values and beliefs involving (1) the conceptualization of values; and (2) the organization of a value system.

examine	
clarify	create
systematize	integrate

5. *Characterization:* This refers to the learner's highest of internalization and relates to behavior that reflects (1) a generalized set of values; and (2) a characterization or a philosophy about life.

internalize	
review	resolve
conclude	judge

The psychomotor domain

Psychomotor objectives are those specific to discreet physical functions, reflex actions and interpretive movements.

Traditionally, these types of objectives are concerned with the physically encoding of information, with movement and/or with activities where the gross and fine muscles are used for expressing or interpreting information or concepts. This area also refers to natural, autonomic responses or reflexes.

As stated earlier, to avoid confusion, if the activity is simply something that is physical which supports another area — affective or cognitive — term the objective physical rather than psychomotor. This goes to instructional intent. A primary example of something physical which supports specific cognitive development and skills might be looking through a microscope and identifying and drawing cells. Here the instructional intent of this common scientific activity is not to develop specific skilled proficiency in microscope viewing or in reproducing cells through drawing.

The key intent in this activity is that a physical action supports or is a vehicle for cognitive growth and furthering recognition skills. The learner is using the physical action to achieve the cognitive objectives — identify, recognize, and differentiate varied types of cells. If you are using a physical activity to support a cognitive or affective function, simply label it as something physical (labeling the objective as kinesthetic, haptic, or tactile is also acceptable) and avoid the term psychomotor.

Reflex movements

Objectives at this level include reflexes that involve one segment of the spine and movements that may involve more than one segmented portion of the spine (e.g., voluntary muscle contraction).

Fundamental movements

Objectives in this area refer to skills or movements or behaviors related to walking, running, jumping, pushing, pulling and manipulating.

Perceptual abilities

Objectives in this area should address skills related to kinesthetic (bodily movements), visual, auditory, tactile (touch), or coordination abilities.

Physical abilities

Objectives in this area should be related to endurance, flexibility, agility, strength, reaction-response time or dexterity.

Skilled movements

Objectives in this area refer to games, sports, dances, and/or the arts.

Nondiscursive communication

Objectives in this area refer to expressive movement through posture, gestures, facial expressions, and/or creative movements.

CURRICULUM PLANNING MODELS

Higher Education continues to face a host of significant challenges meeting the needs of our learners. Meeting these challenges requires a strategic planning model that provides a focus on the learner through the curriculum. The strategic planning process presented here is designed to do just that, helping ensure that the highest quality learning environments are available to those we serve. The Curriculum-Centered Strategic Planning Model presented here, is preceded by the Strategic Decision Engine also developed by the author and published in Working Toward Strategic Change.

The Curriculum-Centered Strategic Planning Model provides a framework for strategic planning in higher education. In fact, it is built specifically for higher education, and centers as the name suggests, around the curriculum. It is designed to import whatever planning has already occurred in an institution avoiding the unpleasant prospect of starting over. It integrates seamlessly with accreditation self study processes and if implemented in time, can become the core of the accreditation process.

The Curriculum-Centered Strategic Planning Model can also integrate academic program review into the overall institutional strategic planning initiative providing unprecedented cohesion between academic and institutional plans. The planning process is designed to run continuously, refreshing itself each cycle and providing an effective communications process resulting in clear understanding among the array of institutional constituents.

The Curriculum Centered strategic planning Model is built around our Learner-Centered Curriculum framework. Together they form the core of our online strategic planning system called Eplanedu. The Curriculum-Centered Strategic Planning Model has proven to be a powerful tool to help address the challenges higher education will face in meeting learner needs. We stand ready to assist you and hope our Curriculum-Centered Strategic Planning Model contributes to your success.

The Curriculum-Centered Strategic Planning Model

The Curriculum-Centered Strategic Planning Model is conducted through five interlocking planning activities including:

(1) the identification and definition of Key Performance Indicators;

(2) the detailing of a Learner-Centered Curriculum Architecture;

(3) conducting an External Environmental Scan;

(4) an Internal Environmental Scan; and

(5) culminating in an Action Planning Process.

The continuous process of evaluation is embedded across all five activity areas. Action Planning is used to develop specific organizational, tactical and operational plans such as a Financial Plan, a Strategic Enrollment Management Plan, a Marketing Plan, an Assessment Plan and so on.

Key Performance Indicators

— Key Performance Indicators establish the frame of reference for the planning cycle by specifying the primary numbers used to monitor institutional performance.

— The classic enrollment management funnel illustrates an ideal initial family of Key Performance Indicators upon which to build a strategic plan.

— While we illustrate Key Performance Indicators using the enrollment management funnel, Key Performance Indicators can be added for any measure of institutional performance including such measures as financial status, learning outcomes, successful accreditation, etc.

Learner-Centered Curriculum Architecture

There are seven interlocking components (more detail on Learner-Centered Curriculum Architecture in the following section) to the Learner-Centered Curriculum Architecture that provide for structured inquiry, they include:

— the deep understanding of the populations that can be served by programs and services;

— knowledge of the objectives that learners in those populations seek;

— an evaluation of learning provider models available to them;

— a comprehensive integration of learning theory, methods and principles appropriate to successful learning and student success;

— a strategic reconceptualization of the overall curriculum architecture providing a full scope of programs and approaches to the populations the institution seeks to serve through its programs and services;

— a synthesis of specific curriculum configurations designed to meet the specific needs of the array of learners served; and finally

— the design, development and deployment of the array of services required by learners to meet their objectives.

External Environmental Scan

— An External Scan involves examining trends and events in the external environment that have impacted or have the potential to impact the key performance indicators, and the curriculum. This activity is conducted continuously and includes (but not limited to) such things as:

An analysis of trends including

- — Political
- — Economical
- — Educational
- — Social
- — Technological

An analysis of learner markets including

- — Market forces at play
- — Market dynamics shaped by market forces
- — Competitor initiatives
- — Existing and potential collaborators
- — Higher Education at large

An analysis of consumers including

- — Learning Populations
- — Learner Objectives
- — Learner Restraints

— Learner's Key Performance Indicators

— Learner Options

Continuous Self Study Process

— The continuous self study process examines institutional aspects and incorporates the findings into strategic, organizational, and operational plans. To begin, take an inventory of existing reports and self-study documents to help build the foundation for strategic planning.

— Self study includes processes such as accreditation self study, annual budget development, employee performance evaluations, annual report development, work-plan development, and a host of others.

— Together, such activities provide a continuous flow of information regarding organizational performance as related to Key Performance Indicators , the curriculum, and the external environment.

Action Planning

— The Action Planning Process involves a series of steps that develop the organization's action agenda that will capitalize upon opportunities, mitigate threats, make strengths stronger and weaknesses weaker.

— Action planning is the process of generating ideas; formulating mission, strategies, goals and objectives; and establishing an implementation and evaluation schedule.

— Action Plans may include unit plans, tactical plans, project plans etc. Specific action plans are not included in this proposal. The recommendations will be developed using our action planning methodology.

— The Eplanedu online strategic planning system includes an online action planning module to facilitate this process.

The Learner-Centered Curriculum Approach

The Learner-Centered Curriculum provides a framework for the identification, design, development, deployment, and evaluation of curriculum. It frames curriculum in the broadest strategic context then guides academic leaders and curriculum designers in drilling down to the most discrete curricular component. The comprehensive nature of the framework makes it ideal for sustaining design integrity across multiple curricular elements. Design integrity helps maintain cohesive strategies within the curriculum processes.

The seven interlocking components ensure that curriculum fulfills institutional and fiduciary missions, they include:

(1) the deep understanding of the populations to be served;

(2) knowledge of the objectives they seek;

(3) an evaluation of learning provider models available to them;

(4) a comprehensive integration of learning theory, methods and principles appropriate to successful learning;

(5) a strategic reconceptualization of the overall curriculum architecture providing a full scope of programs and approaches;

(6) a synthesis of specific curriculum configurations designed to meet specific learner's needs; and finally

(7) the design, development and deployment of the array of services required by learners to meet their objectives.

Two views of the Learner-Centered Curriculum Approach follow. The first is the Simple Round Diagram and the second details the full approach in seven columns.

The Learner-Centered Curriculum Approach forms the core of the Curriculum-Centered Strategic Planning Model and methodology. Together they form the core of the online strategic planning system called ePlanedu. The Learner-Centered

Curriculum approach has proven to be a powerful tool to help address the challenges faced in meeting learner needs.

As a framework the Learner Centered Curriculum Framework provides a systematic way of focusing the curriculum development process in seven essential and interlocking areas. The diagram on the opposite side sets forth seven columns moving the process from left to right systematically through components one through seven. Each component frames the response to a specific set of questions regarding the curriculum and its design.

Learner Populations

— The very first set of questions encountered in the model revolves around the learner themselves. Who are the learners of the 21st century? Whom does the institution now serve? Who could or should the institution be serving? Understanding who the learners are is an essential and often overlooked component of shaping curriculum for a changing society.

— The foundation of the Learner-Centered Curriculum approach is to fully understand learning demand as segmented by population characteristic and identify gaps between those present in society and those an institution now serves.

— The approach becomes more useful if an open discourse occurs regarding the learner populations found in target market areas and society at large.

— To fully understand, one must describe learner population characteristics including preferred venues, constraints, and learning preferences. It is also important to determine the size of the learner population segments.

— For example, we know that of the 461,937 population of Sedgwick County, Kansas there are an estimated 159,368 adult learners. One can determine these populations for all states, their counties and even census track units to provide a consistent view of learner numbers.

Learner Objectives

— The second set of questions encountered in the model revolves around the objectives of the learner populations identified in the first component. What do the learners of the 21st century seek? What are their objectives? How do objectives change in the course of person's life? This is a most fundamental component of the overall structure and intent of an institution's curriculum. Understanding learners' objectives are an important element for motivation and sequencing of learning events.

— Learners seek a vast array of learning objectives.

— Understanding the array of learning objectives will enable an alignment between learner populations and their various learning objectives early in the program and curriculum review, design, and development processes. It is essential to develop effective marketing, recruitment, and even retention programs.

— This alignment is a most fundamental component of the overall structure and intent of an institution's curriculum and programs. Understanding learners' objectives are also an important element for motivation and sequencing of learning events as well as a marketing and recruitment foundation.

— The point here is not to be "everything to everybody" but to be fully informed as to the variety, type and characteristics of the objectives learners seek so that various programs can be aligned with the learning populations needs.

— To further our example: Of the estimated 461,937 population of Sedgwick County, Kansas we estimate that 72,409 participate in work related learning, 68,944 participate in learning for personal development, 21,134 seek credentials, while 4,157 seek basic skills.

Learning Provider Models

— The third set of questions in the model revolves around the models and various providers a 21st century learner has access to. What options are open to 21st century learners as they seek their objectives? What are the various curricular models, business models and assessment models in play? The 21st century is the age where learning opportunity will come to the learner. Leaning will occur wherever learners have need. A complex network of learning resources is already emerging and we must begin to embrace the concept of learning systems to meet the demand for learning across multiple venues. Faculty, Curriculum Leaders, Strategic Planners and Curriculum Designers must fully explore, describe and understand these various models in order to adequately assess the emerging learning landscape. Such an assessment enables the understanding of the competitive environment for enrollments and emerging best practices that develop as the models mature and reveal their strengths, weaknesses, values and deficiencies.

— There exist in the learning marketplace a wide variety of learner provider models and competitors in the learning marketplace.

— They include traditional models, cohort models, open learning models, mini-term models, online models, and a host of others.

— Each model holds particular value for a specific learner population and the objectives they seek.

— Examining the models already available and linking them to the populations for whom they have value builds deep insight into the learner-centered approach.

— To continue our example: Of the estimated 461,937 population of Sedgwick County, Kansas, we can further estimate that 43,156 will receive their learning from commercial providers; 14,771 from postsecondary institutions; 8,037 from trade organizations; 4,779 from private commercial or church related sources and finally 3,144 from elementary and secondary institutions.

— The point here is to fully understand the choice 21st century learners have in meeting their learning objectives. Because the context has been set in the first and second components an examination of the models available begins to paint a cohesive picture of learner options in a 21st century learning marketplace. Decisions regarding what individual institutions 21st century curriculum will look like will emerge from the synthesis of populations, objectives and models present across society.

Learning Theories and Methods

— The fourth set of questions revolves around the learning process. What learning theories are appropriate for the learners we serve and the objectives they seek? What learning methods help inform us of the appropriate curricular approach to take with specific learner populations? How do we focus the curriculum on the individual learner? The learning process becomes extremely important in the Learner-Centered Curriculum. An illustrative list appears in the full Learner-Centered Curriculum Diagram. It is not intended to be definitive. The Learner-Centered Curriculum builds upon effective curriculum design, delivery, and deployment methods.

— The American Psychological Association developed a 14 point learner-centered framework that provides an effective baseline in design.

— There are more than 50 major learning theories, each focused on a different aspect of learning or learner population.

— There is an inexorable link between learning theory and teaching/learning methodologies deployed in the classroom or online.

— Synthesizing effective curriculum requires the matching of theory and practice to learner population characteristics and objectives.

— For example in a study by R. Maki titled: Course: I. Learning and Satisfaction in on-line versus Lecture Courses. Published in Behavior Research Methods, Instruments, & Computers "Increased content knowledge was greater for students in web sections, as was in-class examinations performance. Use of the WWW and use of computers for academic purposes increased more in the online sections, and on-line students showed a greater decrease in computer anxiety. Students in the on-line sections expressed appreciation for course components and the convenience of the source, but lecture sections received higher ratings on course evaluations than on-line sections."

— The point here is to systematically build the curriculum to incorporate effective learning methods.

Learner-Centered Curriculum Architecture

— What does Curriculum Architecture mean? The architecture of a curriculum describes the style, method of design, basic construction, key components and underlying philosophies used to build the modules, courses, and programs that make up a curriculum. Across an institution's entire curriculum, many different approaches are represented.

— The overall architecture of the curriculum is a significant asset and should be considered in the overall plan.

— An institution's curriculum architecture details all of the specific models used to design, develop, deliver, assess, warrant, and market the curriculum.

— The curriculum architecture can also be used to synthesize an institution's comprehensive academic master plan.

— The architecture of a curriculum describes the style, method of design, basic construction, key components, and underlying philosophies used to build the modules, courses, and programs that make up the entire diverse curricula.

Learner-Centered Curriculum Configuration

— A particular curriculum configuration is drawn from the overall architectural options of the institution.

— The configuration is where all of the components of the model are used to construct a specific curriculum for a specific population seeking specific objectives using specific teaching, learning, and assessment methods.

— A particular curriculum configuration is drawn from the overall architectural options of the institution. As design, development, and deployment of new programs occurs we will want to enhance the process through what we learn in this engagement.

— Configuring curriculum also involves the deployment aspect meaning scheduling, pricing, locating, etc.

— Across an institution, a wide variety of curriculum configurations are deployed.

Learner-Centered Support Services

— Services are as important in the learner-centered curriculum as design. Advising, counseling, and assessment are among the most important processes that must be integrated into the curriculum. Too often they are add-ons and not built into the curriculum model.

— The curriculum alone is not sufficient to deliver effective and efficient learning. Services are also required to enable the learner to successfully engage and complete the learning process or processes.

— For example, assessment, advising, counseling, financial aid, and a host of other services are extremely important to the process of creating learner success.

— Appropriate services must be integrated (fused) with the curriculum design, development, and deployment processes.

ASSESSMENT PLANNING

Effective teachers constantly use assessment information in their daily interactions with students when making decisions about teaching and learning needs. It is recognised however that students need sufficient time and opportunities for learning to take place before decisions are made about their levels of achievement.

Teachers should also keep in mind the particular assessment and reporting needs of all students.

Teaching and learning strategies and assessment measures should allow differing groups of students to relate learning to their own experiences, knowledge and interests. This will enhance each student's ability to demonstrate learning outcomes.

At all levels, and particularly in the primary years, many of the key learning areas are taught in an integrated way. Nevertheless, teachers need to ensure that the approach to the eight key learning areas across the P-10 years is balanced and sequential. Planning for assessment is an essential part of this process. In planning for assessment, teachers need to ensure that they:

— include a variety of assessment strategies in their teaching programs to provide multiple sources of information about student achievement

— develop a manageable system of keeping records that can provide a rich mixture of observations of student learning

— use the data they have collected to make judgements about student achievement

Within schools, common interpretations can be developed by teachers discussing their assessments of students' work, developing assessment criteria together or keeping files of representative student work. Across schools common interpretations can be developed by teachers discussing and assessing sample student work together.

Planning For Extension

How do Teachers identify gifted children?

— Initially use the range of available checklists –parent – teacher – underachiever

— **Very important to consider the checklist for gifted underachievers because...**

— Many gifted students hide their ability and are therefore difficult to identify

— Have already shut down

— Don't want to stand out and so appear to 'fit in' with classmates

— May need formal assessment to determine the level of intellectual potential. Necessary with underachievers who may be functioning well below their capacity. Sometimes the student with the highest scores in the class can still be working significantly below their capacity.

How should Teachers develop individual classroom program?

— Encouragement of children to pursue a chosen interest in depth

— Teach on from what the children know. Using pre testing helps identify prior knowledge and thus avoids repetition.

  — activities that are more complex and require more abstract and higher-level thinking processes

  — greater flexibility in the use of material, time and resources

— Higher expectations for independence and persistence to task

— Provision of more opportunities to acquire and demonstrate leadership abilities

— Greater encouragement for creative and productive thinking, including higher level thinking

— More emphasis on interpreting the feelings and behaviour of self and others

— More opportunities to broaden the base of knowledge and enhance language abilities

— Encouragement of exploratory behaviour and risk taking.

Gifted students may study the same concepts, units and themes as the entire class. They simply require opportunities to become engaged with the curriculum on a more sophisticated level. At the same time you are creating instructional activities for the entire class, you may use a critical thinking model to develop alternative activities for gifted students that provide more challenge.

Why do Teachers need to "above level" test?

— Eliminates the chance of teaching children what they already know

— Helps teachers plan effectively

— Appropriately challenging curriculum helps reduce behaviour problems

— Pre-testing is essential, preferably before teachers commence planning for the following term or their next unit of work

Planning For Students With Disabilities and Impairments

In planning and developing an individual program for a student with a disability or impairment the Program Support Group will follow these five steps.

1. Understanding the student and the school

This will include:

— Sharing existing information and any previous reports or assessments.

— Identifying existing student skills and strengths.

— Identifying the most appropriate learning styles.

— Review of the school environment and identification of specific physical requirements.

2. Goal setting

The important issues in setting educational goals for the student are to:

— ensure all parties are in agreement with the goals;

— ensure the goals are a priority for the student;

— build on the strengths and skills of the student;

— understand the difference between long and short term goals, eg a long term goal may be to live independently while a short term goal may be to understand the value of numbers up to 10;

— ensure the goals are achievable, measurable and have a review date.

3. Program Planning

Schools have been provided with an educational planning format in the companions to the Course Advice for Students with Disabilities and Impairments. These companions were published during 1996-98 and are available within your school.

4. Implementation

The key question is how the program plan is to be implemented?

— What existing resources are available within the school?

— What other resources are available to assist the school in implementing the program plan?

— What additional resources need to be purchased to achieve the educational goals and implement the program plan?

5. Evaluation

It is essential that the educational goals set for the student are evaluated on the stated review date. This will allow program support group meetings to be planned in advance. The evaluation process will lead to the setting of new educational goals and programs and may involve a change in the resource mix to best meet the changing needs of the student.

Planning With Student Welfare in Mind

Teachers, student support staff and families have long shared the goal and challenge of helping students to learn and develop in a safe and supportive environment. In every educational institutions the well being of students needs to be considered foremost, both to encourage students' readiness to learn and engage with others and to ensure that curriculum content is relevant to students' personal, intellectual and social development.

The chief emphasis is on primary prevention and early intervention as the most effective means of building resilience in young people and minimising the problems of well being which may otherwise persist into adulthood.

Student Welfare and Support develops policy advice and assistance to schools in a wide range of areas which affect student well being and which in turn impact on students' capacity to benefit from school curriculum programs:

The Student Code of Conduct

— Child protection from abuse and neglect, including protocols and mandatory reporting responsibilities of schools

— Bullying and violence

— Student Attendance

— Alternative/ancillary programs

Student Welfare and Support also undertakes the active promotion of student well being and primary prevention via some particular initiatives which emphasise whole school approaches, partnerships and continuity of care:

Health Promoting Schools

Health Promoting Schools are essentially those which actively seek to promote health and positively enhance the well being of students and staff. Health Promoting Schools Project of Deakin University aims to establish an interactive network of Health Promoting Schools and to strengthen the capacity of schools to be healthy settings for living, learning and working, through the process of organisational development towards health. A key idea underlying this HPS initiative is that schools have considerable potential to provide opportunities for students, staff, parents and community members to lead healthy lives and become participants in the improvement of society's health.

The HPS Project has provided 100 pilot schools with:

— funding for regional based professional development concerning the Health Promoting School concept as well as specialist health issue workshops;

— opportunities to make links with other schools;

— support in establishing links with community agencies;

— the opportunity to be part of a Health Promoting Schools network;

— resources such as the Health Promoting Schools Video and Atlas: Mapping the Health Promoting School. Curriculum & Standards Framework and Beyond.

School Focused Youth Services (SFYS)

These initiative aims to assist the implementation of an integrated service model to provide coordinated health and welfare services to 'at risk' young people within local schools and community clusters.

Student learning cannot be separated from student welfare and we as teachers all share responsibility to actively promote student well being. Effective curriculum planning needs teachers to help generate a positive learning environment where students feel valued, supported and connected with the school community. Factors that place young people at risk of harm, alienation and behaviour problems can be moderated if students experience a sense of attachment or connection to the school.

Every teacher has a vital role as a source of support and determinant of success for students. "The most frequently encountered positive role model in the lives of resilient children outside the family circle, was a favourite teacher who was not just an instructor for academic skills for the youngsters, but also a confident and positive role model for personal identification". Teachers are in a prime position to pick up and act on 'early warning signals' eg passivity, persistent low spirits, agitation, withdrawal, aggressiveness. A teacher's concern and interest are a powerful starting point for response. The added support and perspective of other teachers, student support staff, other students, family and community-based services can often make the vital difference to ensure that planned curriculum hits the mark with all students.

INCORPORATING LEARNING TECHNOLOGIES IN CURRICUMLUM PLANNING

When planning curriculum for students, Education Boards inform teachers' planning and provide a framework for determining the content of the curriculum.

Other considerations include providing for:

— Different learning styles,

— Metacognitive thinking,

— Authentic learning,

— Integrated learning,

— Reflective learning,

— Cooperative learning,

— Active learning,

— Inquiry learning,

— Digital literacy,

— Integration of ICT

The teacher's role is one of a guide, co-learner, constructor and facilitator. There are a number of digital resources now available to support teachers planning new ways of learning.

Tomorrow's workforce requires people who :

— can apply maths and science principles at work

— are comfortable with new information technology

— are willing to retrain continually and upgrade skills

— are team players

— can think logically and critically

— can solve problems

— are entrepreneurial and innovative

— can manage people and information, and

— are effective communicators

Skills that students require are:

— Literacy and numeracy

— Technological capabilities

— Resiliance and flexibility

— Communication skills and exchange of ideas

— Awareness and appreciation of cultures

— Vision and open mindedness

— Critical thinking skills and adaptability

— Teamwork and community service

— Awareness of one's own choices

— Commitment to personal and community growth

INTERDISCIPLINARY CURICULUM PLANNING

In his literature class, Mr. Cline gives students the dates of the birth and death of a famous author, and asks them to figure out how old the author was when she died. Silence falls over the class as students scratch their heads in frustration. One student exclaims, "It's hard to do math in English class!"

How often do we find our students reluctant or unable to recognize and use knowledge they already posses to help them solve new problems or understand new, related concepts? This phenomena can be directly tied to the ways in which students initially learn information. In an educational era where tremendous emphasis is placed upon specialized knowledge, the segregated clustering of subject area instruction often prevents students from identifying important interconnections among the subjects they study. The challenge for teachers is to find a healthy and meaningful balance between curricular breadth and depth. The long history of research on the ways in which students learn provides a strong rationale for the value of interdisciplinary instruction. In the 17th and 18th centuries, predecessors of modern psychology, including and Hartley, speculated that meaningful learning involved the formulation of associated between concepts. More recent research in cognitive science strongly supports this view.

The work of Ausubel, Neisser, and others in the 1960's and 1970's led to our current notion of schematic structures in the brain. These schematic structures, composed of hundreds, sometimes thousands, of interconnected bits of information, serve as a framework for our knowledge. The goodness of our schematic structures is highly dependent upon the way in which we initially process information presented to us. Ausubel referred to these associations as 'cognitive hooks'. Instruction which provides students with links to connect otherwise discrete bits of knowledge enhances their ability to recognize and apply prior knowledge to new, related learning situations.

Obstacles

Although the development of integrated learning experiences is important, we teachers often find it difficult to plan such experiences for our students. While a current emphasis on a 'whole language' orientation in the elementary curriculum assists us as we help students understand relationships among reading, writing, and oral language, most middle and secondary school curricula retain a nonintegrated approach to subject matter instruction. Textbooks and teachers' guides rarely emphasize relationships between the subject area of major concentration and other disciplines.

As a result, teachers have neither the information nor the time needed to realistically include interdisciplinary experiences in curricular planning. While we cannot always change the existing middle and high school curricular materials rapidly or directly, we can employ a planning process which will allow us to periodically incorporate cross-disciplinary ideas and activities into our repertoire of instructional strategies.

Guidelines for Planning

While each of us has particular subject matter expertise, we have also accumulated knowledge and developed interests in other areas. Additionally, we have access to colleagues whose subject matter concentrations differ from our own. Using these resources, we can conceptualize and construct instructional lessons which help students understand important and interesting relationships between the disciplines.

The guidelines below can help us as we develop interdisciplinary lessons.

Formulate a goal statement which indicates the principle(s) or concept(s) to be understood at the completion of the lesson. What are the primary pieces of information or concepts that you want students to understand? Often, interdisciplinary lessons do not concentrate on the mastery of specific skills. By their very nature, these lessons usually focus on the application of skills and knowledge to novel situations. For this reason, goals of interdisciplinary lessons will usually involve helping students understand how the skills and knowledge they possess can be combined to accomplish a task, discover a solution, or explain a situation.

Select the primary content base which will serve as the catalyst for instruction. Often, the content base will be determined by the text. There are times, however, when your goal necessitates the use of other, ancillary materials. In either case, determine the primary vehicle which will drive the instruction (e.g., a work of art or literature, a scientific or mathematical principle, an event or era in history, etc.)

Identify events, discoveries, and writings within other disciplines that relate to the primary content base in a meaningful way. Through talking with colleagues and brainstorming on your own, consider information in other disciplines that seem to relate to the primary content. At this point, you may find it helpful to look at the table of contents in the textbooks you will be using. However, don't discount your own expertise, the films or plays you've seen, the books or magazine articles you've read, and your life experience.

Determine the key points of intersection between the disciplines which correspond to the established terminal goal of instruction. As you investigate each cross-discipline idea in more depth, keep your terminal goal well in mind. It is often the case that we become so enthralled in the idea itself that we lose sight of our major instructional intent. While this is intellectually enjoyable, it is a time-consuming luxury that few of us can afford. Some ideas will probably need to be discarded, either because they are too complex, or because they do not fully address the goal. Other ideas may be so compelling and enlightening that you may want to revise the terminal goal to reflect new insights you have gained.

Formulate instructional objectives. Again, it should be noted that most interdisciplinary lessons will not focus on the mastery of specific skills. Nevertheless, it is important to determine what you expect your students to be able to do when they have completed the lesson. As in other instructional planning, objectives serve as the springboard for the development of the instructional strategies and activities you will use.

Identify the necessary prerequisite knowledge that students must possess in each discipline area you will address. Interdisciplinary instruction can fall apart if students lack knowledge of key principles or concepts within each discipline. Carefully consider the prerequisite skills students must have before they can successfully accomplish the objectives you have set forth. Sometimes, missing skills or pieces of information can be taught rather quickly. However, when this is not the case, it will be necessary to revise the interdisciplinary content.

Formulate instructional strategies which will compel students to use their knowledge in one discipline to better understand and appreciate another. Students are not used to activating their knowledge in one discipline while studying another. For this reason, it is important to develop activities which require this transfer in a purposeful way. Depending upon the content and timeframe of instruction, you may want to use conceptual mapping, in-class debates, group projects, and/or a variety of discovery techniques to accomplish your goal. The critical component of interdisciplinary lessons, as in most instruction, is active and invested participation.

4

FACTORS INFLUENCING CURRICULUM PLANNING

The term curriculum is used in a number of different ways by parents, educators, and businesses. Some see curriculum as the "academic stuff that is done to children in school." Others view it as teacher directions and student activities that can be purchased from any number of curriculum publishers. Teachers themselves use the term in different ways depending on their views and needs. In any school staff room one may hear statements about curriculum such as the following:

— "There's not enough time in the day to get through the curriculum!"

— "The reading curriculum's great but I hate that math curriculum."

— "I found this great curriculum website the other day that has all kinds of ideas for science lessons!"

— "The kids are really making progress since I began modifying the curriculum to better meet their needs."

Webster's concisely defines curriculum as, "A course of study offered by a school". Curriculum is also often referred to as learning content, activities, and structures as experienced by students. Ronald C. Doll, in his book, Curriculum Improvement: Decision Making and Process, goes further, stating that:

> The curriculum of a school is the formal and informal content and process by which learners gain knowledge and understanding, develop skills, and alter attitudes, appreciations, and values under he auspices of that school.

It is this last definition that is perhaps the most useful to educators who wish to affect and improve student learning. Partially this is because it lacks the vagueness that many definitions have, and partially it is because curriculum, as Doll has defined it, can have outcomes that may be measured, allowing for the curriculum to be acted upon and improved.

CURRICULUM-INSTRUCTION RELATIONSHIP

Instruction is the creation and implementation of purposefully developed plans for the teaching of curriculum content. It is what teachers often concisely refer to as "planning" and "teaching." The relationship between curriculum and instruction is so intimate that "curriculumandinstruction" is frequently spoken as if it were one word (perhaps we should refer to it as "curstruction" or "instriculum"). With curriculum being the content of what is taught along with an overall process of how that content is to be taught, and instruction being the more detailed plans and the way those plans are implemented in order to teach the curriculum content, it becomes easy to understand that the two must be compatible in order to maximize student learning.

The case of multiage classrooms illustrates this close tie that exists between curriculum and instruction. Currently the most common classroom structure in American elementary schools is the single-grade classroom. This structure is meant to make instruction more efficient, allowing students of the same age to move through curriculum content at the same pace. In these classrooms the most prevalent teaching method is whole-class direct instruction. Because of the dominance of this structure nation-wide, commercially available curriculum and state learning standards are designed to be implemented in this type of learning environment. Some educators in their efforts to improve education have switched from a single-grade classroom structure to a multiage one.

The multiage structure purposefully places students of different ages together in the same classroom while supporting an individualized continuous progress instructional model. While changing the structure of the classroom, multiage educators also change the instructional methods they use in order to better match the needs of their diverse group of students. They have found that "curriculum designed for use in single-grade classrooms is not always adaptable to environments in which whole-class direct instruction is not the norm. Allowing for flexible groupings, academic diversity, and individual pacing are needs that are central to multiage practices". The instructional methods used by these teachers necessitate that curriculum be organized in a compatible manner.

BASES FOR CURRICULUM PLANNING

When planning for curriculum improvement, two categories of bases should be understood, those that are institutional in nature and those that affect people directly. The institutional bases for curriculum planning include planning domains, the context or characteristics of the school situation, the impact of current trends and issues, and the use of strategic planning. Those bases of curriculum planning that affect people directly include student and teacher needs, local curriculum problems to be addressed, competencies of the planners, and pressures from inside and outside the school. All of these bases affect the curriculum planning process in various ways and to differing degrees. They can also vary with each situation over time.

As of this writing, a current educational issue in the United States is that of student performance and preparation for the workplace. The trend is for state governments to create standards of competence that are tested at various points in students' educational careers and to make schools and students accountable for their performance on these tests. Test scores are frequently reported in the local media and this may lead to pressure from the local population being brought to bear on the school to improve its curricula.

The context of the school may be that it is within a district that hasn't passed a school levy for a number of years and thus has not been able to budget money to work on improving the curricula during that time. This not-uncommon scenario shows how a combination of factors can become the bases for, and can influence the curriculum planning process.

CRITERIA TO PLAN, DEVELOP, AND IMPLEMENT CURRICULA

Ronald Doll lists eleven principles of decision making and process as it relates to the evaluation of curricula and projects. These principles form the criteria of a quality curriculum development process that includes the stages of planning, development, and implementation. Curriculum decisions should be made:

— for valid educational reasons.

— on the basis of the best available evidence.

— in a context of broadly conceived aims of education

— within a context of previously made decisions and of needs for additional decision making so that balance and other important curriculum considerations may be safeguarded.

— by achieving a resolution of forces originating in the nature and development of learners, the nature of learning processes, demands of the society at large, requirements of the local community, and the nature and structure of subject matter to be learned.

— cooperatively by persons who are legitimately involved in the effects of the decisions.

— taking into account new facts of human life such as the proliferation of knowledge and a need for a new sense of unity within the diversity.

— taking into account the many differences among learners.

— with a realistic view of certain organizational or engineering matters that can affect the quality of the decisions themselves.

— with some forethought about ways in which they may be communicated and shared.

— only with reference to subject matter and pupil experiences that cannot be offered as satisfactorily outside the school.

INFLUENCE OF VALUES ON CURRICULUM PLANNING

Social forces that can influence curriculum planning come from far and wide. The ideas and values of various groups of people may include their social goals, ideas about cultural uniformity and diversity, social pressures, ideas about social change, their plans for the future, and their concepts of culture. An example of this can be seen when contrasting the CYFERNet and the Catalyst: Voices of Chicago School Reform websites. The Children, Youth, and Families Education and Research Network website, CYFERNet is designed to provide "...program, evaluation and technology assistance for children, youth and family community-based programs".

The website is a collaborative project that "...is funded (by) the U.S. Department of Agriculture's Cooperative State Research, Education, and Extension Service and the Cooperative Extension System". Because of this, many of the curriculum links are to agricultural and 4-H educational activities. In contrast, the CATALYST: Voices of Chicago School Reform website sponsored by the Community Renewal Society, works "...to create racially and economically just communities". Its focus is on Chicago area urban educational issues, especially in regards to race and the economically disadvantaged. It provides information to help influence educational decision making as it relates to the organization's mission.

On the one hand is a group that wishes to influence educational policy (and thus curriculum) to better meet the needs of children in an urban environment, and on the other a group trying to do the same for rural children. Although there may be a few communities where the two groups compete with one another, they do illustrate how the values and issues of various social groups can try to influence curriculum planning.

CURRICULUM FOUNDATION

At the foundation to every curriculum, including the planning, design, and implementation stages, is the educational philosophy of those directly involved in the process. Often this can influence to a great extent the direction a school or school district takes with its curriculum and instruction. At the school district this writer has been employed with, the philosophy has allowed for a diversity of instructional styles as a way of meeting a diversity of children's learning styles.

This has led in the elementary school to several educational options available for students and parents: single-grade, single-grade clusters, multiage, looping, and home-school hybrid educational environments. Because some of these educational structures have different instructional designs than others, there are available different curricular materials. Other nearby schools offer only a single choice and a single curriculum. The basis for these decisions can be found in the above mentioned factors as well as in the educational philosophies of the decision makers.

DEVELOPING THE CURRICULUM

Many different resources are employed to achieve an effective teaching-learning environment. One important resource consists of curriculum materials, which are often synonymous with instructional materials. These materials play a key role in helping to motivate, teach, and evaluate students. Some individuals even go so far as to say that curriculum materials are the crucial factors in determining whether an individual learner succeeds, not the instructor. Whereas arguments could be made against such a statement, educators must not underestimate the role that quality curriculum materials can have in an effective teaching-learning environment.

Even with the variety of career and technical and technical curriculum materials available today, the curriculum developer is often faced with the need to produce new materials. This need becomes evident when materials are required for a certain instructional situation and are not available. Furthermore, a need may be established when the available materials are not appropriate for an intended audience or when their use is limited by other factors that might prohibit an instructor from using them with established instructional objectives. During the development process, consideration must be given to factors such as time and dollars available, the audience, and the development alternatives. In addition, the actual development process must take on a logical and orderly format to assure that usable materials are produced.

ROOTS OF HEALTHY CURRICULUM

Public education has always had the goal of helping to both maintain and to recreate a healthy democracy. Individual students are helped to learn the values of society as well as ways they can be personally successful and contribute to the success of their nation. Sometimes the emphasis has been on the economic health of the country, sometimes the political health, and sometimes the technological health of the society.

Roots of educational curriculum in the twentieth century

During early 20th century curriculum delivery was centered around the recitations. It was considered the focal center towards which all school activities converge. Basically this was when the teacher used a combination of conversation, lecture, and questioning to teach new information while tying it to previous lessons and preparing students for future lessons. Its design consisted of four parts: the introduction, the development, the drill, and the summary. Its usefulness was to impart selected knowledge from the teacher to the student, this at a time when "graded schools" were just making their presence known.

The introduction of the graded school, in which students were separated by age into sequential groups or classes (know then as classification), was considered the most modern and scientific approach to education. It created a model through which children progressed in efficient steps throughout their education, which, for most children near the beginning of the twentieth century, ended before the eighth grade. In 1918 only about six percent of the children entering elementary schools in the United States reached the eighth grade. States published books outlining the curriculum, including content, that students were to learn in each grade. This lock-step approach to structuring education has been termed the factory model of schooling. This design brought with it more than the arrangement of students around an age-based curriculum.

This approach was characterized by top-down management in which the administration designed, monitored and inspected work, rather than relying on the knowledge and abilities of the people doing the work. As a result, teachers made decisions based on rules and procedures found in textbooks and curriculum guides, on tests, and in grading and promotion policies. These guidelines were developed and handed down by others rather than based on the teacher's own understanding of learning and teaching strategies appropriate for diverse learners.

Throughout the industrial period, a time in which the majority of working adults held blue collar jobs, the factory model of education worked relatively well. It helped maintain the health of the democracy, in general providing students with the skills and values necessary for success in the society of that age. It must be noted that during this time, from the beginning of the century through its middle, more and more children attended and completed higher levels of education than ever before.

Educational curriculum in the twenty-first century

As the world has moved out of its industrial age, new skills become important for individual success as well as for economic and technological health. This transitional period has of course found its reflection in the educational arena. Pressure from the economic sector as well as the political sector has been brought to bear on educators. The cry is for higher standards, perhaps what is really meant is different standards.

Blue collar jobs that the majority of people once held will make up only 10 percent of total employment, and the jobs that are replacing them require levels of knowledge and skill previously taught to only a few students. The education challenge facing the United States is not that its schools are not as good as they once were. It is that schools must help a larger number of young people reach levels of skill and competence once thought to be within the reach of only a few.

Curriculum is currently changing as we pass through this age of transition. The aspect of educational life that is reflective of society is being asked to catch up with what is current. The aspect of education that is a driver of society is being drawn along by representatives through the use of standards and high-stakes testing. As this happens, the curriculum, the structure of schooling, and the role of the teacher goes through a process of change.

As always, students will need to gain the ability to think, to use knowledge they have acquired to solve problems, and to attain a level of wisdom appropriate for their maturity. Although memorizing the multiplication tables will likely never go out of style, the emphasis of curriculum will move away from factual knowledge to conceptual understanding and to skills needed to locate and use knowledge for any variety of purposes.

The structure of public education will also change. It is generally recognized that at least a certain part of every child's day in school should be given over to the child's own plans and purposes, and that an opportunity should be made in this period for help in carrying out such plans and purposes. In the twenty-first century, after education has moved through the present transition, the barriers to individual pacing for students will be lifted. Students' own plans and purposes will again be important within the framework of educational road maps. Technology's promise of open communication and dialogue will help to decentralize the schools. Virtual classrooms will allow small groups of students access to courses that may be initiated from anywhere in the world.

The move over the past fifty years to centralize students into ever larger schools in order to efficiently and economically offer more classes will no longer be an issue. Schools will once again be community or neighborhood based geographically and physically being comprised of much smaller student bodies, thus supporting closer connections between students and adults.

Teachers in this new structure will still be important, their job description will simply change. In US, a recent public agenda poll asked, "What is the most important thing public schools need in order to help students learn?" The top response by far was "good teachers". What the people polled in this survey meant by "good teachers" varied, however it might be summed up as follows: knowledgeable managers of students, ideas, and learning experiences that help develop compassionate links between all of these elements.

In the future the teacher may lose much of the student management aspect of the job, at least in the way we currently view it. Students will not be limited by age or geographical location to learning opportunities, instead they will likely be engaged in small fluid learning groups organized around specific educational needs or interests. The learning experiences that best match their group will be available through the use of technology, a technology that will seem as invisible as a pencil is today, it will simply be a tool of learning.

In 1959 West Virginia Governor Cecil H. Underwood submitted his predictions for the future of education to the NEA. These were placed in a time capsule that was opened 50 years later. His predictions for the dawn of the twenty-first century sound similar to those many educators now foresee for the future of the mid-twenty-first century.

> ...the erosion of "rigid schedules, formal classes, and arbitrary norms and standards of pupil achievement." He painted a picture of a world of seemingly unlimited human knowledge, which students would be helped to explore rather than digest, the goal being "the pursuit of truth-not its capture."
>
> And although he couldn't have had the Internet in mind, Mr. Underwood wrote that the "barriers to communication-which, in a direct way, affect the educational opportunity of many of our people," would by 1999 be reduced to "insignificance" by technology.

In the 21st century, public education will be different. Education will be more individualized yet more community based. Public education will be less about a fixed location and fixed schedule, and much more about learning anytime and anywhere. Technology or E-learning will penetrate every aspect of education and change it. n the future, schools will be more fluid, teachers more adaptable and flexible, and students will be more accountable as the task of learning becomes theirs.

DEVELOPMENTAL TRENDS

It was once believed that children were simply new people that only lacked the knowledge of adults in order to be mature and wise. If this were really true, education would simply be the passing down of knowledge from one generation to the next.

Now we understand that people think and reason differently during different stages of their lives. The way a child of three thinks is qualitatively different than the way a child of fifteen does. Further, as has been stated by Piaget, the stages that people pass through are followed in a sequential order, with none of the stages being skipped or followed in a different order. Children from birth through eleven or more years of age go through four cognitive stages. Basically these stages show that the way children learn and make sense of the world changes from concrete manipulation to abstract manipulation of objects and information as they move through these stages.

Teachers strive to have all of their students be academically successful throughout their school years and beyond. This most often manifests itself through educators determining what it means to be a successful student and then trying to find ways to help diverse sets of students reach those expectations. Embedded within those expectations and driving many of the strategies employed by teachers is a knowledge of the cognitive stages of development as outlined above. However, when looked at from the students' perspective, there is a different agenda of tasks that must be accomplished in order for the student to feel successful at different stages of their development. A study reported by James E. Gay, Robert B. Williams, and Joan B. Flagg-Williams found the following examples of developmental tasks.

1. Examples of developmental tasks of a girl in kindergarten included:

   — Being accepted by adults.

   — Dressing in ways pleasing to adults.

   — Being accepted by a significant adult (e.g., teacher) outside of the home.

   — Seeing herself as a contributing member of the class - helping other kids.

   — Developing reading and writing skills.

— Speaking before the class.

— Developing relationships with peers/classmates.

— Developing socially acceptable ways of expressing her emotions rather than crying.

— Self-evaluation skills in relation to academics.

2. A second-grade boy's developmental tasks were identified as:

— A desire to feel loved.

— Intending to improve his skills.

— Needing to have successful and rewarding school experiences.

— Developing appropriate coping mechanisms.

— Relating to and obtaining nurture from significant adults (e.g., teacher).

— Being able to tell people when he is hurting.

— Developing a relationship with his parents.

3. Some developmental tasks a sixth-grade girl was thought to be working on included:

— Academic survival -avoiding failure.

— Getting caught up in school work.

— Seeking positive attention.

— Attempting to please teachers.

— Gaining acceptance of peers.

4. An adolescent male's developmental tasks were identified as:

— Establishing a personal and unique identity.

— Planning for his future education and work.

— Developing work habits.

— Collaborating with peers to establish a living arrangement away from his family.

When looked at together, these developmental tasks and the cognitive developmental stages discussed earlier can provide educators with a picture of child development as students pass through the school years. Although, as implied above, there are some general age spans that can be determined for each developmental stage, students often move through these stages at different rates. For instance, "...because gifted children often begin understanding and using concepts at an earlier age, they are said to be more adept at understanding and using abstraction" while they also seem to move more rapidly within and frequently between stages.

Developmentally appropriate educational practices

What does this mean to educators? How can an understanding of cognitive developmental stages and developmental tasks help educators plan and implement a curriculum that is developmentally appropriate, one that helps insure student success and promotes life-long learning?

First of all a commitment to a child-centered (or student-centered) educational program is important. A child-centered program is one in which educators first strive to meet student needs. The antithesis of this would be a curriculum-centered approach which places the mastering of predetermined curriculum goals over that of meeting student needs. In order for a child to be successful, they need to meet the needs of their own developmental tasks. As they do this they will be grounded and ready to be engaged by a developmentally appropriate academic curriculum.

Because people think qualitatively different at different stages of their development, learning activities need to match the way each child successfully gains understanding and makes connections. In order for students to be actively engaged with their learning, the educator should assess their cognitive levels and determine their strengths and weaknesses. From this information the teacher should then individualize instruction as much as possible. Those students in the earliest developmental stages will need to manipulate real objects in ways that help them learn patterns and see connections. Students in later stages will need the chance to abstractly manipulate information and be given "...opportunities to communicate with one another, to argue and debate issues...to make mistakes and learn from them".

Although this looks as if the best educational structure would be to group students by developmental level, it is not. The work of Lev S. Vygotsky shows that there are other factors that need to be considered by educators when structuring classrooms and planning for instruction. A student's "...actual developmental level refers to all the functions and activities that a child can perform on his own, independently without the help of anyone else. On the other hand, the zone of proximal development includes all the functions and activities that a child or a learner can perform only with the assistance of someone else.

The person who intervenes in this scaffolding process could be an adult (parent, teacher, caretaker, language instructor) or another peer who has already mastered that particular function". It is in this zone of proximal development, while social interaction is happening, that substantiative learning occurs. One way to effectively take advantage of this is to structure classrooms heterogeneously, to insure a diversity of skills and abilities. Since the boundary between any two developmental levels is not absolute and since a child can simultaneously exhibit traits from two different developmental levels, a heterogeneous mix of students will likely include children with developmental traits from two or more levels.

When studying factors that make up exemplary programs for limited English proficient (LEP) students, researchers found that "...(m)ost sites emphasize cooperative learning in untracked classes, in which students with different proficiency levels work together in groups. The exemplary schools demonstrate the power of cooperative learning as a tool to unleash students' ability to learn from one another. Some schools use practical strategies for keeping students with the same teacher(s) for several years. These students develop a sense of identity with their group; moreover the teachers are more easily able to coach them through their development as learners.

Instead of placing students who lag behind in remedial classes, some schools assume that all students can learn to high levels and use an accelerated learning environment to get students on track quickly". These practices that work so well for students learning a new language also work well with students in any learning endeavour.Just as structure looks different for developmentally appropriate practices, so do classroom lessons. The following list of learning activities are examples illustrating appropriate strategies for students at various developmental levels.

Primary - Teddy Bear Picnic

> Primary aged students need to manipulate real world objects in order to learn. This mathematics lesson has kindergarten aged students physically grouping their own teddy bears based on attributes that they come up with.

Intermediate - Seed Dispersal

> This science lesson has elementary aged children create and test model seeds, comparing them to those found in nature. Children at this age need to make connections between the real and the abstract by observing and manipulating both. The way this learning activity requires students to look closely at real plant seeds and at the same time create mental abstractions that they turn into models, lends itself well to this developmental level.

Secondary - Collaborative Poetry!

> Secondary students generally can learn abstractly and are working on establishing their unique identity. This language

arts learning activity, in which students collaboratively write poetry, lends itself to the developmental needs of this age group .

Other developmentally appropriate practices can be found in structures defined as multiage, nongraded, differentiated, and student-centered or child-centered. Whatever the label, educators striving to include developmentally appropriate practices as a part of their curriculum decisions should consider the following guidelines:

A. Developmentally appropriate curriculum provides for all areas of a child's development: physical, emotional, social, linguistic, aesthetic, and cognitive.

B. Curriculum includes a broad range of content across disciplines that is socially relevant, intellectually engaging, and personally meaningful to children.

C. Curriculum builds upon what children already know and are able to do (activating prior knowledge) to consolidate their learning and to foster their acquisition of new concepts and skills.

D. Effective curriculum plans frequently integrate across traditional subject-matter divisions to help children make meaningful connections and provide opportunities for rich conceptual development; focusing on one subject is also a valid strategy at times.

E. Curriculum promotes the development of knowledge and understanding, processes and skills, as well as the dispositions to use and apply skills and to go on learning.

F. Curriculum content has intellectual integrity, reflecting the key concepts and tools of inquiry of recognized disciplines in ways that are accessible and achievable for young children, ages 3 through 8. Children directly participate in study of the disciplines, for instance, by conducting scientific experiments, writing, performing, solving mathematical problems, collecting and analyzing data, collecting oral history, and performing other roles of experts in the disciplines.

G. Curriculum provides opportunities to support children's home culture and language while also developing all children's abilities to participate in the shared culture of the program and the community.

H. Curriculum goals are realistic and attainable for most children in the designated age range for which they are designed.

I. When used, technology is physically and philosophically integrated in the classroom curriculum and teaching.

Helping all students be successful during their school years by engaging them in a developmentally appropriate and student-centered program can insure their success as life-long leaners after they graduate. When a person views them self as a learner, understands that learning is a key to attaining their goals, and finds learning enjoyable, then they will seek out learning opportunities throughout their life. Developmentally appropriate practices in school can provide a foundation to support this.

All of this may lead one to wonder at the current trend in the United States to enact school reform through standards and accountability methods. This trend encourages a curriculum-centered rather than a child-centered approach to education. Current methods based on standards are the result of a three-pronged government approach to school reform. First are the creation of standards. These standards in many states have become the foundation to grade specific frameworks, detailed lists describing what academic skills a child should master at any particular age. Rarely do these frameworks allow for the reality of students who are differently-paced than the age level norm.

The second part of the approach is to measure academic progress with standardized testing. These tests are either criterion referenced in which student scores are compared relative to a set standard deemed adequate for success, or they are norm referenced in which student scores are compared with other same-aged students who took the test. Although standardized testing may allow for success of the average developmental level of the students who are being tested, they do not necessarily allow for success of students whose developmental pace is different.

The third part of this reform movement has to do with accountability. Consequences are created, both positive and negative, based on student test scores. It is this aspect that changes standardized tests from a tool that can inform instruction to high-stakes tests that can move schools away from child-centered approaches and towards curriculum-centered ones. Increasingly early childhood experts say, that (the solution to increasing a school's scores) becomes that school's need to downplay exploration, hands-on learning, and flexible curriculum to drill students in specific, structured academic content...'We're comfortable with the idea that kids walk and talk at different ages, but we're not comfortable with that happening with reading, writing, and arithmetic,' says Gronlund. 'It's accountability that's the crux of the problem, not standards'".

5

Curriculum Effectiveness and Efficiency

The new information and communication technologies has profoundly affected education in the twenty-first century. Due to its availability, there has been a major shift from teacher-centered learning to student centered learning. The teacher is no longer the primary source of information for the student who now has access to indefinite sources of information. The role of the teacher has moved from that of *sage on the stage* to that of *guide on the side.* The student no longer depends primarily on the perceptions of the teacher but develops his/her perceptions and constructs his/her learning from multiple sources. More than ever before students are being encouraged by effective instruction that integrates the World Wide Web to be independent, life-long learners who are skillful in communication and collaboration.

Although strategies for teaching have changed in the Internet Age, the process of developing curriculum for onsite and online learning is fundamentally the same. Curriculum is a plan for learning that includes targeting a student population, conducting a needs assessment, and writing a mission statement. It includes developing goals, objectives, content, teaching strategies, and assessment tools. Alignment is critical in curriculum development from purpose and philosophy, to goals and objectives, to content and activities, and to assessment and evaluation. Working through a process of asking and answering who, what, where, why, when, how questions is important in designing and developing curriculum.

Some of the essential questions to be asked and answered include the following: Who are the *students or the audience in online learning?* What are their needs? What can teachers learn from a review of relevant educational about meeting the education needs of the specific students? How can they develop rubrics that outline how individual and group assignments are to be evaluated?

A review of current onsite and online educational courses reveals student inquiry should be at the center of learning, not the teacher. The instructor facilitates and moderates the coursework. The learning community is especially significant. Students need to participate in interactive, collaborative, participatory activities either onsite and/or online. Participants need to be involved in authentic learning, problem solving, critical thinking, decision making, and online projects. Small classes are broken down into smaller working groups. Students are required to be familiar with minimal technologies.

A review of onsite and online educational course models reveals that goals for learning should be demonstrable and objectives need to be measurable. Instructional units include two major components: basic information with links to resources and activities, assignments, and discussion questions. Rubrics that specifically outline how individual and group assignments are to be assessed should be available.

In onsite and online teaching there is a tendency to develop learning activities prematurely. There is a tendency to avoid mission statements and planning assessments until the end of the process. However, the order of the process of curriculum development is significant. The students must be identified, their needs should be assessed, and measurement evaluation ought to be considered early in the process. Goals, objectives, content, and teaching strategies should be carefully developed and aligned. Alignment is critical in curriculum development from purpose and philosophy, to goals and objectives, to content and activities, and to assessment and evaluation.

Curriculum design involves working through a process of asking and answering who, what, where, why, when, how questions. Effective onsite and online courses are designed for small classes that are divided into smaller working groups. The instructor functions as a facilitator or moderator with a constructivist or inductive approach. In this process the student constructs his/her meaning as the instructor guides, facilitates, or moderates the learning.

Student inquiry is at the center of the educational process. Students are often involved in interactive, collaborative, participatory project or problem-based learning. More than ever before students are being encouraged by effective curriculum design to be independent, life-long learners who are skillful in communication and collaboration.

CONCEPT-BASED CURRICULUM

A concept is an idea that is timeless, abstract, broad and can be shown through a variety of examples. Conflict, change and perspective are concepts. Examples of the concept change can be found in social studies (historical events), science (erosion), literature (characters) and mathematics (trading).

Two jobs that concepts have are to focus the study of topics and integrate the curriculum. Looking at a topic through a concept gives the study a focus. For example, the topic fairy tales can be looked at through the concept culture. With this focus, students can study fairy tales from different cultures. They can find similarities and differences in fairy tales in order to understand the effect that culture has on literature. Without the focus of a concept, only factual learning takes place.

Concepts, due to their broad nature, provide opportunities for curriculum integration. Culture could be used to integrate language arts (fairy tales from different countries) with social studies (geography). Also, because concepts are timeless, they are relevant to students' lives. The study of topics, guided by the focus of culture, allows students to develop an understanding and hopefully acceptance of people of different cultures.

Skills are embedded in the study of a topic. For example when studying fairy tales through the concept of culture, map skills can be taught. As students notice cultural elements in fairy tales, they can locate the countries from which the fairy tales originated. Language arts skills can be taught as students write their own fairy tales and compare and contrast versions of fairy tales from different cultures.

When teachers base their instruction on concepts, they can expect their students to learn more than just facts. During a concept-based unit of study, students are given many examples of concepts. Through these examples of concepts from the topic, students notice common elements. Discussion, guided by carefully planned and also spontaneous questions, helps students form generalizations.

A generalization is a statement that shows a relationship between two or more concepts. The formation of a generalization by students is the objective a teacher strives for in her lessons. The ability to generalize using examples from a topic shows that students have achieved genuine understanding. In teaching a fairy tale unit, the teacher would strategically present students with appropriate examples of cultural elements found in fairy tales. Then after discussion, the teacher would guide students to form the generalization, "Literature reflects elements of a culture."

Instruction based on conceptual generalizations is an effective way for students to genuinely understand topics, but more importantly, it is an effective way to teach students to think.

Importance of concepts-base curriculum

Teachers are faced with the task of covering an enormous number of topics during the school year. Just because a topic has been "covered" does not mean that understanding has taken place. A week after the topic has been covered, students may remember almost nothing or only a few unrelated facts about the topic.

Lynn Erickson is an educational consultant who works with schools and districts, including District 118, around the country with curriculum design. In her book; Stirring the Head, Heart, and Soul, she states, "Under the older fact-based paradigm, depth of instruction meant teaching more facts about a topic. In the newer paradigm, depth of instruction means teaching higher level thinking related to a significant concept and theme, problem, or issue by connecting ideas across disciplines to extend understanding, find answers, foster generalizations, and create new knowledge.... Content serves not as an end product but as a tool for thought and action."

Implementation

Eight Step Concept-Based Model

The following is an explanation of an eight step model that was designed to help teachers implement a concept-based unit of study. The explanation is in question form. The purpose of the questions is to help teachers think about each step in the planning process. This model is based on the work of Lynn Erickson Ed D and has been classroom tested. Along with the explanation is a specific example of a concept-based unit of study.

— Choose a topic to study.

What topics do I teach at my grade level?

What topics lend themselves to an in-depth unit of study?

Do I have or can I get materials to create an in-depth unit of study on this topic? How can I sequence the topics so that they logically connect to each other in order to enhance understanding for my students?

— *Decide on a concept.* What concept will focus the study? What concept will give the study a focus that will promote thinking beyond the factual level? What concept do examples from the topic lend themselves to? What concept will allow for integration of the curriculum?

— *Brainstorm areas of the curriculum that can be integrated in the study of the topic.* What disciplines can be connected to the topic using the concept? How can I create an in-depth study by tying in topics from other disciplines?

— *Create generalizations.* What generalizations related to the topic do I want my students to form? What generalizations can be formed from examples from the topic? How can I put two or more concepts together to form a relationship that will help my students achieve genuine understanding? How can I sequence my lessons so that they build toward the formation of a generalization by my students?

— *Think of questions and use charts.* How can I turn the generalizations that I planned in step four into questions? What questions will focus my students on the concepts that they will need in order to form generalizations? What column headings for my chart will focus my students' thinking in order to form a generalization? What examples from the unit of study will build on each other toward the formation of a generalization as I record them on my chart?

— *Identify skills.* How can I help my students develop skills in acquiring, organizing and presenting information during the unit of study? What skills lend themselves to instruction during this unit of study? How can I incorporate instruction in reading, writing, listening, speaking, critical thinking, problem solving and mathematics skills? How can technology skills be used to help students acquire, organize and present information?

— *Plan lessons.* What lessons can I create to help my students learn how to acquire, organize and present information using skills in comprehension, grammar, punctuation, capitalization, spelling, etc. skills? What lessons can I create that will develop higher level thinking skills?

— *Develop a performance task.* How can I develop a task that will require my students to demonstrate an understanding of a concept used in the study of the topic? What task that my students will present will show that they have acquired and organized information about the topic? What understandings and skills do I want to assess in the performance task? What criteria should I include in a rubric to assess my students' performance task?

DEVELOPING AN EFFECTIVE CURRICULUM

Students who are gifted and talented are found in full-time self-contained classrooms, magnet schools, pull-out programs, resource rooms, regular classrooms, and every combination of these settings. No matter where they obtain their education, they need an appropriately differentiated curriculum designed to address their individual characteristics, needs, abilities, and interests.

An effective curriculum for students who are gifted is essentially a basic curriculum that has been modified to meet their needs. The unique characteristics of the students must serve as the basis for decisions on how the curriculum should be modified.

It is difficult to generalize about students who are gifted because their characteristics and needs are so personal and unique. However, as a group they comprehend complex ideas quickly, learn more rapidly and in greater depth than their age peers, and may exhibit interests that differ from those of their peers. They need time for in-depth exploration, they manipulate ideas and draw generalizations about seemingly unconnected concepts, and they ask provocative questions.A program that builds on these characteristics may be viewed as qualitatively (rather than quantitatively) different from the basic curriculum; it results from appropriate modification of content, process, environment, and product.

Modifying Content

Content consists of ideas, concepts, descriptive information, and facts. Content, as well as learning experiences, can be modified through acceleration, compacting, variety, reorganization, flexible pacing, and the use of more advanced or complex concepts, abstractions, and materials. When possible, students should be encouraged to move through content areas at their own pace. If they master a particular unit, they need to be provided with more advanced learning activities, not more of the same activity. Their learning characteristics are best served by thematic, broad-based, and integrative content, rather than just single-subject areas. An entire content area arranged and structured around a conceptual framework can be mastered in much less time than is traditionally allotted. In addition, such concept-based instruction expands opportunities to generalize and to integrate and apply ideas.

Middle and secondary schools are generally organized to meet student needs within content areas. Providing an interdisciplinary approach is another way of modifying curriculum . Jacobs and Borland found that gifted students benefit greatly from curriculum experiences that cross or go beyond traditional content areas, particularly when they are encouraged to acquire an integrated understanding of knowledge and the structure of the disciplines.

Modifying Process

To modify process, activities must be restructured to be more intellectually demanding. For example, students need to be challenged by questions that require a higher level of response or by open-ended questions that stimulate inquiry, active exploration, and discovery. Although instructional strategies depend on the age of the students and the nature of the disciplines involved, the goal is always to encourage students to think about subjects in more abstract and complex ways. Activity selection should be based on student interests, and activities should be used in ways that encourage self-directed learning. Bloom's TAXONOMY OF EDUCATIONAL OBJECTIVES offers the most common approach to process modification. His classification system moves from more basic levels of thought, such as memory or recall, to more complex levels of analysis, synthesis, and evaluation. Parnes, Taba, and others have provided additional models for structuring thinking skills. Every teacher should know a variety of ways to stimulate and encourage higher level thinking skills. Group interaction and simulations, flexible pacing, and guided self-management are a few of the methods for managing class activities that support process modification.

Modifying Environment

Gifted students learn best in a receptive, nonjudgmental, student-centered environment that encourages inquiry and independence, includes a wide variety of materials, provides some physical movement, is generally complex, and connects the school experience with the greater world. Although all students might appreciate such an environment, for students who are gifted it is essential that the teacher establish a climate that encourages them to question, exercise independence, and use their creativity in order to be all that they can be.

Modifying Product Expectation and Student Response

Teachers can encourage students to demonstrate what they have learned in a wide variety of forms that reflect both knowledge and the ability to manipulate ideas. For example, instead of giving a written or oral book report, students might prefer to design a game around the theme and characters of a book. Products can be consistent with each student's preferred learning style. They should address real problems, concerns, and audiences; synthesize rather than summarize information; and include a self-evaluation process.

Assessing Curriculum Effectiveness

In their synthesis of curriculum effectiveness studies and effective practice, VanTassel-Baska et al. suggested that differentiated curriculum would respond to diverse characteristics of gifted learners in the following three ways:

— By accelerating the mastery of basic skills through testing-out procedures and reorganization of the curriculum according to higher level skills and concepts.

— By engaging students in active problem-finding and problem-solving activities and research.

— By providing students opportunities for making connections within and across systems of knowledge by focusing on issues, themes, and ideas.

Curriculum development is a dynamic, ongoing process. Special attention needs to be paid to articulation, scope, and sequence to avoid gaps and repetition through grade levels; ensure that the understandings and skills teachers expect children to develop fit together; and assure that children are provided with the knowledge and skills that will prepare them for the future. Periodic evaluations of curriculum effectiveness allow corrections to be made when needed, and they are essential if curriculum is to meet the long-term needs of gifted students for increasingly complex and challenging opportunities.

EVALUATING CURRICULUM EFFECTIVENESS

When evaluating the effectiveness of a curriculum, assessing the performance of the learners is but a part of the whole. There is a step-wise approach to evaluation that can assist in performing effective evaluations that can improve the curriculums. Some performance evaluation tools are included in the handout.

Stepwise approach

— Identify the decision makers

This will vary from institution. Are the decision-makers those in administrative positions in the department or hospital that affect the rotations? Are they those who provide funds through a residency grant? Are they the residents and/or medical students? It is important to identify these people before establishing the evaluation program.

— Specify purpose and objectives

The educational intents must be written down if there is to be an adequate evaluation. These objectives may state the behaviors teachers desire their students to acquire. Other purposes may be directed toward changes in institutions or towards revenue generation. Educational programs can have multiple purposes; each purpose warrants evaluation.

— Select indicators of success

Clarify the performance criteria you will use to indicate success. Are these personal or standard criteria? Do they cover parameters such as program soundness (i.e. educationally well-designed), learner satisfaction, acquisition of knowledge or skills, and philosophical and actual commitment to change (i.e. use of new knowledge and skills in patient care).

— Develop data gathering materials

— Determine approaches to be sued to document evidence that the defined purposes/objectives are being successfully attained. With something like participant satisfaction, an opinionnaire might be used; for resident knowledge, achievement tests; for philosophical commitment, a personal interview would be appropriate. Does the method provide you with inferential or direct information?

— Collect data

Determine your collection procedures – from whom do you collect data? How often? Remember to train evaluators regarding your criteria for success.

— Analyze data

— Distribute results

— Solicit feedback

— Make revisions

DESIGNING CURRICULUM EFFECTIVENESS STUDIES

Curriculum products in every subject area and for every grade level abound in today's educational contexts. In addition to textbooks adopted by school systems and locally determined curriculum, multiple resource books and on-line lesson plans are available for teacher use. However, many of the curriculum products on the market have not been tested with students for effectiveness in promoting student learning, and although they may be interesting or attractive, there is limited documentation supporting their use.

In a society increasingly focused on accountability in education, there is an ever greater need to demonstrate the effectiveness of the materials and instructional methods students are experiencing in classrooms. Over the last decade, the Center for Gifted Education has been engaged in ongoing curriculum effectiveness research investigating various outcomes related to the use of the curriculum units in classrooms across the country. Results of these studies, demonstrating learning gains for students in science and language arts, have been published in several journals, and additional results of the most recent work appear in this issue of *Systems*.

In addition to contributing to the ongoing curriculum development agenda, work to refine the research efforts has also helped to develop a template for designing curriculum effectiveness research, whether that research is to be conducted on a small scale, such as an action research project conducted by one or two teachers, or on a large scale across a school system or multiple systems. At the 2001 convention of the National Association for Gifted Children, Dr. Joyce VanTassel-Baska and Dr. Catherine Little from the Center, with Dr. Karen Rogers of the University of St. Thomas and Virginia Tucker of Montgomery County Public Schools, presented a Master Class exploring this template with participants interested in conducting curriculum effectiveness research. A summary of the highlights of that presentation follows.

The first step in any research study is the determination of an area of focus and tentative questions of interest. This should be followed by an investigation of the existing educational literature related to the subject, including emphasis on related theories and previous research conducted. Research questions may then be formalized, growing from the tentative questions of interest and the exploration of existing literature. At this point in the study planning process, one important challenge is the need to specify the scope of the assessment planned and to ensure that the scope is manageable a single study does not need to answer every possible question about a curricular program's effectiveness. Sample research questions that may underlie a curriculum effectiveness study include the following:

— Do gifted learners participating in a specific curriculum intervention outperform gifted learners not participating on relevant measures?

— Does the grouping approach affect performance on relevant measures?

— Do gender, age, or socioeconomic status relate to performance on relevant measures?

— Do observed teacher behaviors relate to student performance on relevant measures?

— What developmental or other patterns are evident in student products?

In addition to these types of questions, school-based curriculum research studies also frequently involve an evaluative component, exploring curriculum in use to support maintaining or changing it or investigating to what degree a curriculum deemed effective in other contexts is appropriate for a given local population. Some sample questions that might frame an evaluation study are as follows:

— To what extent are the learning goals and outcomes of the curriculum addressed and fulfilled in classroom implementation?

— To what extent is the curriculum meeting the needs of identified students, as perceived by relevant groups?

— What evidence exists to document positive student performance trends for students participating in specialized curriculum?

— What are the strengths and weaknesses of the existing curriculum in relation to the state of the art or best practices in gifted education?

The remaining aspects of the study design then grow out of the research and/or evaluation questions. Depending on the results to be explored, the researcher must identify specific curriculum outcomes, teacher behaviors, or perspectives to be assessed. Particularly when designing research studies around curriculum for the gifted, student outcomes should be focused at higher levels of thinking and must be measurable. Teacher behaviors should also include methods that support higher level thinking and demonstrate attention to differentiation. Moreover, the specific outcomes to be assessed should be linked directly with the goals and outcomes of the curricular program being studied.

The research design emerges from the questions of interest and the types of outcomes to be assessed, keeping in mind that the design selected must be feasible, given the resources available, and appropriate to answer the types of questions asked. In measuring curriculum effectiveness in real-world classroom settings, the most powerful design that is practical for use is a pre-post quasi-experimental one. In this design, two similar groups of students are defined and established as the treatment group and comparison group.

Both groups take pre- and post-assessments related to the outcomes of interest; between the assessments, the treatment group participates in the curriculum under study, while the comparison group does not. Student gain scores are then compared statistically. If the groups are sufficiently similar and if the treatment group's gains are larger than the comparison group's gains, then student growth on the outcomes of interest may be attributed to the curriculum treatment. This type of design has been the main focus of the Center's curriculum effectiveness studies.

However, other types of studies are also useful in exploring aspects of curriculum effectiveness, depending on the research questions. Researchers may conduct an observation study of teacher behaviors, again relying on a pre-post design or perhaps using a qualitative observational approach instead. A qualitative study of student products developed in the course of a curriculum unit or a case study of a classroom or school using a given curriculum are also design possibilities, as is a descriptive study of student learning effects or other perceived effects.

A critical part of preparing a curriculum effectiveness study is the determination of data sources and instrumentation. Studies are stronger if they utilize multiple sources of data and if the instruments selected are demonstrably valid and reliable. Measures of student and teacher performance, perception surveys, and interview protocols are among the sources possible to tap. Wherever possible, existing instruments aligned with the intended outcomes should be used, assuming that these instruments have been published with relevant technical adequacy data.

The issues of instrument reliability and validity are key questions to consider, because any findings will rely on the strength of the instruments used. On the other hand, the instruments chosen must be appropriate for the questions of interest and logistically practical for use in the study, so sometimes no appropriate instrument exists. If instruments must be created for a study, they should be piloted and revised to strengthen technical adequacy.

With these elements in place, study procedures, participants, and timeline should be determined, and then an action plan moved forward. In addition, with any educational research study, proper approval for human subjects research should be sought from relevant authorities; most school districts and universities have existing procedures and committees for review prior to study implementation, and generally most require attention to alignment with existing programs and to obtaining parental permission.

The implementation of a curriculum effectiveness study may encounter many challenges and delays along the way, and researchers must be prepared for the impact of extraneous variables. Several recommendations to smooth the path of a curriculum effectiveness study follow. These recommendations apply primarily to studies to be conducted across multiple classrooms and perhaps multiple schools, but aspects of them also apply to smaller action research studies:

— Assign a research coordinator to facilitate the process.

— Pilot the curriculum with a small number of teachers and schools and examine the data from the smaller sample before a large implementation study.

— Communicate the purposes and intended use of the data collection efforts to relevant audiences, using multiple modes and venues for communication.

— Provide appropriate professional development on the curriculum intervention, including follow-up opportunities during implementation.

— Assign sufficient resource time for monitoring (to allow 2-3 visits per classroom)

— Assess selected outcomes within curriculum and use performance-based measures that meet technical adequacy requirements.

— Administer pre-post measures directly.

— Institute double-blind scoring procedures, but provide teacher training in the process as well.

— Schedule a student exhibit day for products.

— Use external reviewers for product review.

Curriculum effectiveness research, whether conducted on a small scale or a large scale, should be promoted as a critical aspect of the educational process. If student learning is the ultimate goal of education, then discovering whether what to do is helping to achieve that goal is fundamental to the educator's role. Teachers, school and central office administrators, and university personnel should work together to conduct curriculum research in order to strengthen the effectiveness of what happens in classrooms each day.

RESEARCH PROGRAMME ON EDUCATIONAL EFFECTIVENESS

A research programme favors the systems approach of the comprehensive model of educational effectiveness. This approach allows for the identification of different research issues at different levels of the educational system. Because of this differentiation of research problems, the research programme is organized into three coherent thematic groups of problems, each with its own group of researchers:

(1) problems of learning and instruction at the classroom level; the group is particularly interested in knowledge of how to learn effectively and how to instruct effectively;

(2) problems at the school level; the group is particularly interested in school factors pertaining to school organization, curriculum and school governance, that are regarded as conditions for effective instruction and effective learning;

(3) problems related to the contexts of the schools; the group is particularly interested in the effects on school and instructional effectiveness of contextual conditions, such as educational policies, socio-economic contexts determining the intake of students.

Each group is involved in solving problems and interested in dealing with issues at different levels of the educational system. The topics of particular interest for each group respectively are described in the following sections.

Effectiveness research on learning and instruction

The research group on learning and instruction focusses on the effectiveness issues of instructional design. Their theory driven research of learning and instruction focusses on the classroom and student level of the comprehensive model and on alternatives in terms of adaptive and cognitive instruction. So doing they hope to improve instructional design for different groups of students (different in terms of prior knowledge, motivation, cultural backgrounds, and learning strategies) and for different kinds of goals (different kinds of skills; different subjects).

Due to the expertise of the participants the research group limits the range of school subjects mainly to the Dutch mother tongue, to foreign language education in the English and German languages, and to mathematics and science. The effectiveness concept is treated empirically: which kinds of instruction are effective for which kinds of goals in which subjects? The concrete research tasks that are undertaken have regard to the following topics.

Implementation and effects of curriculum materials

Questions to be answered are to which degree text books are used and implemented as is intended by the designers of the materials, and which effects on learning strategies and achievement may be observed as a consequence of the use of different text books. GION has a long tradition of this kind of quality assessment of text books for different subjects in primary, secondary and vocational education.

Next to the effectiveness research of the text books themselves also effectiveness research takes place of teacher training in a better use of text books.

Quality requirements of curriculum materials for adaptive instruction

Different groups of students may have different quality requirements for the curriculum materials they use. Research is oriented to making explicit the requirements of good, as well qualitative as useable, curriculum materials. Quality assessment of curriculum materials may make use of the explicit requirements. Quality requirements are mainly being derived from the direct instruction and the cognitive instruction models.

Several research projects have dealt with quality assessment of text books for primary and secondary education making use of the procedure of expert judgement: experts were asked to judge text books on the quality requirements that were made explicit for their use.

Quality requirements of curriculum materials for higher order skills

In line with a recent research project into the use of new educational technology and it's influence on mathematical problem solving, new research in mathematical problem solving, particularly in science education is taken up. Especially the relationships between the use of curriculum materials and the use of computer aided instruction will be investigated with a view to producing knowledge on learning strategies of weak learners in the second phase of secondary education. Computer aided instruction may benefit from this knowledge.

Opportunity to learn and the students' processing of the contents

In relationship with opportunity to learn questions are investigated about dosage of practical exercises, pacing of the instruction and of the learning processes, and the students' processing of the learning contents. Differences in opportunity to learn may be related to differences in students' processing of the learning contents. The investigation is important for differentiated instruction (differentiation in goals and in content) in primary education.

Longitudinal research into English as second language and the curricula in primary and secondary education is being prepared in line with international comparative research in English examinations, that has been carried out.

Students' motivation, attributions, and choices

In line with a long tradition of research and partly as a consequence of evaluations of educational policy programmes questions are investigated about the impact of students' motivations to learn on their learning achievement. Motivation to learn seems, for example, next to ability the best predictor of achievement after some years. Students are differentlt motivated to learn in different subjects, so one has to distinguish between an 'achievement motivation' in general and 'subject specific affect' of students.

Also investigated are the interactions between students' motivations and teachers' instruction in their impact on achievement. Examples are the indirect effects of the meachanisms of evaluation, feedback and corrective instruction on the students' achievement by a probable impact on their motivation. Attributions of successes and failures to circumstances under the students' control versus attribution to their own ability are another example of a research issue within the complex interrelationships between teacher feedback, student motivation and learning achievement.

Effectiveness research on school organization and curriculum

The research group on school organization and curriculum focusses on conceptual issues of school effectiveness, on issues of schools providing support to effective classroom processes of teachers and students, on issues of evaluation as quality assurance, and on issues of effective school improvement.

The concept of schooleffectiveness

The size and the stability of school effects is one of the most important conceptual issues in effectiveness research, that may be analyzed in many of the research scheduled by this research group. It will be a routinely performed task in each longitudinal data set on school effectiveness.

Although most research project will probably limit themselves to measurement of basic skills, whenever it is possible, higher level cognitive skills and/or attitude measurements will be included in the research in order to test the validity of the effectiveness model for attaining other than basic skills.

The school providing support to effective classroom processes

Comparisons of school-level and classroom-level determinants of achievement are rare, especially such comparisons in which effectiveness treatments are actively controlled by researchers.

The support the school level characteristics in fact provide for the classroom level characteristics is, whenever possible, routinely tested in the analyses of data.

In the research programme as a whole emphasis is given to the impact of classroom level factors. Focussing on school level characteristics this research group tries to demonstrate the supportive function of these characteristics. The supportive function of the school level characteristics is one of the relationships between the classroom level and the system levels above the classroom. In secondary and tertiary education also characteristics at the department level are studied and compared to the supportive function of school level characteristics.

Evaluation, feedback and reinforcement

The mechanisms of evaluation, feedback and reinforcement are mechanisms of control at the school level. Without such mechanisms schools have no control of their effectiveness. The specifics of these mechanisms are determined by the evaluation policy and the evaluation system at the school level, both of which indicate the educational quality factors in the comprehensive model of educational effectiveness. Whenever possible these mechanisms will be included in research projects.

Curriculum and educational effectiveness

Curriculum refers to indicators - at the school level - of opportunity to learn. Schools are responsible for the school curriculum and for the purchase of curriculum materials. Curriculum research mostly compares curriculum documents (the school curriculum and the curriculum materials) with curriculum implementation. Curriculum research is therefor typically directed towards the way teachers implement the curriculum as provided by the school, i.e. towards problems at the interface between school and classroom levels. The way a curriculum is im[illegible] determines the effectiveness of the curriculum concerned.

School governance

The way schools are governed may have impact on the achievements of students. This relationship is demonstrated particularly for schools in the Netherlands. Building on the tradition of research in school governance this phenomenon is studied further, especially as to the processes and mechanisms responsible for this relationship between governance and student learning.

Effective school improvement

Two kinds of activities will be undertaken in this context, viz. a theoretical analysis of the problems involved in the issue of combining the improvement and the effectiveness paradigms; and the development of an effective school improvement programme. An international cooperative project has been prepared. Funding is being requested of the European Commission.

Effectiveness research on contextual conditions of schools

The contextual conditions of school effectiveness are particularly studied in evaluation research of educational policy programmes. Educational policy programmes are mostly programmes of government policy. The programmes are implemented in primary and secondary education. The evaluation of educational policy programmes is mostly government sponsored. The programme evaluations mostly have a longitudinal as well as a multilevel design. They are conducted in great samples of schools. They gather data on students, teachers and schools. Because many of the programme evaluations are large scale evaluations, next to the general assessment of the programmes' effectiveness, several other issues are investigated and analyzed.

Educational policy as effectiveness context

The evaluations of educational policy programmes compare the stated policy with (variations in) it's implementation at school and classroom levels. They also assess the general effectiveness of the educational policy programme.

Environment as effectiveness context

Many educational policy programmes aim at the improvement of education for specific groups of students. This is either the main goal of the programme, as in the educational priority programme or in the programme for children with learning handicaps, or one of the programme goals, as in basic education.

The concept of educational effectiveness

The size and the stability of school effects and of programme effects is one of the most important conceptual issues in effectiveness research, that may be routinely analyzed in the large scale longitudinal programme evaluations.

Differential effectiveness of educational programmes

The effects of educational programmes may differ, not only from one group of students to the other, but also from one school subject to an other, or from one type of goals to an other type. This differential effectiveness also may be routinely analyzed in large scale evaluations.

Impact of students' motivation, attributions, and choices

Large scale longitudinal evaluations that study - among others - cohorts of students, are typically adequate to include - and some in fact do include - longitudinal data on motivation, attributions and individual choices of students.

Economy of education

The comprehensive model of educational effectiviness is primarily interested in theoretical explanations and practical improvements of school and classroom effectiveness. The model is not interested in the costs of the improvements as such. The model may be supplemented with an analysis of costs and benefits of the - configurated - factors that influence effectiveness. So doing the actual decisions of schools and policy makers in order to improve educational quality may be understood and explained.

CURRICULUM AND FACULTY WORKLOAD PRODUCTIVITY

The significant reduction in state funding over the next two years will profoundly affect the capability to respond to emerging issues in all programmatic areas. With fewer resources teachers must position themselves to retain quality and access and strong relationships with current and emerging clientele. Their challenge is to focus on high priority areas, maintain existing and build new revenue streams while at the same time maintaining quality.

The first responsibility of each academic unit is to serve students well. This may require some reallocation of faculty, staff, and financial resources in each unit to address student needs. Success will require ongoing emphasis in every academic unit on restructuring academic work to achieve broader access, better learning outcomes, higher scholarly productivity, and commitment to university service with balanced and fair workloads for the faculty and staff.

Planned improvements in each college need to include multiple initiatives in the following areas:

— Initiatives to strengthen academic program viability ? quality and efficiency

  — Redesign viable programs to improve focus and efficiency

  — Streamline and simplify curriculum to facilitate timely student degree completion and success

  — Share foundation, core and elective courses across multiple majors

— Eliminate non-essential courses including those not offered regularly

— Redesign curriculum to improve student learning, reduce faculty contact time, and accommodate different learning styles

— Design efficient and effective use of all learning resources including undergraduate and graduate teaching assistants

— Reduce the minimum credit hour requirements for degree completion

— Consolidate majors and options for greater efficiency

— Offer courses in a predictable sequence (e.g., each semester, every other year)

— Review, change and in some cases phase-out less viable programs

— All degree programs that average fewer than 10 undergraduate, 7 masters and 3 doctoral graduates per year, and those with under-enrolled upper division, masters and doctoral courses need to be reviewed for quality and efficiency. Degree programs with few majors and graduates may be efficient if they are highly integrated with other degree programs in the department, or use few resources.

— Large, as well as small, programs of marginal quality need to be reviewed and changed (improved or reduced).

— Identify and resolve bottleneck problems in the undergraduate curriculum

— Priority in curriculum assignments should be need rather than faculty preference

— Teaching assignments may need to be flexible and adjusted according to student demand

    - College and unit resources may need to be voluntarily reallocated to resolve bottlenecks
    - Within the major
    - In service to Core and other electives to serve other majors
    - University strategic priorities including diversity

- Mechanisms to address efficiency and balance in faculty workload
    - Implement mechanisms in the college to encourage, support and reward departments and faculty to transform curricula ?including information technology to support learning
    - Review current policy and practice with respect to consistency and equitability in course assignments across the university
    - Faculty in departments will small or no graduate programs should have higher average teaching loads per year
    - Faculty in departments with growing graduate programs should have moderate average teaching loads per year
    - Faculty in departments with large graduate programs, especially the Ph.D. program, should have lower average teaching loads to support higher advising numbers and other activities associated with a large graduate program.
    - Assign instruction, scholarship and service responsibilities differentially across and within units. Assignments will vary according to need, interest and expertise of the faculty and the program. For example, faculty with lower scholarship expectations should be teaching more than average. Faculty evaluation must recognize and reward excellence in performance in different assignments.

CREATING METHODOLOGY TO IMPROVE CURRICULUM EFFICIENCY

The hottest educational issue of the past 10 years has not been whole language versus phonics. It runs much deeper than that, primarily because whole language and phonics can be taught concurrently, if allowed. What, then, is the disparity that has widened the chasm within the educational system? In order to fully understand, teachers must analyze the issues carefully.

It began with this premise: children have a language base, thus reading should be predicated on a child's natural language usage. Therefore, reading books that do not sound like the natural language of a child should be avoided. (Good-bye basals, hello literature.) As children are involved in print rich literature, they will automatically pick up the phonemic patterns of speech, so phonemic awareness does not need to be taught directly. (Good-bye phonics, hello sight vocabulary.) In connection with this, if children are listening to print rich literature and are writing authentic student text, children will naturally pick up the spelling patterns in the written word. (Good-bye spelling, hello high frequency words.)

The only thing that was forgotten in this whole decade of "natural education" was the child's brain and how it processes information. It does not like random information and stores it poorly.

The educational field allows more pendulum swings than any other profession. Perhaps it is the constant search for new ideas that leads to drop one teaching method or program to follow another. With the whole language movement, teachers have virtually thrown the baby out with the bath, rather than artfully combining all the wonderful aspects of whole language and phonemic awareness. (It really wasn't "whole" without phonics.) You don't have to negate a child's language base and self discovery because you highlight and teach a certain phoneme in your lesson plans.

It is easy to see that the whole language movement has had a positive impact on several areas in curriculum development: it forced to become more imaginative as teachers, to integrate the curriculum and to provide children with authentic reading and writing opportunities, rather than "busy" work. It also helped to move away from inane little stories and, instead, brought wonderful books, rich with vocabulary and artwork into the children's experiences.

It is upon this positive literature-based foundation that teachers must build excellent curriculum and teaching strategies. Their job, then, is to,

1) be trained to integrate the concepts of whole language and direct phonetic instruction so children have the advantage of both schools of thought.

2) be aware of how children learn most efficiently, and implement effective teaching in the classroom,

3) masterfully teach, reaching young minds so that they fully understand all concepts taught, not neglecting one skill for another.

Jeanne Chall said it so well: "Both the direct instruction and whole language models are concerned with enhancing student achievement in reading. Both are equally concerned that the students develop a love of reading. Both want children to read good literature as well as expository texts. Both combine reading and writing. Both want all students to achieve their potential, and both want to reduce the number of students who fail. Whole language proponents tend to view learning to read as a natural process, developing in ways similar to language.

Therefore, like language, most whole language proponents say it is not necessary to teach reading directly. Direct instruction models, on the other hand, view reading as needing to be taught, and taught systematically. Indeed, an often used rationale for the need to teach reading is that all people on earth speak a language while, according to UNESCO, nearly a billion are illiterate, mainly because they do not attend schools where reading is taught and learned.

This is where teachers need to start:

1) Teachers must take back to their profession. They are educational experts and know (or should know) how children learn best. If something does not feel right, they must be strong enough in the convictions and training to speak up. Never again should teachers see themselves as only facilitators or implementers!

   Research shows again and again that the teacher is a major variable in how well a child learns to read and spell. Yhey must fully research the premises behind each educational philosophy, and cognitively assess the long term effects it will have on students' academic progress.

2) Schools must adopt methods and strategies that handily teach children how to read and spell through a curriculum that presents the richness of literature, creative and informative writing, critical thinking and phonetic analysis at the same time. There must be harmony and continuity of thought in order for changes to be implemented at all levels of the school system.

3) Teachers must teach children to become reading and spelling experts. College requirements must be restructured, adding many specific classes in these areas. They need to learn how to teach children phonetic skills to decode and encode text with books that are readable, in addition to exposing them to the joy and enrichment of fine literature. Teachers must learn the various sounds of every phoneme in the English language in order to teach it, as well as how to tie it into the reading and writing curriculum.

   a) Teachers must understand the nature of language acquisition. Children are in a language acquisition mode both before and after birth, and language development is crucial to their reading and writing success. Speaking to them, asking and answering questions and reading to them is essential to their future literacy. So important are hearing and perception in this endeavor that if language is delayed, so is literacy.

Guessing what the words are and struggling to find meaning within context is not an efficient way to read. Give them the phonetic code to the language. The sounds that they have heard from birth can be decoded and later, written down

b) Teachers must be taught how to reach EVERY child in the classroom, not allowing any child to slip through the cracks. All teachers must have the tools, materials, strategies and training similar to special education training. They no longer have the option of homogeneous classrooms. Classrooms are cultural, social, economic and academic melting-pots, especially with more and more full-inclusion taking place. Teachers must be highly skilled in pacing the academic work load, creating lesson plans that reach 100% of the children, regardless of language or ability.

c) Teachers need to fully understand how a child's brain functions. From birth to around seven or eight years of age, a child must, approach text using right hemisphere strategies. Research found that, "The principal components of the potentials, while analyzed in relation to a number of independent variables, revealed significant associations between reading proficiency and right hemispheric activity at early ages, to shift to significant associations between reading proficiency and left hemispheric activity at later ages." Based on this research they must reach young learners through methods that easily teach the concepts needed for literacy. Traditional approaches passed down from generation to generation have often put up educational road blocks, unwittingly, for the child, because of t heir abstract nature.

Since the alphabet is made up of symbols, which are abstract and left- brained, how do teachers reconcile this with four, five and six year olds whose brains are not yet ready for assimilating this type of information? To make matters worse, teachers expect a kindergarten child to not only know the letter names (a), but teachers expect them to recognize them by sight, know the sounds they make (a), and know their upper and lower case counterparts, (A, a). This is just too much information for most five year old children to handle.

4) Teachers must commit to the education of pre-school children. Continuity is needed with feeder pre- schools, Head Start and K-3 grades throughout the school district. They can do this by encouraging feeder pre-schools and Head Start Programs to tie into the local school curriculum and to participate in staff and curriculum development.

5) Teachers must help parents to learn how to work appropriately (playfully and non-stressfully) with their children, readying them for the language arts process. If pre-school children enter kindergarten with essential pre-reading, spelling and writing skills, the kindergarten teacher could then continue readying them for the academics needed as well as to prepare them for first grade.

Problems with the traditional approach

1) *Too much information is given*: When teacher say to the child, "This is a capital "A," this is the lower case "a," the letter name is "a" and the usual sound it makes is "a," the child, becomes confused and does not fully understand, because the information holds little, if any, meaning. Now multiply these tasks by the 26 letters of the alphabet and the child becomes overwhelmed.

2) *Not enough information is given*: When teacher fragment the alphabet, children do not see the alphabet as a whole entity. Unless they see the complete alphabetic picture, they

will not understand its purpose. If they do not understand, they cannot utilize the information in reading or writing.

3) *Children are expected to learn from abstractions*: Teachers give children abstract symbols which they should understand and relate to a specific sound. Additional obstacles are found with similar letter shapes: show a child a "b" and a "d." Can you imagine visually distinguishing this at five years old? Try these: "p" and "q." Or, try to distinguish auditorily the difference between the sounds of "e" and "i"?

Solutions to the problems

Commit to a curriculum that provides strategies that present the alphabet and the formation of words with a brain-efficient, right hemispheric method.

1) Teach, first, the sounds and shapes of the entire alphabet in the daily presentation, postponing letter names and capital letters. Traditionally the alphabet is presented by showing a letter a week to kindergartners, it being divided into 26 weeks. When the alphabet is fragmented in this way, the brain cannot perceive a whole picture. What, then, happens to the child who is out with the cicken pox for two weeks (two letters unlearned), or a cold or the flu? How is his/her understanding of the alphabet affected?

   According to many researchers, "knowing the letter names is the best predictor of beginning reading achievement." We would like to propose, again, in the interest of brain-efficient teaching, that teachers treat the letter names as secondary in importance to learning the sounds of the letters. Since teachers do not read with them, letter names provide no real purpose for the early reader. Therefore, it should follow that the sounds need to be taught first.

2) Teach lower case letters first. Teachers have been taught, societally, that teaching the upper case letters first to the child is proper. They have justified it by saying it is easier

for a child to form an upper case letter than it is to form a lower case letter. This is just not so. Some capital letters (E for instance), take more strokes than its lower case counterpart. Each time a young writer has to pick up a pencil to locate another point on the letter for formation, the child loses his or her place. There are more pencil pick-ups with uppercase letters than lowercase letters. The reasons for teaching lower case letters first are these:

a) Books are mainly written with lower case letters. When Mom is reading The Napping House, by Don and Audrey Woods, with her child snuggled in her lap, the letters are in lower case form. If the child has been taught his capital letters first, the child is denied the opportunity of participating in the text. If the child, though, that has been taught the sounds and shapes of the lowercase letters, then the child can recognize the letters while mom and dad are reading. The opportunity to participate gives him/her the confidence to explore text in other areas.

b) First and second grade teachers have to spend much of their time breaking the children's habit of writing with capital letters. Teach them correctly the first time around!

c) Each time a young writer has to pick up the pencil to locate another point on the letter for formation, the child looses his or her place. There are more pencil-pickups with upper case letters than lowercase letters. d. Teaching both lowercase and uppercase (two totally different forms multiplied by 26) is overwhelming to the child. It is desired that a child not only exit kindergarten with a full understanding of the sounds and shapes of the alphabet, but have capital letter and letter name mastery as well.

The following paragraph will help explain how to teach the sounds and the shapes of the letters for alphabet mastery:

3) Because there is nothing inherent in the visual symbol that suggests its name or sound, one must develop that "something" that causes the child to make the letter/sound connections. If a teacher uses pictures that relate to the sounds of the letters and uses the child's modalities to learn and remember the sounds, these techniques will provide a safety net for memory and retrieval. Without these connection there will be no understanding. Without understanding, there is no retention, usage or transference.

4) Attach a motor movement, (also a mnemonic, right brain stimulus), which is directly related to the picture/letter, establishing the sounds to the letters. The brain uses this device to cement the information into memory, then uses the same device to retrieve the information from the brain when needed for reading and spelling activities.

5) Teach spelling as a vital part of the school curriculum. Because spelling/writing are a watermark of success (read a job application from an average high school graduate), writing and spelling are the factors that separate the person from higher education or the profession of choice. A person may have all the talent, intelligence and/or creativity in the world, but without mastery of written language, this person is not able to accomplish his/her goals.

   a) Spelling can no longer be treated as an incidental activity. Many teachers in California expressed that they don't teach spelling. Often word lists (if given at all) are sent home for study.

   b) Spelling must be taught as a vital, consistent and integrated part of the reading curriculum. It should be supported by the literature used in the daily presentation. This gives a child a reason for studying spelling.

   c) Word families, rather than high frequency words, should be taught to first and second graders. Think about a first grade child trying to words such as, "of,""said," "there," "was," "because," etc., in one week's spelling lesson. Teaching random information (abstract and left-brained) makes it difficult for students to assimilate this type of information for future use. Many can memorize a list for the spelling test on Friday, but on Monday, there is little transference when writing in journals. There is no meaning nor connection. Research states that children are pattern seekers and pattern makers. After the child has mastered the alphabet and can identify the sounds in text, the next logical step is to combine the letters (still in the picture/letter form for right hemispheric strategies) to form words. If the children see the pattern (remember, it will be introduced with the pictures and placed into memory with a body signal), memory will take place more easily.

It is crucial that children understand the purpose behind the phonemic analysis being presented. The teacher must tie the "a-z's" into all text (tying initial, medial, and ending sounds into literature, other textual experiences and classroom environment); and when broadening reading and writing skills, the teacher should tie the phonemes into the literature and other text.

6) Give children books that they can read. First and second graders must have reading books that they can read independently. Ask any first grade teacher and s/he will tell you that their emerging readers are not able to learn how to read from literature books. The text is too difficult and unpredictable. These students need readers so that they can experience successful independent reading. It is necessary for students to be taught decoding so that they are able to sound out unfamiliar words that may already be in their oral vocabulary.

7) Reading and spelling errors must no longer go uncorrected. Teachers should allow room for young writers to write

without fear of making mistakes. Inventive spelling was encouraged for this very reason and the results have been positive in that students are writing more freely. But many interpreted it to mean that spelling need not be corrected or taught. But if spelling is taught, high frequency words have often been used as spelling lists. The brain does not easily store such random information. The same philosophy reigned in reading. It has been believed that children's reading should not be interrupted by the teacher to correct mistakes. If the child continues to repeat the same mistake, it becomes a problem. Teachers must remember how the child's brain stores information. Mistakes left uncorrected are remembered.

6

CURRICULUM DEVELOPMENT VERSUS CURRICULUM TRANSACTION

COLLABORATIVE VS COOPERATIVE LEARNING

Collaboration is a philosophy of interaction and personal lifestyle whereas cooperation is a structure of interaction designed to facilitate the accomplishment of an end product or goal.

Collaborative learning (CL) is a personal philosophy, not just a classroom technique. In all situations where people come together in groups, it suggests a way of dealing with people which respects and highlights individual group members' abilities and contributions. There is a sharing of authority and acceptance of responsibility among group members for the groups actions. The underlying premise of collaborative learning is based upon consensus building through cooperation by group members, in contrast to competition in which individuals best other group members. CL practitioners apply this philosophy in the classroom, at committee meetings, with community groups, within their families and generally as a way of living with and dealing with other people.

Cooperative learning is defined by a set of processes which help people interact together in order to accomplish a specific goal or develop an end product which is usually content specific. It is more directive than a collaborative system of governance and closely controlled by the teacher. While there are many mechanisms for group analysis and introspection the fundamental approach is teacher centered whereas collaborative learning is more student centered.

Spencer Kagan in an article in Educational Leadership provides an excellent definition of cooperative learning by looking at general structures which can be applied to any situation. His definition provides an unbrella for the work cooperative learning specialists including the Johnsons, Slavin, Cooper, Graves and Graves, Millis, etc. It follows below:

> "The structural approach to cooperative learning is based on the creation, analysis and systematic application of structures, or content-free ways of organizing social interaction in the classroom. Structures usually involve a series of steps, with proscribed behaviour at each step. An important cornerstone of the approach is the distinction between "structures" and "activities".
>
> "To illustrate, teachers can design many excellent cooperative activities, such as making a team mural or a quilt. Such activities almost always have a specific content-bound objective and thus cannot be used to deliver a range of academic content. Structures may be used repeatedly with almost any subject matter, at a wide range of grade levels and at various points in a lesson plan."

John Myers points out that the dictionary definitions of "collaboration", derived from its Latin root, focus on the process of working together; the root word for "cooperation" stresses the product of such work. Co-operative learning has largely American roots from the philosophical writings of John Dewey stressing the social nature of learning and the work on group dynamics by Kurt Lewin.

Collaborative learning has British roots, based on the work of English teachers exploring ways to help students respond to literature by taking a more active role in their own learning. The cooperative learning tradition tends to use quantitative methods which look at achievement: i.e., the product of learning. The collaborative tradition takes a more qualitative approach, analyzing student talk in response to a piece of literature or a primary source in history. Myers points out some differences between the two concepts:

> "Supporters of co-operative learning tend to be more teacher-centered, for example when forming heterogeneous groups, structuring positive inter- dependence, and teaching co-operative skills. Collaborative learning advocates distrust structure and allow students more say if forming friendship and interest groups. Student talk is stressed as a means for working things out. Discovery and contextural approaches are used to teach interpersonal skills."
>
> "Such differences can lead to disagreements.... I contend the dispute is not about research, but more about the morality of what should happen in the schools. Beliefs as to what should happen in the schools can be viewed as a continuum of orientations toward curriculum from "transmission" to "transaction" to "transmission". At one end is the transmission position. As the name suggests, the aim of this orientation is to transmit knowledge to students in the form of facts, skills and values. The transformation position at the other end of the continuum stresses personal and social change in which the person is said to be interrelated with the environment rather than having control over it. The aim of this orientation is self-actualization, personal or organizational change."

Rocky Rockwood describes the differences by acknowledging the parallels they both have in that they both use groups, both assign specific tasks, and both have the groups share and compare their procedures and conclusions in plenary class sessions. The major difference lies in the fact that cooperative deals exclusively with traditional (canonical) knowledge while collaborative ties into the social constructivist movement, asserting that both knowledge and authority of knowledge have changed dramatically in the last century. "The result has been a transition from "foundational (cognitive) understanding of knowledge", to a nonfoundational ground where "we understand knowledge to be a social construct and learning a social process". Rockwood states:

"In the ideal collaborative environment, the authority for testing and determining the appropriateness of the group product rests with, first, the small group, second, the plenary group (the whole class) and finally (but always understood to be subject to challenge and revision) the requisite knowledge community (i.e. the discipline: geography, history, biology etc.) The concept of non-foundational knowledge challenges not only the product acquired, but also the process employed in the acquisition of foundational knowledge."

"Most importantly, in cooperative, the authority remains with the instructor, who retains ownership of the task, which involves either a closed or a closable (that is to say foundational) problem (the instructor knows or can predict the answer). In collaborative, the instructor—once the task is set— transfers all authority to the group. In the ideal, the group's task is always open ended."

"Seen from this perspective, cooperative does not empower students. It employs them to serve the instructor's ends and produces a "right" or acceptable answer. Collaborative does truly empower and braves all the risks of empowerment (for example, having the group or class agree to an embarrassingly simplistic or unconvincing position or produce a solution in conflict with the instructor's)."

"Every person, Brutee holds, belongs to several "interpretative or knowledge communities" that share vocabularies, points of view, histories, values, conventions and interests. The job of the instructor id to help students learn to negotiate the boundaries between the communities they already belong to and the community represented by the teacher's academic discipline, which the students want to join. Every knowledge community has a core of foundational knowledge that its members consider as given (but not necessarily absolute). To function independently within a knowledge community, the fledgling scholar must master enough material to become conversant with the community."

Rockwood concludes:

> "In my teaching experience, cooperative represents the best means to approach mastery of foundational knowledge. Once students become reasonably conversant, they are ready for collaborative, ready to discuss and assess,...."

Myers suggests use of the "transaction" orientation as a compromise between taking hard positions advocating either methodology.

> "This orientation views education as a dialogue between the student and the curriculum. Students are viewed as problem solvers. Problem solving and inquiry approaches stressing cognitive skills and the ideas of Vygotsky, Piaget, Kohlberg and Bruner are linked to transaction. This perspective views teaching as a "conversation" in which teachers and students learn together through a process of negotiation with the curriculum to develop a shared view of the world."

It is clear that in undertaking the exercise of defining differences between the two ideas we run the risk of polarizing the educational community into a we versus them mentality. There are so many benefits which acrue from both ideas that it would be a shame to lose any advantage gained from the student-student-teacher interactions created by both methods. We must be careful to avoid a one-size-fits-all mentality when it comes to education paradigms.

CURRICULUM TRANSACTION

The NCTE has formulated norms and standards for various teacher education programmes (TEPs). These are used to grant recognition to teacher education institutions for offering TEPs. This process of granting recognition to TEI is to ensure the minimum level of infrastructure, academic facilities and the human resources of requisite qualifications. Availability of these facilities and resources in TEI is an assurance to enable it to create curriculum transaction processes of certain standard. However, actual quality of curriculum transaction in a TEP would largely depend upon the effectiveness of utilisation of resources by teacher educators individually and collectively for creating conducive training environment and supportive synergetics. This calls for professional competence of teacher educators and their ingenuity.

Further, for encouraging the TEIs to offer innovative programmes and courses in teacher education, NCTE has provided for necessary regulations to recognise such TEPs. The B.El.Ed. of Delhi University and B.Ed. (Enriched) of Banasthali Vidyapith, Rajasthan, are instances of such TEPs recognised by the NCTE.

During the last few decades, the system of TE has expanded in most parts of the country. The incidence of untrained teachers that exists in some States is mainly due to reasons other than teacher training avenues. Therefore, 'access' to teacher education facilities, or, to put it in different words, quantity of these is no longer a crucial problem. However, the quality of teacher preparation at all stages of education presents a serious challenge. In fact, it has persisted through the entire post-Independence period.

The theme 'curriculum transaction for quality teacher education' included for discussion at this conference suggests that perhaps, a renewed effort can be made while the endeavour of 'accreditation and assessment' is in its initial stage. In this context it may be relevant to mention that the basic intent of accreditation involves the following:

— To take the TEI beyond the minimum level of performance, and make it proceed towards excellence in the tasks of teacher preparation.

— The products of TEIs, namely, trained teachers must fulfil the expectations of stake holders in a larger social system.

— The TEI places itself in a self-initiated and self-accepted process of making its performance referents known not only to itself but also to other stake holders for its distinctive features of performance.

— It seeks greater linkage between the quality attributes of teachers and curriculum transaction.

It is with reference to these broader goals of accreditation, curriculum transaction in teacher education needs to be viewed. In the section to follow, a few considerations and concrete actions are presented with a view to exploring feasible ways of improving curriculum transaction in TEIs.

As mentioned earlier, concerns of qualitative improvement in teacher education have persisted. The concerns are well articulated and documented. Significant ones are the following.

a) Theory of education as taught through courses in TE is not integrated with practices of schooling.

b) Teaching-practice as organized generally for student-teachers is not in consonance with emerged view of teaching-learning.

c) The nature of 'professional development process' is not sufficiently focused in preparing teachers.

Substantial efforts have been made by national level institutions like NCERT and state level institutions like SCERTs, with active support of teacher education system in the country, for capacity building of teachers through pre-service and in-service programmes of TE. Yet, the system of teacher preparation in TEIs leaves much to be desired. What could be done in the present context is the focus of the next sections.

So far three National Curriculum Frameworks in TE have been brought by NCTE. Another similar exercise was carried out by the UGC in 1989. In all these national documents, the position taken is that the 'Frameworks' have to be treated as broad guidelines and actual curricular details be worked out by TEIs under different systems. While certain changes in teacher education curricula and its transaction are noticeable here and there, general pattern of teacher preparation still needs to be changed further. Let us consider a few other points to make teacher preparation more responsive and feasible.

Perhaps, a more feasible approach to introduce a change in TE curriculum would be to develop quality material in TE, keeping in view the major thrust in teacher preparation. And, the material thus prepared could be discussed in fora of teacher educators and others concerned with TE. It may enrich the discourse in TE and also provide concrete referents for shaping the curriculum at various stages of school. It may consequently lead to a process of change in TE curriculum by teacher educators in more concrete terms. With this major consideration the NCTE has developed an approach to teacher preparation at secondary stage.

Features of the approach

— Theoretical inputs are drawn from cognate disciplinary areas like psychology, philosophy, sociology, economics, political science and history. These are converged around "pedagogical themes." This is to facilitate the process of integration between theory and practice of education.

— Convergence of varied theoretical inputs is sought to be made in the perspective of education which is derived from the nature of education, namely, it is purposive; it is practice/ activity oriented; it is socially contrived; it is human endeavour; it has its own establishment and organisatin.

— Theoretical inputs from cognate disciplines when combined with considerations arising from educational perspective, undergo a translation and turn into 'conceptual inputs', relevant to education. Such 'conceptual inputs' are basic or foundational to the development of 'professional competence' in student-teachers.

— Conceptual inputs' are derived from teacher roles, viz.,

  — Teacher and instructional process.

  — Teacher in school.

  — Teacher and the community.

— Teacher in socio-political and cultural context.

— Teacher as a professional.

These roles when analysed led to certain concepts, concept clusters and other conceptual formulations. Also, interconnections across teacher roles and conceptual inputs were discerned and identified. We visualized that the 'conceptual inputs in TEP could be presented in integrated manner if roles related 'themes' were brought into focus.

— Knowledge-base in pedagogical process is primarily 'professional knowledge-base.'

  The pool of conceptual inputs identified was further clustered on the basis of their similarity, purpose to be served and utilized in teacher preparation. Appropriate titles of pedagogical themes were given to the clusters. As many as 30 themes were identified covering all of the above mentioned role areas.

The reading materials on instructional role of teachers have been prepared. The themes covered under this role are the following :

— What is teaching? (Conceptualizing teaching)

— How does learning occur?

— How to teach ?

— Curriculum Dimensions

— Knowing how much is learnt.

Each chapter consists of 60-80 computer processes pages. The reading material in these chapters has been reviewed by ten experts, two for each theme. For remaining themes the reading materials would be developed in the next phase of the project.

If these materials are discussed in advance level workshops of teacher educators, the curricular materials suited to their TEIs could be developed for use in curriculum transaction. This could be carried out by assessing the relevance of the material, adapting it and augmenting it wherever required. The greatest advantage visualised in the process is two fold. One, NCTE mobilises the expertise available across the country; it gets the quality curricular inputs developed; and enriches discourse in TE through interactive fora. Two, the main responsibility of developing curriculum and determining transaction strategies remains with teacher educators in the field, which legitimately is theirs.

Need to reorganize teaching practice

The approach to teacher preparation presented at '6' above, has direct implication to reorganise practical experiences that are offered to student-teachers generally in the form of lesson-based teaching practice. Theoretical inputs drawn from cognate disciplines are varied across disciplines as well as within a discipline. These inputs enlighten a student-teacher about various view points. The reading materials on pedagogical themes referred to under 6 enable him to converge these view points around pedagogical themes and internalise them to form educational perspective for his understanding and action as a practitioner in education. This involves three stage development, viz.,

— conceptual understanding

— specific skills and action abilities

— composite professional competence

Towards the goal of helping student-teacher acquire composite professional competence, teaching practice as a component of teacher preparation need to be orgnaised in a more flexible way. This composite competence is suggestive of certain attributes to be developed in a student-teacher, viz., reflection, creative and appropriate use of skills and insights, and decision-making to act.

For this purpose, varied experiences about teaching under different conditions would be qualitatively more appropriate exposure for developing 'experiential inputs' and stable insights in student-teacher to become effective teacher. This may require flexible way of organizing school-based experiences and assessing their adequacy for enabling student-teacher to internalise professional knowledge as part of his overall competence. For similar reasons, the formating of 'lesson plan' and its placement in teacher training may have to be reorganized.

Towards change in mind-set

Often a question is asked whether TEIs through their teacher preparation programmes offer inputs to student-teachers for developing attitudinal make-up and value inculcation needed in them as professionals. Answer to this is in affirmation; we do talk and discuss about attitudes and values during teacher training. However, that the intended change in student-teachers takes place cannot be asserted. There are several reasons for that, viz., the very nature of these attibutes, conditions needed for effecting such behavioural changes, organisational and instructional inputs required, etc. Let us see if anything could be done under the present conditions in which TE system is situated. Towards that a few consideration could be as under.

TEPs prepare teachers for teaching and participation in other activities related to educational development. For this purpose, teacher must have appropriate professional orientation. Towards achieving this considerable inputs are included in curriculum of TE. However, these are generic and varied. These inputs make the student-teacher wonder as to what he should do in actual educative process. It becomes more complicated and complex when this academically dilemmatic situation is seen in relation to what obtains in social environment in which the school is 'situated' for its functioning. In this context, let us consider the following.

Education is directional; so is teaching. This 'direction' is derived from the parameters of social development in general.

This limits the choice of academic inputs; some of them become more relevant and certain others less. This is very handy and convenient in education organisationally. We may follow it. But 'how' to do that remains a question yet. More about it in the next para.

The Constitution of India as an organic instrument provides directions for overall societal development. It has specific directives, articles and other supportive provisions and explanations in respect of education and its operations. They emphasise inter alia very specific attitudes and values that need to be nourished and developed through educative processes. Fundamental Rights and Fundamental Duties and other specifications in the Constitution are clear directions for organising educative processes.

Teachers need to be made conscious of them, practise them and help students acquire them. Towards this goal appropriate inputs may have to be offered through teacher preparation. In this regard what could be done is explicated next.

Relevant curricular inputs could be prepared through participative process by competent teacher educators. NCTE, perhaps, should initiate such exercises. Care needs to be taken that the inputs prepared are of good quality. They can be utilised for discussions in advance level seminars and workshops, and refined. Such inputs may form the basis of organising curriculum transaction on values and attitudes during TEP. Emphasis in these interaction may be on what a teacher and students have to reflect in their behaviours.

The expected outcomes may not be development of attitudes and values to a high pre-determined degree. However, one can expect that the student-teachers will get initiated to viewing educational processes and the problems encountered in a professional way. It is this 'mind-set' that needs to be developed through teacher training.

NATIONAL COUNCIL FOR TEACHER EDUCATION

Norms and Standards For Elementary Teacher Education Programme

Preamble

The elementary teacher education programme is meant for preparing teachers for elementary schools (primary and upper primary/middle).

Duration and Intake

a) The elementary teacher education programme shall be of a duration of two academic years.

b) For effective curriculum transaction and for ensuring optimum utilisation of physical and instructional infrastructure and expertise of the teaching staff, there shall be a unit of 50 students for intake each year.

Eligibility

a) Candidates with at least 45% marks in the senior secondary examination (+2), or its equivalent, are eligible for admission.

b) Admission should be made either on the basis of marks obtained in the qualifying examination or in the entrance examination conducted by the State Government, as per the policy of the State Government.

c) There shall be reservation of seats for SC/ST/OBC, Handicapped, Women, etc. as per the rules of the concerned State Government.

Curriculum

Transaction and Requirement of Teaching Staff

a) There shall be at least 150 teaching days in a year exclusive of period of admission, examination, etc. Besides, every teacher trainee shall be required to undergo internship in teaching (including practice teaching/skill development) at least for 30 days in nearby elementary schools.

b) Apart from teaching of foundation subjects, there shall be provision for teaching of methods subjects relating to primary and upper primary curriculum, namely, Regional Language/Mother Tongue, English, Mathematics, Science and Social Studies.

c) For a unit of 50 students or less (with combined strength of 100 or less for the two-year course), the full-time teaching faculty shall comprise of the Principal/Head and at least five lecturers. For intake of students in excess of the prescribed unit, the number of full time teachers shall be increased proportionately.

d) Appointment of teachers should be so distributed as to ensure the required nature and level of expertise for teaching methodology courses and foundation courses.

e) For teaching subjects such as physical education, art, work experience, music, information technology literacy, etc., part-time instructors may be appointed.

Qualifications of Teaching Staff

a) Principal/Head

   i) Academic and professional qualification will be as prescribed for the post of Lecturer.

   ii) At least five years' experience of teaching in elementary teacher education institutions.

b) Lecturer

Good academic record with M.Ed./M.A. (Education) with 55% marks, preferably with specialisation in elementary education.

OR

Good Academic record with Master's Degree with 55% marks in the relevant school subject and Bachelor of Elementary Education (B.El.Ed.), or B.Ed. preferably with specialisation in elementary education, and with five years' teaching experience in recognised elementary schools.

c) A relaxation of 5% may be provided, from 55% to 50% of the marks, at the Master's level for SC/ST Category.

d) Qualifications for other academic staff for teaching physical education, art, work experience, information technology literacy, etc. shall be as prescribed by the concerned State Government.

Administrative Staff

The administrative and other support staff may be provided as per the norms prescribed by the concerned State Government.

Infrastructural Facilities

a) There shall be provision for adequate number of classrooms, hall, laboratory space for conducting instructional activities for approved intake of students, rooms for the principal and faculty members, and office for the administrative staff and a store. The size of instructional space shall not be less than 10 sq.ft. per student.

b) There shall be a library equipped with text and reference books relating to prescribed courses of study, education encylopedia, year books, electronic publications (CD-ROMs) and journals on teacher education and other software relevant to the elementary stage.

c) There shall be games facilities with playground. Alternatively, the playground available with the attached school or local body may be utilized and where there is scarcity of space as in metropolitan towns/hilly regions, facilities for yoga, indoor games may be provided.

d) To provide these facilities, the Management / Institutions shall, at the time of making application, have in its possession adequate land / land and building on ownership basis free from all encumbrances. Govt. land acquired on long-term lease as per the law of the concerned State / UT will also be considered valid for the purpose. Pending construction of permanent building in the above land, the institution may provide these facilities in suitable temporary premises up to a maximum period of 3 years, before expiry of which the institution should shift to its permanent building.

Instructional Facilities

a) There shall be a multi-purpose educational laboratory with psychology and science sections, and a workshop attached to it.

   i) The science section shall have the apparatus and chemicals required to demonstrate all the experiments as per the syllabus of elementary schools.

   ii) The psychology section shall have facilities for conducting the following tests : Sensory-motor, Intelligence (Performance, Verbal and Non-verbal), Aptitude, Personality and Interest Inventories including Projective Tests : provision for conducting simple Piagetian and Brunnerian experiments.

b) There shall be hardware and software facilities for language learning.

c) There shall be an Educational Technology laboratory with hardware and software required for imparting Information Technology (IT) literacy.

Terms and Conditions of Service of Staff

a) The appointments shall be made on the basis of recommendations of the Selection Committee constituted as per the policy of the Central/concerned State Government.

b) All appointments are to be made on full-time and regular basis.

c) Government institutions/Government-aided institutions, may make appointments on deputation or contract basis as an interim measure, in the absence of availability of suitable candidates recommended by appropriate bodies set up by the concerned government.

d) Appointment of part-time instructors and other staff can be made as per the norms of the concerned Government.

e) The academic and other staff of the institution (including part-time staff) shall be paid such salary as may be prescribed by the concerned State Government from time to time.

f) The management of the institution shall discharge the statutory obligations relating to pension, gratuity, provident fund, etc.

g) The age of superannuation of staff shall be determined by the policy of the concerned Government subject to maximum age not exceeding 65 years.

Financial Management

a) The tuition fees and other fees shall be charged at rates as prescribed by the concerned State Government.

b) In case of private and unaided institutions, there shall be an endowment fund of Rs.5.00 lakh to be operated jointly by the authorised representative of the management and an officer of the concerned Regional Committee, and a reserve fund equivalent to three months' salary of the staff.

Relaxation in eligibility/duration of the course

As in some States, the duration of the elementary teacher education course is one year only and the eligibility for admission to such course is a pass in class ten, such States are given time up to the end of academic session 2004-2005 to switch over their programmes for bringing them in conformity with the NCTE Norms and Standards.

Meanwhile, recognition for reduced duration of the course, which shall not be less than one year and/or lower eligibility criteria, which shall not be less than a pass in class ten with at least 50% marks in aggregate, may be given subject to the condition that the certificate given by the State authorities in respect of such a course will be valid for employment within that State only and such courses including their duration and admission criteria are those that have been in existence in that State on the date when the NCTE Act, 1993 came into force.

7

Instruction and Learning: Basic Concepts

Instruction can be defined as "the purposeful direction of the learning process" and is one of the major teacher class activities (along with planning and management). Professional educators have developed a variety of models of instruction, each designed to produce classroom learning. Joyce, Weil, and Calhoun describe four categories of models of teaching/instruction (behavioral systems, information processing, personal development, and social interaction) that summarize the vast majority of instructional methods. Each model differs in the specific type or measure of learning that is targeted. Therefore, as we make decisions about "best educational practices" we must be certain that we connect recommended practices with specific desired outcomes. This point is often omitted; discussion of best practices then becomes a debate about desired outcomes rather than a discussion of how to achieve them.

Another important point is that the different models and methods of instruction have been developed based on specific interpretations of concepts and principles of teaching and learning. While it is important to learn and practice the approaches developed by others, it is even more important to understand the concepts and principles upon which they are based.

The most often used measures of student achievement in are scores on standardized tests of basic skills. Using this criteria as the desired student outcome, one set of models, labeled direct or explicit instruction, has developed overwhelming research support in the past 25 years. Several principles of direct instruction, such as more teacher direction and student-teacher interaction, provide the foundation for this approach.

INSTRUCTIONAL CONCEPTS

Teaching sailing requires the instructor to have a good understanding of a variety of concepts and techniques. There are no set answers about how to run a course or teach a particular part of the syllabus because the situations and student's requirements are infinitely variable.

A good, experienced instructor will have a range of approaches in their took box that they can utilise as they are called for. If ever you reach the stage where courses are all the same. you should start to experiment and try something new at least once a week. If you can do this, not only will you learn a lot as an instructor, but your courses will be fresh and fun for your students.

S.E.L.

S.E.L stands for Safety, Enjoyment then Learning. Whatever we do, safety is of prime importance. This means balancing the risks of the situation against your and the crew's experience and abilities.

When students are enjoying what they are doing they will learn with very little effort, the job of the instructor is to keep the tasks challenging at the correct level for the student. They must also feel that they are progressing. If you focus on students enjoying themselves and the tasks they are set, you will find it easy to help them learn.

E.D.I.C.T.

E.D.I.C.T. Stands for Explanation, Demonstration, Imitation, Correction, Testing or Training. This is the normal teaching approach. However, not all subjects lend themselves to this method.

A good example is teaching boat handling, if you explain the task, then give a good demonstration the students will have a clear picture of what they should perform. If your demonstration is not exactly what you intended, do not by afraid of admitting it. Then re-demonstrate it correctly!

Ideally, students should have at least three attempts at a task. If they get it right first time, it may be luck! If you do not give them several attempts, it would be like learning to play darts by only throwing a dart once a day-it would take a long time! In practice this has to be balanced against the time available, and keeping the task interesting.

When you offer correction, remember that most of what the student did was probably correct. Offer help in positive ways. An example is: The line you took was perfect, let's try it again a little slower/faster. Another approach is to ask them how they felt about their performance, they usually know what went well and what did not, and they do not need it pointed out in front of everyone else on board!

Only correct one aspect at a time. When they have a second attempt, only offer advice on that aspect. Avoid suddenly changing the focus on to some other element. An example could be when a person is not stopping at a mooring buoy correctly because they approaching it too fast, when they get the speed correct but not the direction-praise the correct speed-that is where their focus should have been! At the end of this you may decide that they need more training or that the student is ready to be tested. The best approach to doing this is to set a task that uses the skills they have been practising. Giving the student full command whilst entering an actual berth at the end of the day, is a good example.

K.I.S.S.

K.I.S.S. Stands for Keep It Simple and Stupid. What is the minimum we can say, to get our point across? More information does not mean more learning!

Teach a Little Well, Not a Lot Badly

One of the most common problems when you first start teaching is knowing when to stop. You should not be trying to pass on all your knowledge that took years to gain, in one week. It is far better to teach the minimum that the students need, then add extras on at a later date. An example is teaching how to take and plot a three point fix. All the students need is some time handling a hand bearing compass, some plotting of bearings on a chart and the concept that they are on each position line. Variation can be explained very simply as a correction that they must apply each time, they do not need to know much more about it at first.

Teach in Short Bursts

After 30 minutes teaching you will lose your effectiveness. Students will learn more from several short lessons. Try breaking up teaching sessions with a tea break (try heaving too), or go for a sail and give them a chance to absorb the information.

Brief Thoroughly

Before every activity brief the students on what will happen, if they are skippering, cover what you expect of them. Pay special attention to any likely difficulties. The briefing should include any special problems you think they may encounter. An example may be entering Portsmouth Harbour; the trainee skipper should have been prepared for the ferry traffic and the local regulations. They must have some idea of the tactics they could be employing before they get in to a situation where they need to act decisively.

Debrief Thoroughly

After every activity debrief on what occurred. Good points, weaker areas and other approaches if relevant. This debriefing is probably the most important part of training, especially when a student is struggling. It must be done in a positive way so that the student has a clear picture of what they should be doing to perform better next time.

Often the best debriefing approach is to ask the student how they think they performed, then ask leading questions if they do not raise the points you consider important. This could be by asking them how they would deal with a particular situation if they had to do it again.

Ideally a debrief should be done individually and in private, especially if there may be any negative aspects. However, some parts of training lend themselves to group debriefs. An example is when the skipper is not communication or controlling the crew effectively. Try asking the crew about how they experienced the particular exercise, could they hear any orders? Did they know what they were supposed to do? A group debrief needs very careful handling, it could quickly degenerate in to an argument, the instructor must control the session and ideally inject a little humour.

Accept a Rough Form

No one will perform perfectly, be prepared to accept a good try, and then build on that. Praise the best parts of their actions, give them some advice on where to focus their attention and then give them another go at some time. If they could do things first time-they would not need an instructor to guide them!

Approach To Errors

If a student cannot do a task there is a reason: They may not be experienced enough-Chose a different task. They may not understand-Find a different explanation! This may mean drawing the situation; this is ideal with boat manoeuvres. Remember they are there because they cannot yet do the tasks they have come to learn!

P.E.T.

P.E.T. Stands for Perception, Emotion, and Technique. When correcting weaknesses. Check students Perception of the task, do they understand it the same way you do? The best means of checking this is to ask them to describe the task to you, as if you do not know anything about it.

Consider their emotional state, when people are very nervous they do not perform well. Imagine entering Cowes marina on a busy Saturday afternoon for the first time. A novice skipper will probably think that everyone is watching them, this in itself can cause them to not act effectively. If this is a problem-try reducing the stress by practising the manoeuvre first in a simple situation where there is no audience.

Once you are sure that the student understands the task and is not under undue pressure, it is safe to offer correction to technical elements.

Find Something to Praise

Concentrate on praising the attempt, rather than focusing on the negative. It is very easy to come across to students as always criticising their performance. If you praise their attempts and focus their attention on those part that are done well, the weaker area often improve on their own.

See Your Students Where You Want Them to Be-Not Where They Are Now

Our views of people tend to be self-fulfilling; if you think negative thoughts about your students you will find lots of things to criticise, and vice-versa! People will rise to your expectations- or sink to them! Give them a reputation to live up to.

An example is to say something like-"You are always very good at briefing the crew before a passage." Frequently they remember that you think they are good at it, and then find they have to live up to how you think of them.

Asking questions

Asking questions, which lead students in the right direction, can aid the retention of information. People remember much better when they have thought a subject through for themselves, than if you spoon-feed them everything.

An example is when learning to spring a boat off a pontoon. Try asking them how to do it rather than telling them. Provided that boat will not be damaged, it is worth letting them try incorrect approaches occasionally. The contrast with a better technique will then be very obvious.

Talk Through Actions First

Getting the student to describe what they are about to do can help then clarify the best sequence of events. This is especially important when the action is complicated. A crew overboard recovery exercise is a good example. Try asking the student to talk through each step they intend to carry out immediately before starting.

A good time to try this is before organising putting a reef in the main sail.

Visualisation

Virtually all serious athletes use visualisation techniques because of the proven results in improving their performance. Get students to visualise all the actions that will take place before attempting a complex manoeuvre, the more detail the better. This is particularly valuable with students who find boat handling difficult. You could get them to include; each of their actions, the boat's movements, the individual crew actions, possibly even sounds of the engine.

This can be done from a viewpoint of an observer outside the boat, or from the helming position. Frequently people who struggle with boat handling do so because they do not have a clear picture of what they are trying to achieve, this technique can help those people enormously if they will buy in to it.

As a minimum, you will replace the negative pictures that some people have in their mind, they may be focused on where they do not want to go or the the other boats they could hit on the way out!

Communication

Develop different means of communication with students. Verbal, Visual, Demonstrations, Ask Questions and Group Discussions. Remember 90% of good communications is in LISTENING.

Chaining

Building up the whole task from small segments. Example: Man over board recovery under power.

— Start with the drill under power with no sails.

— Gradually add in; appointing a pointer, throwing the lifering, sending a Mayday, pressing the MOB button on the GPS, preparing a line with a loop.

— Try the drill under power but starting with the main sail up.

— Practice heaving too.

— Start the drill from sailing, heave too, check for ropes, start engine, lower headsail, motor round to pick up casualty.

All of the above would take place over 4 or 5 days. In this way, the students get lots of practice, but there are no steps where they need to learn a lot of new actions in one go.

Whole Part Whole

Start with the whole task, and then work on any weaker parts separately, before reintroducing them to the whole. Example: Man over board recovery under sail.

Try demonstrating the whole manoeuvre. Then if the students struggle with the positioning of the vessel for the return leg, try covering the backing and filling technique under main sail alone. Once they can do this part, reintroduce it to the whole manoeuvre.

Coaching

The task is attempted, then coaching advice given to tweak the performance in the right direction. Example: Execution of a short passage.

Instructional concept resources available to faculty

Instructional concepts are the application components of the critical content of a course or module. These instructional concepts may be:

1) concepts that have been historically difficult for students and/or

2) critical course concepts, which students must know to function in real-world situations.

Once developed, these instructional concepts can become a part of an integrated learning experience where critical content is first presented to the student followed by the presentation of the instructional concept. Students are given the opportunity to work with the concept as many times as needed before completing a performance assessment, which may lead the student back into the learning cycle for supplemental relearning and reassessment

NEW PARADIGM OF INSTRUCTIONAL THEORY

It is important to encourage instructional theories in a wide variety of different areas—not just in the cognitive domain, where we need theories for fostering understanding, building higher-order thinking skills, developing metacognitive skills, designing problem-based and interdisciplinary or thematic learning environments, and tailoring instructional guidance to specific content-area idiosyncrasies, but also in the affective domain, where we need guidance for developing what Daniel Goleman calls "emotional intelligence" and for what Thomas Lickona calls "character education," as well as how to develop attitudes and values and so forth. Instructional theory has been construed much too narrowly in the past.

The following are three points that may be particularly worthy of discussion:

1. Some of the "key markers" that should distinguish the new (information-age) paradigm of instructional theories from the old (industrial-age) paradigm are:

Industrian Age	*Information Age*
Standardization	Customization
Centralized control	Autonomy with accountability
Adversarial relationships	Cooperative relationships
Autocratic decision making	Shared decision making
Compliance	Initiative
Conformity	Diversity
One-way communications	Networking
Compartmentalization	Holism

Parts-oriented	Process-oriented
Teacher as "King"	Learner (customer) as "King"

To get a feel for what these key markers mean for instructional theory, the first key marker could be stated as: instructional theories should provide guidance for customizing learning for each learner, as opposed to "one size fits all" instruction. And the fifth and sixth markers could be stated as: instructional theories should provide guidance for giving learners initiative and responsibility for their own learning, while still providing support that makes the learning process more effective, efficient, and appealing. This is in contrast to instructional theories that resulted in instruction where compliance and conformity were emphasized.

2. We need to recognize the existence of two major kinds of instructional methods: basic methods, which have been scientifically proven to consistently increase the probability of learning under given conditions (e.g., for given types of learning and/or learners), such as the use of generalities, examples, and practice with feedback for teaching a skill, and variable methods, which represent alternatives from which you can choose, as vehicles for the basic methods (e.g., it doesn't matter very much whether you use print, computer, or audio tape, as long as you use one of them). For example, if someone wants to learn a skill, then demonstrations of the skill, generalities about how to do it, and practice doing it, with feedback will definitely make learning easier and more successful. Behaviourists recognized this, and called them examples, rules, and practice with feedback. Cognitivists also recognized this, but naturally had to give them different names, such as cognitive apprenticeship and scaffolding. And, yes, constructivists also recognized this, and even radical constructivists "walk the walk," even though they may not "talk the talk." An analysis of instruction designed by some radical constructivists reveals a plentiful use of these very instructional strategies.

We have learned much about the basic methods in the old paradigm of instructional theory. Now we need a new paradigm of instructional theory that provides flexible guidelines about when and how learners:

- should be given initiative;
- should work in teams on authentic, real-world tasks;
- should be allowed to choose from a diversity of sound methods;
- should best utilize the powerful features of advanced technologies; and
- should be allowed to persevere until they reach appropriate standards.

The Learning-Focused instructional theory must offer guidelines for the design of learning environments that provide appropriate combinations of challenge and guidance, empowerment and support, self-direction and structure. And the Learning-Focused theory must include guidelines for an area that has been largely overlooked in instructional design: deciding among such variable methods of instruction as problem-based learning, project-based learning, simulations, tutorials, and team-based learning.

3. Instructional theory should result in designs that allow learners to make more decisions about their instructional methods, by allowing them to choose from among sound alternative approaches. This reflects the "user-designer" concept in systems design theory. There are several ways in which this could be done. In one scenario, design teams (including all stakeholders) create flexible, computer-based, learning tools, like intelligent tutoring systems, that learners can use—while they are learning—to create or modify their own instruction. This concept is like adaptive instruction, except that the learners have the capability to request the computer system to use some instructional strategies, as well as the computer deciding on some strategies based on learner input. As Winn put it:

This means that the role of instructional designers will involve less direct instructional decision making and more concentration on the mechanisms by means of which decisions are made. ...It follows that the only viable way to make decisions about instructional strategies that meshes with cognitive theory is to do so during instruction using a system that is in constant dialogue with the student and is capable of continuously updating information about the student's progress, attitude, expectations, and so on.

Learners are able to make decisions (with varying degrees of guidance) about both content (what to learn) and strategy (how to learn it) while the instruction is in progress. The work of Dave Merrill and associates on "transaction shells" could well lead to this type of tool and has shown that such a tool is feasible to create.

A major shift in the paradigm of ISD that this scenario of the concept of user-designers represents is the notion that much of the analysis that is now done by a designer for a whole "batch" of learners well ahead of the actual instruction will soon be done during the instruction as the computer system continuously collects information from an individual learner and/or a small team of learners and uses that information to present an array of sound alternatives to the learner(s), both about what to learn next and how to learn it. Also, the teacher or trainer is afforded the opportunity to modify the system in ways s/he thinks are important. The systems concept of "equifinality" reflects the reality that there are usually several acceptable ways to accomplish the same end. The new paradigm of ISD will allow for such diversity of means, as well as a diversity of ends, for learners.

In another scenario of the concept of user-designers, computers play a relatively minor role in some instructional situations, so the users must—ahead of time—design the framework or support system within which the instruction will occur. Rather than this being done in a designer-based team, in which an instructional designer plays the leading role, it is done in a user-based team in which the designer plays a facilitating role and the users—teachers or trainers, along with learners—play the leading role This user-based approach recognizes the need to put better design tools and knowledge in the hands of those who generally create and deliver the instruction anyway. In order for this to occur, we believe a new paradigm of ISD is needed that will empower the users to play a greater role in designing their instruction than our current conception of ISD allows.

This empowerment is particularly critical in the case of teachers. Teachers are a unique type of clientele for instructional designers. They share with us a (somewhat) common knowledge base in educational theory, as well as powerful perspectives in regards to what typifies appropriate instruction. Teachers also have been empowered, both through formal preparation and classroom practice, to feel a great deal of ownership regarding the instruction they create and deliver. Also, teachers are the ones closest to the learners. Rather than using pre-constructed instructional products, teachers use and create a wide variety of materials that support their own instructional activities. Other than perhaps novice teachers, most teachers tend to take pre-constructed instructional products, deconstruct them, and then use the resulting resources in unique ways during instruction. This raises the question, why do we continue to make complete instructional products for a clientele that doesn't want them nor will use them the way we, as instructional designers, intend for them to be used? Have we been out of touch with the real needs of our clients? We propose that in fact we, as a field, have not fully recognized the need to support trainers, and particularly teachers, in designing their own instruction. And this should expand to include learners. Thus, our responsibility as a field is to conceive of and develop a whole new type of instructional design theory—one which assists trainers, teachers, and learners in meeting their own instructional needs.

CONCEPTS OF LEARNING

Although different schools of psychology define the learning process in their own ways, there is a general agreement among most psychologists on this definition: "Learning may be defined as a process in which behavior capabilities are changed as the result of experience, provided the change cannot be accounted for by native response tendencies, maturation, or temporary states of the organism due to fatigue, drugs, or other temporary factors".

Runyon interpreted the nature of learning, and differentiated the learned behavior and random behavior in his book. He wrote:

> The difference between the diffuse, random behavior of a small child and the organized, purposive behavior of an adult is largely attributable to learning. Cultural values, attitudes, instrumental behaviors, knowledge of the environment, concepts, ideas, many motives, and ways of satisfying personal and social needs are all the consequence of learning. Parents, teachers, industrial managers, training directors, rehabilitation workers, marketers, and many others constantly face the problem of how to control learning to achieve their goals and objectives. All of us spend our lives "learning", yet we often understand little of the basic process through which learning occurs. In view of the ubiquity of learning in human behavior, we can understand the contention of stimulus-control theorists that all behavior is learned.

Learning Theories

Many psychologists believe that the development of contemporary communication theory was influenced by the nineteenth-century natural science. Behaviorism, a branch of psychology, perhaps is the most experimentally oriented of the schools of psychology which flourished in the early years of the twentieth century, applied the model of the natural sciences sketched above to the study of human beings.

Psychologists have studied learning using a variety of approaches, and have tried to explain learning with a variety of different accounts. On the modern scene, these different approaches can be roughly organized into two broad categories, behavior theory or learning theory, and cognitive theory. These two approaches to learning are often regarded as quite separate from each other. Each has its own complexities, emphases and methods. They were concerned with entirely different problems and topics.

The study of learning and behavioral modification principles pushed ahead vigorously from the 1920s to the 1950s. So-called "learning theory" became a central concern of behaviorism, which accounted for human learning and behavior in terms of reinforcement schedules. Learning theory came to be a dominant school of psychology at the time investigators began to study communication scientifically. Scholars developed some basic learning principles, relying heavily on what has been labeled the stimulus-response family of learning theories. In the most basic form of the stimulus-response model, as advocated by Thorndike, all that is necessary for learning is the temporal contiguity of a stimulus and a response. To the extent that a direct connective relationship ("associated bond") exists between a stimulus and a response to that stimulus, learning is said to have occurred.

In more recent and elaborate stimulus-response theoretical formulations, the individual is considered active in his environment, and the basic learning model can be summarized as drive, cue, response, and reinforcement.

Learning theory is based on these four components: Drive, Cue, Response, and Reinforcement.

(1) *Drive:* Drive refers to an internal state of tension which calls for action.

(2) *Cue:* A cue is an environmental stimulus.

(3) *Response:* Response represents the person's reaction to cues within his environment.

(4) *Reinforcement:* Reinforcement happens to the extent that a response is rewarded. When reinforcement happens, the probability of a response being duplicated is increased—habit formation occurs. However, if the responses is not reinforced over time, the learned habit may cease—extinction occurs.

Besides those four components, forgetting is another important related notion in learning theory. Many scholars mentioned the concept of forgetting in their publications. "The theoretical basis of the process of forgetting information rests in Pavlov's notion of extinction. When Pavlov ceased rewarding his dogs as they salivated at the sound of bell, they eventually appeared to "unlearn" the association".

Amsel also mentioned the concept of forgetting. He wrote:

> When the "cognitive revolution" was already well underway, the lines that were drawn by the neo-cognitivists were indeed between investigations involving humans and animals as subjects. When the work involved people as the laboratory subject, psychologists were, of course, concerned with processes they regarded as primarily human: remembering and forgetting of verbal material—and later of visual and auditory material... ; it is subjects such as these that still define human cognitive psychology.

Runyon defined forgetting as "the extinction or loss of some skill or cognitive material that has been learned." He provided further interpretation that "once a consumer has learned something, he cannot "unlearn" it, although it may drop out of consciousness and no longer be available for voluntary recall. Occasionally, forgotten material is brought back into consciousness without further experience".

Behavioral Learning Theory

John B. Watson was one of the first American psychologists to question the narrow scope of psychology. He became the "pop" psychologist in the 1920s by publishing a series of manifest and self-help manuals that promoted his vision of a world perfected by behavioral engineering. He published his first Conditioned-Reflex data in 1916 and the beginning of learning theory.

Solomon explained behavioral learning theory as:

> Behavioral learning theories assume that learning takes place as the result of responses to external events. Psychologists who subscribe to this viewpoint do not focus on internal thought processes. Instead, they approach the mind as a "black box" and emphasize aspects consist of things that go into the box (stimulus, or events perceived from the outside world) and things that come out of the box (response, or reactions to these stimulus)"

Three theorists have major contributions to behavioral learning theory are Pavlov, known for salivation experiments with dogs, Thorndike, known for the law of effect, and Skinner, who developed operant conditioning.

Pavlov: Classical Conditioning: The beginning of the modern, scientific study of learning may be found in the work of Ivan P. Pavlov, a Russian physiologist . Pavlov, known as the "Father of Learning Theory," was the first to make the relationship between stimulus and response explicit. He is primarily responsible for the theory of classical conditioning.

Classical conditioning occurs when a stimulus that elicits a response is paired with another stimulus that initially does not elicit a response in its own. Over time, this second stimulus causes a similar response because it is associated with the first stimulus. Pavlov's famous experiment in which a dog is conditioned to salivate in the absence of food:

> He noticed that his dogs would salivate at the sight of food at feeding time. Thus, Pavlov spoke of an unconditioned stimulus (UCS) (food) eliciting an unconditioned response (UCR). He conducted a number of conditioning trials by pairing a neutral stimulus (a bell) with a stimulus known to cause a salivation response in dogs. Over time, his dogs learned to salivate at the sound

> of the bell alone. This bell is a conditioned stimulus (CS), and the salivation a conditioned response (CR).

Classical conditioning utilizes an innate response. ... Learners are essentially passive, since they do not consciously control the emission of the response. ... Reinforcement is also important in classical conditioning. While the subject is learning to give the conditioned response, a reinforcement is presented.

Thorndike: Instrumental Conditioning: In addition to classical conditioning, instrumental conditioning is the other major approach to learning. Laboratory and theoretical analyses of instrumental conditioning begin in earnest with the work of E. L. Thorndike in 1898. Thorndike's original intent was to study animal intelligence. He conducted an experiment to investigate animals' response in certain situations. "He would place a hungry cat (or dog or chicken) in the puzzle box with some food left outside in plain view. The task for the cat was to learn to escape from the box and obtain the food". On the basis of the evidence, Thorndike concluded that the animal did not suddenly realize what was going on, but that the process was one of repudiating incorrect responses and repeating correct ones.

Thorndike interpreted the results of his studies as reflecting the learning of an association. He believed that such successful escapes led to the learning of an association between the stimuli inside the puzzle box and the escape response. As the association, or connection, between the box and the successful responses became stronger, the cat came to make those responses whenever it was confined in the cage. The consequence of the successful responses—escaping the cage—strengthened the association between the box stimuli and those responses.

Thorndike also studied the effect of punishment, but seemed to feel that "positive rather than negative incentives were the key to learning". On the basis of his research, Thorndike proposed a mechanism called the law of effect. The law of effect states that "if a response in the presence of a stimulus is followed by a satisfying event, the association between the stimulus and the response is strengthened. If the response is followed by an annoying event, the association is weakened".

Kerby explained:

> The major element of Thorndike's theory is that people learn by forming connections between stimuli and responses. When rewards are provided, these connections become stronger; when punishments are imposed, they become weaker. Under this system, learning requires repetitive associations. If this theory has any validity, marketers should expect their customers to learn purchasing patterns through associations such as those created when a product in a distinctive package provided expected, or greater than expected, satisfaction, or is consumed in especially agreeable surroundings. Not only do customers learn about product performance, they learn to associate both the product and its performance with the purchase and the usage environment

In summary, in all instrumental conditioning situations, the subjects' behavior results in some type of environmental consequence. Instrumental conditioning procedures can be categorized according to the nature of the environmental event controlled by the behavior. Instrumental conditioning fundamentally involves three elements: a response, an outcome (the reinforcer), and a relation, or contingency, between the response and the reinforce.

Skinner: Operant Conditioning: Another famous theorist is B. F. Skinner who contributed to behavioral learning theory by developing operant conditioning. The term "operant" is used because the behavior actively operates on, or has an effect on , the environment for learning to occur. Skinner demonstrated the effects of operant conditioning by teaching animals to dance, play Ping-Pong, and so on by systematically rewarding them for desired behaviors. He identifies two types of learning, respondent behavior and operant behavior. Operant behavior is very important, primarily because the bulk of human behavior is of this type.

The core development of operant conditioning was accomplished through experimentation with rats. This experiment is described as following:

> Experimentation with rats generally involves the use of a Skinner box, which in its simplest form consists of a box equipped with a lever that, when passed, activates the release of a food pellet from an attached dispenser. ... Part of the exploratory behavior will bring the rat to press the lever, thereby releasing a pellet of food. At later times, the rat will repeat the lever-pushing (known as operant) and ultimately make the association between the operant and the reinforcement (food).

Operant conditioning occurs as the individual learns to perform behaviors that produce positive outcomes and to avoid those that yield negative outcomes or punishment. Operant conditioning is sometimes called instrumental conditioning, because the response emitted by the learner is instrumental in procuring a positive reinforcement or reward.

Differences between Classical and Operant Conditioning: There are two differences between operant and classical conditioning. They are that operant conditioning reinforces responses that are presumed to be under the conscious control of the individual, while classical conditioning reinforces involuntary responses, and - classical responses occur as a result of stimuli that occur prior to the response, whereas operant responses are reinforced by consequences that occur after the behavior.

Cognitive Theories

Since 1960 psychology has moved away from behaviorism and has welcomed a new branch of study, called cognitive psychology. Cognitive theories constitute the second major approach to the study of the learning process. Unlike stimulus-response theories, these theories do not view learning as the establishment of a connection between a stimulus and a response. Instead, they argue that learning is a more complex process that utilizes problem-solving and insightful thinking in addition to repetition of a stimulus-response chain.

Cognitive learning theory has roots in the classical work of Kohler, who experimented with a caged monkey. Bananas were placed outside of the cage, out of monkey's reach, and a stick was placed inside the cage. The monkey had to solve the problem of reaching the bananas by using the stick as a tool. In this case learning did not occur as a result of merely associating a stimulus and a response. Rather, insight intervened between goal recognition (procurement of food) and goal achievement.

Cognitive psychology has been concerned primarily with the processes of learning, memory, and thinking, but has also explored many other domains as well. Cognitive psychology is characterized by a willingness to explain observable behaviors by means of complicated but hidden processes.

Cognitive learning occurs as a result of mental processes. In contrast to behavioral theories of learning, cognitive learning theory stresses the importance of internal mental processes. This perspective views people as problem solvers who actively use information from the world around them to master their environment.

Cognitive theory emphasizes events that take place inside the learner. That is, cognitive research seeks to describe the role of the person's own mental activity in learning and remembering. This approach has centered on learning as the acquisition of new knowledge, rather than focusing on behavioral change

Differences between Behaviorism and Cognitive Theories: As discussed earlier on, learning theories, at both the individual and group level, can be broadly divided into behaviorism and cognitive theories. However, as Hendry wrote:

> These are linked by the principle of feedback. In behavioral conditioning, feedback works to reinforce particular responses through a system of rewards supposedly without a conscious mind intervening. In the various forms of cognitive theories, people form plans and images based on their needs, motives, values, and beliefs about themselves; they act on these; get feedback about the effects or consequences; and then actively modify perceptions, plans, and behavior accordingly.

Applications of Learning Theories

Learning theory applies to many consumer phenomena, ranging from the creation of a distinctive brand image to the perceived linkage between a product and an underlying need. In this section, the discussion will focus on its application to consumer behavior and advertising.

Some basic concepts of learning theory long studied by psychologists have direct relevance to the field of consumer behavior. Robertson wrote: "Most consumer behavior is learned behavior, which means that consumer behavior is based on previous experience under similar circumstances". The consumer's tendency to respond on the basis of habit introduces considerable efficiency into the purchasing process".

Learning is an unconscious activity; consumers don't usually even know when it is happening. It is impossible for consumers to learn all the products in the market. "Consumers are interested in learning about the products they plan to purchase, and their interest extends from the product to the outlet, the manufacturer, and the possible reactions of associates who are expected to see the item in use".

Without learning something about the product to be purchased, it is difficult to make an intelligent purchase decision. However, it would appear that the learning approach employed depends to some extent on the type of product involved . "The information source predicted on the basis of product type was selected by respondents more frequently than would be expected by chance alone. This indicates that people tend to learn about products differently, depending upon the nature of the product".

Robertson indicated in his book that the learning plays an important role in consumers' purchase decision-making processes. He wrote:

> It would be time-consuming and require vast amounts of mental energy if each and every purchase were a "new" purchase, and if prior experience and learning could not serve as a buying guide. Yet, even though most consumer behavior is habitual, a reasonable amount of brand switching, trying new products, and buying items for the first time or after extended lapses of time does occur, and consumers may make such purchases our of a desire for novelty.

Understanding how consumers learn is very important to marketers. In marketing, "all learning designed to provide the learner with a means of making more effective buying decisions with the smallest possible effort". From the marketer's point of view, "learning becomes "teaching," which means that marketers must have some understanding of the way in which learning is accomplished". After all, the statement is based on "the assumption that consumers are continually accumulating information about products, and that these people can be "taught" to prefer some alternatives over others".

Classical Conditioning Applications

Solomon gave the examples of using classical conditioning in marketing:

> The transfer of meaning from an unconditioned stimulus to a conditioned stimulus explains why "made-up" brand names like Marlboro, Coca-Cola and IBM can exert such powerful effects on consumers. The association between the Marlboro Man and the cigarette is so strong that in some cases the company no longer even bothers to include the brand name in its ad. When nonsense syllables

> (meaningless sets of letters) are paired with such evaluative words as beauty or success, the meaning is transferred to the nonsense syllables. This change in the symbolic significance of initially meaningless words shows that complex meanings can be conditioned.

Retention of Advertising: Marketers or advertisers are concerned about how long advertising messages are retained and what value repetition has on retention. A considerable amount of experimental work in psychology has dealt with the retention or forgetting of learned material. From those work, Robertson drew a number of conclusions:

1. Forgetting is greatest immediately following learning; thereafter, it declines to a stable level. In advertising practice, the decay of advertising messages is part of forgetting. If advertising for a product is withdrawn, consumers gradually forget the information. However, renewed advertising works very quickly to reestablish the previously learned associations, implying that extinction is rarely complete. Material may be latent or suppressed, but it is not totally forgotten.

2. Retention increases with repetition. However, (a) Repetition distributed over several periods leads to greater retention than repetition concentrated in a single period; (b) variation in form, style, and expression during repetition, together with repetition of main points, may result in greater retention than repetition of the identical message; (c) the greater the complexity and length of the message, the greater the amount of repetition necessary to produce retention; and (d)the greater the interference from competing messages, the greater the amount of repetition necessary to produce retention.

3. More meaningful or more vivid material is better retained than less meaningful or less vivid material.

4. The more completely material is initially learned, the greater is retention.

5. Material presented first (primacy) or last (recency) is better retained than material presented in the middle.

Repetition: The amount of repetition is another factor involved in the learning process. Repetition has important value in retention of advertising and has generally been considered the key to advertising success. "The more repetition, the greater the depth of the learning and the slower the rate of decay. This implies that knowledge of old established brands is less subject to extinction than knowledge of newer brand. Hence, a cutback in advertising for a younger brand would be more detrimental to sales performance. The decay rate can also be reduced by high meaningfulness of the material and high motivation of the consumer".

The critical question here is how many times a consumer should be exposed to an ad before the advertising message is effective. Some advertising researchers argue that "more than three exposures are wasted". They explain that "the first creates awareness of product, the second demonstrates its relevance to the consumer, and the third serves as a reminder of the product's benefits". Solomon supported this argument:

> This approach implies that repetition is needed to ensure that the consumer is actually exposed to (and processes) the ad at least three times. Marketers attempting to condition an association must ensure that the consumers they have targeted will be exposed to the stimulus a sufficient number of times. On the other hand, it is possible to have too much of a good thing: Consumers can become so used to hearing or seeing a marketing stimulus that they no longer pay attention to it. This problem, known as advertising wearout, can be alleviated by varying the way in which the basic message is presented.

The previous findings provide their implications for advertising media scheduling. According to Robertson's conclusion:

> He would suggest that advertising spread out over a year will be more effective than the same amount of advertising concentrated into a three-month period. (This assumes that

> the product's sales are not seasonal.) The superiority of a continuous schedule diminishes and may even be reversed, however, for complex messages requiring learning based on reasoning. Myers and Reynolds (1967) conclude that continuity of advertising is generally best for established products, and that impact (concentrated messages) is best for new products requiring some thought on the consumer's part. Furthermore, Bogart (1967) suggests that advertising featuring new sales points may be most effective when it runs in "concentrated bursts" separated by substantial time intervals, rather than on a continuous basis.

Repetition of a central theme with some variation is generally considered superior to repetition of identical messages. This finding seems to hold across a wide variety of research. In fact, Cox and Bogart suggest that "repetition of identical messages beyond some critical point may actually lead to negative response; that is, over repetition may cause consumers to actively disregard the message, and may even encourage negative feelings toward the product".

Psychologists who work on the learning process view advertising impact in two ways, focusing on the individual level or the aggregate level. On the individual level, the degree of recall (aided or unaided) a consumer has of a particular environment was measured. Alternatively, on the aggregate level, the proportion of a specialized population that recalls the message was determined. In either case, the generalized learning curve applies, The first time advertisement appears, it produces only minimum effect. In fact, it has been proposed that it takes three exposures to an ad before any real impact is generated.

Media Scheduling: In media scheduling, learning theory also has its important implication. As Runyon wrote: "In terms of advertising alone, the frequency and timing of advertisements to maximize learning and minimize forgetting is a major consideration in media scheduling". Zielske conducted an experiment which demonstrates the importance of advertising scheduling on product recall. According to the findings of the study indicates:

> The thirteen-week schedule shows the greatest learning, with 63 percent of the women who had been mailed an advertisement weekly being able to recall the product at the end of period. Forgetting was also rapid, however, Within four weeks of the last exposure, the percentage who could remember the advertising was cut in half. After each exposure, substantial forgetting occurred. However, by the end of thirteen mailings (52 weeks), 48 percent of the respondents recalled the advertising.

Instrumental Conditioning Applications

Principles of instrumental conditioning are at work when a consumer is rewarded or punished for a purchase decision. Business people shape behavior by gradually reinforcing consumers for taking appropriate actions.

Brand Loyalty: Brand loyalty is considered a positive reinforcement of consumption. The assumption here is that it is possible for people to change their attitudes by reinforcing. According to a research finding, about 65 percent of the average company's business comes from its present, satisfied customers. "Consumers over time come to associate with people that reward them, and to choose products that make them feel good or satisfy some need".

Robertson also discussed this issue in his book:

> Many consumer purchases are habitual responses deriving from prior satisfying experience with the products. Habits which develop on the basis of past experience and reinforcement of prior purchase responses therefore lend efficiency to consumer shopping. According to a experimentally study of the development of brand loyalty conducted by Tucker, if the product offerings are identical, loyalty would therefore not be expected. About half of his respondents established brand loyalty, and this loyalty can be considered logical in that it reduces ambiguity in decision making and because the brand responses made were sufficiently reinforced to result in learned behavior.

The tendency of consumers to develop brand loyalties benefits the manufacturers of established brand. However, for the manufacturer of a new brand, it becomes has the usually difficult task of breaking such loyalties and encouraging brand switching—unless existing product offerings are not providing adequate reinforcement. "To the extent that learning and brand loyalty can be gained for a product, the manufacturer achieves a more stable sales profile and is not as subject to competitive inroads").

Breaking brand loyalty is difficult, but it is not impossible. Robertson wrote:

> Habits can be broken when response ceases to gratify (boredom or satiation with a product), or when a new response can be shown to be potentially more gratifying. Deal activity and free sampling are marketing strategies to break response pattern and establish new patterns. Thus, what has been learned can be unlearned—extinction can occur. An individual may prefer a specific brand, but some unpleasant experience may cause extinction of the learned preference. When a response is followed by reward, its probability of recurrence increases; but when a response is followed by punishment or lack of reward, its probability of recurrence decreases. On the other hand, some consumers may be observed to seek gratification through variety—perhaps extending their patronage to several different brands of a product or service in succession

Cognitive learning applications

Marketing is primarily concerned with cognitive learning. Solomon mentioned the application of cognitive learning to marketing in his book:

> Consumers' abilities to learn vicariously by observing how the behavior of others is reinforced makes the lives of marketers much easier. Because people do not have to be directly reinforced for their actions, marketers do not necessarily have to reward or punish them for purchase behaviors. Instead, they can show what happens to

> desirable models who use or do not use their products, knowing that consumers will often be motivated to imitate these actions at a later time. In addition, many applications of consumer problem-solving are related to ways information is represented in memory and recalled at a later date.

Corrective Advertising: If an advertisement is found to be deceptive, the Federal Trade Commission has the power to order the advertiser to use corrective advertising. A question of interest here, then, is how can corrective advertising contribute to changing material previously learned by consumers? Robertson provided his answer:

> In fact, learning theory suggest that change will be affected in two stages. First, consumers must "unlearn" the false or misleading information imparted by the initial advertisement or series of advertisements. Then, new, corrective information must be provided to replace the original message.

NEEDS OF EFFECTIVE LEARNING

Knowing Yourself as a Learner

— Know 'how you learn best and adapt the study' strategies that work best for you.

— Choose the best learning strategy for the task at hand.

— Monitor your understanding and progress as you go along.

— Adjust strategies when appropriate.

— Web sites on learning styles, metacognition (knowing how you know) and learning disabilities.

— Find out more about the Study Skills Course.

Getting the Big Picture & Dealing with Details

— Read the course syllabus for an overview of the course.

- Preview the whole text to get an overview of course content.
- Outline or map each chapter before you read in detail or go to class.
- Read/listen for the introduction and summary.
- Review your outlines or maps before tests.
- Preview the test before starting, then plan your strategy.

Breaking Tasks into Meaningful Chunks

- Break up study into 45 minute to 1 hour chunks.
- Break up reading or study by units of information (i.e., chapters or topics).
- Label information in text books and in your notes.
- Connect new information to maps or outlines to keep it connected with other related information.
- Look for relationships— i.e., categories, cause-effect, similarities/differences, etc. Use cognitive questions and visual organizers to assist understanding and memory.
- Study by reviewing main ideas and details from flash cards and Cornell notes.

Questioning and Using Cognitive Structures

- Determine your purpose for reading or for the task.
- Ask, "What do I already know about this task or subject?"
- Use questions at the end of the chapter or develop questions from headings to focus on important information as you read.
- Monitor your understanding as you read or listen to lectures.

— Use questions at all cognitive levels to help yourself process and remember information.

— Ask: "Does this answer make sense?"

— Ask for help if you need it.

Memory and the Importance of Review

— "Use it, or lose it". Go over material frequently.

— Focus on the material and information that is most important.

— Use index cards and maps or Cornell notes for quick, convenient review.

— Analyze past tests to improve your test-taking skills.

— Use mnemonic devices to assist memory of important information.

8

INSTRUCTIONAL DESIGN

The purpose of instruction is to help people learn. The goal of instructional designers is to make learning easier, quicker, and more enjoyable. Some people view training as a process of finding out who the brightest employees are. But performance in a course is not very highly correlated with the basic ability to be good on the job. So what we need is a knowledge base about methods of instruction to supplement the creative, "art" aspect of training. Such a knowledge base would offer optimal methods for given situations. But what are the important situations that call for different methods? How can we tell what methods to use when? Some of the options are the nature of:

— the learner

— the content

— the goals

— the learning environment

— the teacher

— the resources

KINDS OF LEARNING

Perhaps the most important aspect of the situation is the kind of learning that is to be facilitated. Knowing about the kinds of learning helps us to do a better job of teaching them. The most basic distinction is Benjamin Bloom's three domains:

— Cognitive learning (thoughts), such as teaching someone to add fractions.

— Affective learning (feelings, values), such as teaching someone to not want to smoke.

— Physical or motor learning (actions), such as teaching someone to touch type.

Levels of Cognitive Learning

The major levels of cognitive learning can be classified as memorizing, understanding, and applying. Most content can be learned at any of these three levels of learning. For example, you can memorize a definition of performance-based assessment as indicated by being able to restate it, you can understand what performance-based assessment is by being able to relate it to relevant prior knowledge, and you can learn to use performance-based assessment in your training. Too often we teach at the wrong level or test at the wrong level.

Memorization. This is rote learning. It entails learners encoding facts or information in the form of an association between a stimulus and a response, such as a name, date, event, place or symbol. For example, these are facts: Columbus discovered America in 1492, Pi = 3.1417, 2 + 4 = 6, "B" says "buh", ¶ is the symbol for a new paragraph. The behavior that indicates that this kind of learning has occurred is stating (or "regurgitating"), usually verbatim.

Understanding. This is meaningful learning. It entails learners relating a new idea to relevant prior knowledge, such as understanding what a revolutionary war is. The behaviors that indicate that this kind of learning has occurred include comparing and contrasting, making analogies, making inferences, elaborating, and analyzing (as to parts and/or kinds), among others.

Application. This is learning to generalize to new situations, or transfer learning. It entails learners identifying critical commonalities across situations, such as predicting the effects of price increases. The behavior that indicates that this kind of learning has occurred is successfully applying a generality (the critical commonalities) to a diversity of previously unencountered situations.

Memorization, though sometimes very important, is greatly overused in most training settings. Understanding is very important, but it is relatively complex, and has not received much attention by instructional theorists until very recently. Application is important and has received much attention by instructional theorists. It therefore provides a good place for us to begin.

Application-level Learning

Dave Merrill has proposed that it is useful for prescribing methods of instruction to think of three types of content that can be learned on the application level:

— Concepts

— Procedures

— Principles

The term, "concept", has many meanings. Concept is a group or class of particulars which have something in common. These are concepts:

—Shoe Resistor

—Pencil Paragraph

—Fight Democracy

—Anger Lever

A procedure is an ordered sequence of steps for accomplishing some goal. These are procedures:

— How to write a paragraph.

— How to add fractions.

— How to operate a machine.

The term, "principle", also has several meanings in our every-day language. A principle is a relationship between two or more changes. It can be a causal, correlational, or natural-order relationship. The following are principles:

— An increase in price causes a decrease in demand.

— A train comes whenever ! reach this crossing.

— Plants grow from a seed to a seedling to a plant.

Synthesis

Here's a good rule of thumb for identifying these kinds of content:

— Concepts are concerned with grouping things into categories. What?

Procedures are concerned with how to do something. How?

— Principles are concerned with predictions and explanations. Why?

It is also helpful to keep in mind that these three types of content can be learned at any of the three levels of learning: Many topics can entail all 9 of these kinds of learning. For example, learning what "mastery learning" is could entail learning to apply a concept, apply a procedure, apply a principle, understand a concept, memorize a concept, and so forth for all 9 types.

This is very important to understand, because students have trouble when we teach one kind of learning but test for another, such as teaching them to memorize the concept but asking them to apply the principle on a test. But this distinction is not just helpful for deciding what to teach (and test), but also for deciding how to teach it. Each of these kinds of learning requires quite different methods of instruction.

	Concept	Procedure	Principle
Apply			
Understand			
Memorize			

INVARIANT TASKS

Invariant tasks require memorizing factual information or routine procedures. They do not require any understanding, nor do they require learning how to deal with variation. They require what Ausubel referred to as "rote" learning. There are several quite different kinds of memorization, each of which is learned a bit differently:

— A list is a number of items, mental and/or physical, which need to be memorized. List learning is a rote form of learning, requiring no meaningful understanding of the items in the list and no variation from one performance of the invariant task to another.

— A mental list requires only cognitive learning, such as the names of all the products your company sells, or the mental actions involved in translating quarts into gallons.

— A physical list requires learning physical actions as well, such as learning to change the oil in your car.

If a list needs to be "performed" (e.g., stated or acted out) in a certain order, it is called an ordered list. For example, the "Pledge of Allegiance" is an ordered mental list, sometimes called a "verbal chain". And changing the oil in your car is an ordered physical list, sometimes called a "rote procedure" (the used oil must be drained before the new oil is added). Singing the scales, applying for travel funds in your company, and initializing a diskette are also rote procedures. Keep in mind that in some rote procedures (mental or physical) the order doesn't matter, as long as you do all the "steps."

An association is a one-to-one correspondence between two items, such as a product and its price or a state and its capital. Items can include objects, pictures, sounds, symbols, actions, and much more, but learning names for things is perhaps the most common kind of association learning. Of course it is possible for lists of associations to be learned, such as the capitals of all the countries in South America or the prices of all the products your company offers.

Importance of Invariant Task

Memorization has a bad name in educational circles. Since it is the easiest type of learning to teach and to measure (test), it is overused. We often require our learners to memorize things which don't really need to be memorized, and we fail to teach as many of the higher types of learning as our learners need because we have spent so much time on memorization. But there are some important invariant tasks in the world, and the only way it makes sense to learn them is memorization. Most higher forms of learning are not possible unless certain information has been memorized first, to the point where it is an "automatic" "response-that" is, we don't have to think about it, which frees us to use our cognitive resources on higher matters. The addition facts in math and the sounds of individual letters in reading are cases in point. We also need to memorize the names of things in order to be able to communicate about them.

PRINCIPLES

Before you can figure out how to teach an invariant task, it is helpful to know how invariant tasks are learned. Different learning theories provide different perspectives on how they are learned.

Behaviorist Learning Theory

There are several kinds of behaviorist learning theories. You may be familiar with "conditioned response theory" developed by Pavlov, whereby a response that already occurs in the presence of one stimulus can be "conditioned" to occur following a different stimulus. This learning theory is very important for emotional learning, but has little relevance to most learning of invariant tasks. Far more relevant is "reinforcement theory," first developed by E. L. Thorndike and further developed by B.F. Skinner and others. In reinforcement theory, an invariant task is viewed as a "response" and is learned when it becomes "associated" with an appropriate stimulus. For example, "3.14" is a response that should become associated with "Pi".

This learning process occurs whenever "reinforcement" follows the response. For example, each time a learner responds with "3.14", a reinforcer such as "Right!" or "Good!" or even just a smile with a nod will increase the probability of the learner responding the same way in the future. With sufficient repetition of these stimulus-response-reinforcement events, the response will come to occur automatically in the presence of the stimulus.

Cognitive / Information Processing Theory

There are at least two major kinds of cognitive theory relevant to learning invariant tasks: information-processing theory and schema theory. According to the information-processing model of learning, there is a series of stages by which new information is learned. Information is received by receptors (such as the eyes and ears), from which it is passed to the sensory register where all of it is held, but for only a few hundredths of a second. At this point, selective perception acts as a filter which causes some aspects of the information to be ignored and others to be attended to. For example, the ears (receptors) receive the sounds comprising "Pi equals 3.14," along with various other background sounds, and all those sounds are passed on to the sensory register in the brain. Then through the selective perception process, some of the information (hopefully the "Pi equals 3.14 part) is attended to."

That information which is attended to is transformed and passed on to short-term memory, which can only contain a few items of information at a time (usually identified as 7+2 items, depending on their complexity). For example, if "Pi equals 3.14" is attended to, it is then passed on to short-term memory, where it might be said to "echo" for a few seconds, and the echoing can be prolonged through rehearsal." Items can persist in short-term memory for up to about 20 seconds without rehearsal, but with constant rehearsal they can be retained indefinitely. Finally, the information may be passed to long-term memory. This process is called encoding.

For example, if appropriate encoding processes are exercised to link the "Pi equals 3.14" with prior knowledge, then the information is passed on to long-term memory." It is likely that different types of knowledge are encoded in different ways, which is why they require different methods of instruction. It is typically only this stage which we call "learning", for information which is not passed on to long-term memory is lost (at least, it is not retrievable). It is necessary to turn to other theories, such as schema theory, for descriptions of how the encoding process may occur.

Cognitive/Schema Theory

The other major kind of cognitive theory is schema theory. It proposes that, when new knowledge is encoded, it is organized into schemas, which are networks of related pieces of knowledge. For example, an invariant task can be encoded as a new schema, complete with such contextual factors as conditions for its use, in which case it will be at least loosely related to other schemata, or more typically it can be assimilated into an existing schema. But more importantly for instructional purposes, specific elements of the invariant task can often be learned—or more accurately, retrieved—more easily by relating them to certain carefully selected prior knowledge, especially meaningful knowledge. For example, it is easier to remember the colors of the rainbow and their order (red, orange, yellow, green, blue, indigo, violet) by associating them with the name, "Roy G. Biv."

Constructivist Theory

Constructivist theory views learning as....

An integrated view

There are two major degrees of memorization: recognition and recall. In recognition for a list, the name of the list and an item from the list are both presented to the learner, who indicates whether or not the item belongs to the list: "Which of the following were Presidents of the United States: Abraham Lincoln, Fred Washington,... ?" For an ordered list, two or more items from the list are presented or performed, and you indicate whether or not they are in the right order. In recall for a list, the name of the list is presented, and you have to retrieve the items from your own memory: "List ten Presidents of the United States below" or "Change the oil in your car."

Does association learning occur the same way? An association, in its simplest form, has two elements which must be paired together (associated with each other): a stimulus, which is presented to the learner, and a response (either mental or physical), which is provided by the learner. A state with its capital, a person with her name, a painting with its artist, a symbol with its name, and the letters of the alphabet with the finger movement necessary to type each on a standard keyboard are all cases in point. In its more complex forms, an association can have many elements which are all to be associated with each other, such as a person, a place, a date, and (the name of) an event. In this case, you usually have one stimulus and multiple responses. For example, "the discovery of America" might be associated with "Christopher Columbus," "1492," "Queen Isabel of Spain," and "the Nina, Pinta, and Santa Maria."

In recognition for an association, the stimulus and a response are both presented, and you indicate whether or not they are a correct match, or you match up the correct ones. "Was the Declaration of Independence signed in 1770?" is such an item. In recall for an association, the stimulus is presented, and you have to retrieve the response from your own memory. "When was the Declaration of Independence signed?" is a case in point. In spite of these differences, association learning is similar to list learning in that it is a rote (nonmeaningful) form of learning which is committed to memory primarily by repetition. It is also acquired gradually over time with practice, and it can be learned to the point of recognition or to the point of recall.

Learning a rote procedure may require learning two things: when to do each action, and how to do each action. But in many cases, the learners may already know how to do each action, such as an experienced computer user learning how to use a particular WWW browser to search the Internet. That learner just needs to learn what actions to take when, not how to take them.

What are the obstacles to memorization?

Learning psychologists generally believe from hypnosis experiments that getting information into memory is easy, that the only real obstacle is retrieval from memory. The items on a list are thought of as being stored in memory as individual nodes, in this case, one for each President. Retrieval occurs through links among nodes. The links become stronger each time they are used. The challenge, then, becomes one of creating links which are strong enough that retrieval is quick and effortless.

An obstacle to list learning is presented when there are many items to remember on the list—the more items, the harder the task. Would you try to learn the names of all the Presidents at the same time? Or would you divide up the names and work on a few of them at a time until they are mastered before going on to another set of names? George Miller found that "working memory" has a limit of 7 ± 2 items. In other words, you can only productively work on memorizing up to about seven items at a time. Much subsequent research has shown that learning proceeds more easily if a large list is divided into chunks of about 5-7 items and each chunk is mastered before the next chunk is taken on.

Two additional things have been found to facilitate remembering. Rote information can usually be remembered better if it is related to meaningful prior knowledge. For example, the meaningful phrase, "Every Good Boy Does Fine", makes it much easier to remember the order of the notes (lines) on a staff (in music): E G B D F. It is also easier to remember visual images and musical tunes and rhymes than to remember words. For example, presenting a picture of a boy with a halo getting a pat on the back would likely make it easier to remember "Every Good Boy Does Fine". Similarly, the rhyme, "Thirty days have September, April, June, and November....", makes it much easier to remember the lengths of the months.

Activities in the Development Process

If you were developing a computer program to teach the names of the Presidents of the United States, what activities would you engage in?

1. *Analyze* - identify needs, objectives, and content, and analyze learners.
2. *Design* - select instructional tactics for the type of learning.
3. *Develop/Produce* - write and produce the instructional materials and directions.
4. *Implement* - deliver, manage, and monitor the instruction.
5. *Evaluate formatively* - try it out and revise it.

Although the four activities are somewhat sequential, there are aspects of every activity which are performed during each other activity. It is much more an iterative process than a linear process, as I'm sure you have already come to learn. Of these various activities, design is usually the most difficult and time-consuming to learn how to do well. So let's take a look at how it might be done. In the case of invariant tasks, it might be broken into the following steps:

1. Break the information into chunks if the optimal learning load is exceeded (usually about seven items).
2. Design the presentation for the first chunk.
3. Think up a mnemonic if helpful, and design the presentation for it.
4. Design practice for remembering the mnemonic and relating it to the information (if needed).
5. Design practice for the first chunk of information, complete with prompting and feedback. Design it in a game format if there is a lot of information to be remembered.
6. Plan for repetition of the practice, as needed, including systematic review.

CONCEPT CLASSIFICATION

Design a Concept-Classification Lesson

Pick a concept for which learners need to be able to distinguish examples from nonexamples. Try to pick a concept for which the examples are very different from each other, such as: prepositional phrase or concave lens.

Nature of Knowledge

There are two major kinds of knowledge:

— Knowledge of things (descriptive knowledge) and

— Knowledge of changes in things (productive knowledge).

Each of these kinds of knowledge can occur in either of two forms (Fig.1):

— Particulars are single, unique cases, often referred to as referents, examples or instances.

— Generalities are statements which apply to more than one particular.

	Particulars	Generalities
Descriptive (Things)	Facts, Information, Examples, Instances	Concepts
Productive (Changes)	Facts, Information, Demonstrations, Instances	Rules, Procedures, Principles

Figure 1: Kinds of Knowledge

Things. Particulars of things are instancesof concepts, and include objects (e.g., one particular computer), actions (e.g., one particular debate), ideas (e.g., one particular thought), and symbols (e.g., one particular fraction). Generalities of things are what we usually call definitionsof concepts.

Changes. Particulars of changes are instances of procedures and principles, and include specific events, like the evaporation of a puddle on my driveway last Sunday, the growing of a particular flower from a seed in front of my neighbor's house, and my son's writing of an essay last Tuesday night. Generalities of changes are what we usually call statements of principles and procedures. It is helpful to distinguish between what content is learned and on what level it is learned: Content (what is learned) can be classified in accordance with the type of knowledge. Concepts and facts represent knowledge of things, and principles and procedures represent knowledge of changes.

Level of learning can be classified as memorization, understanding, or application. As defined by instructional designers, a concept is a group or class of things which have something in common, such as plants, animals, reptiles, snakes, essays. But a concept can be a class of events, ideas (including values), or symbols, rather than just a class of things: football game, word processing, justice, compassion, fraction, and % sign are all concepts. Particulars can be grouped in many different ways. For example, trees can be classified according to their genus (birches, oaks, etc.), their age (seedlings, saplings, etc.), their climate (tropical, subtropical, etc.), and so on. So concepts are arbitrary groupings which are *invented*by people. Concepts don't really exist; the only tangible evidences of them are their instances (or examples) and their definitions.

Be careful not to confuse concepts with principles. The term "concept" is often used in common language to refer to principles. When people talk about the "concepts of science", they are usually talking about principles, which instructional designers define as change relationshipsóindications of the relationship between two or more changes.

Levels of Learning for Concepts

There are three major ways that a concept can be learned. You can memorize itóeither its definition, or a particular instance and its name. You can understand itóbe able to describe it in your own words and explain its relationship to other things you know. Or you can learn to apply it in new situations. This third type of behavior is what we call skill application.

Importance of Concept Classification

Concept classification is one of the most common types of learning. Let's look at how concepts are involved in rule-using capabilities. Principles describe changes in things. Those "things" are concepts which are simpler components of the principle and must be mastered before it is possible for a learner to master the principle. For example, the law of supply and demand describes relationships among changes in price, supply, and demand. Those three concepts must be mastered before the law of supply and demand can be mastered.

Procedures describe how to change things (to achieve a goal). Those "things" are also concepts which are simpler components of the procedure and must be mastered before the procedure can be learned. For example, the procedure for dividing fractions indicates that the divisor must be inverted, the resulting numerators must be multiplied to form the new numerator, and the denominators must be multiplied to form the new denominator. The three conceptsódivisor, numerator, and denominatorómust be mastered before it is possible to master the procedure (although it is not necessary to learn those labels). Also, procedures often require the use of tools to perform a step, and those tools are concepts.

Given the importance of concept classification, it is essential that we know how to teach it well. Fortunately, much research has been done in this area, so we understand much about how concept classification is learned and what features instruction should have to best help learners learn it.

Principles for Learning Concept Classification

How is concept classification learned? Consider for a moment your knowledge of concepts. When someone says "dog" to you, what goes on in your mind? Think about it for a minute!... You probably form an image of a dog in your mind, right? What is that dog like? What color is it? It doesn't really have any color, does it? How big is it? About average height for a dog, right? Unless you have a beloved dog of your own, your image is not of one specific dog. Rather it is of a prototype (which literally means pattern or model). It concentrates on the characteristics common to all dogs and tends to ignore the characteristics which vary across dogs, such as color and size and length of hair.

Robert Tennyson has shown that prototype formation is probably the first phase of learning to apply a concept. This is the first principle of learning for concept classification. Once a prototype has been formed, we must learn how dogs varyóthat they can be different sizes, colors, shapes, and so on. So we must learn to generalize beyond the prototype. But the other side of that coin, according to Sue Markle and Phil Tiemann, is learning ways that dogs cannot vary. So we must learn to discriminate them from nondogs.

Discrimination. All dogs have certain characteristics in common, such as being mammals, having a certain type of teeth, a certain type of diet, a certain range of body shapes, and so on. These are called common characteristics. Some of them are easily visible (e.g. body shape) and some of them are not (e.g. diet). Hence, some common characteristics are useful for classifying an animal as being a dog or not, and others aren't. The ones which are useful are called critical characteristics. They are what you need to learn to discriminate dogs from nondogs. This is the second principle of learning for concept classification.

Generalization. Dogs also have certain characteristics which vary from one dog to another, such as their color, size, and so on. These are called variable characteristics. They are what you need to learn to generalize across all kinds of dogs. This is a third principle of learning for concept classification.

Generalization across variable characteristics and discrimination on the basis of critical characteristics are very important aspects of learning to apply concepts. But it is helpful to keep in mind that variable characteristics can have different degrees of variability. Some can be common to almost all of the members of the concept class, while others can be very rare in any of them. The ones that are common to most can sometimes be very useful for classifying. Almost any concept can be broken down into kinds (called "subordinate concepts"), and each of those kinds represents what Joseph Scandura calls a different "equivalence class." The different equivalence classes are sometimes called "dimensions of divergence."

Some concepts are quite complex. That is, they have many critical characteristics. This can make learning to classify very difficult. Lev Landa has identified a technique which people learn to facilitate the process. They develop an algorithm, or procedure, to follow. It is likely to be something like this:

First look to see if it has such-and-such. If it doesn't, it is not a widget. But if it does, look to see if it has either a whatsit or a whosie. If it has neither, then it is not a widget. But if it has either one, then look to see if...." Learning to apply a concept *always*entails learning an algorithm, but for simple concepts the algorithm has just one step. This is the fourth principle of learning for concept classification. Incidentally, "experts" are usually unaware of the algorithm they use.

A final important consideration for learning concept classification is prior knowledge. Robert Gagné has shown that the skill of applying a concept always has some "prerequisite" skills, skills which must be mastered before it is possible to learn any given classification skill. Those prerequisites are the critical (and sometimes variable) characteristics, which are concepts in their own right. This is yet another principle of learning which has important implications for the instructional strategies that will be helpful for teaching concept classification. Given all these principles for concept learning, how should one teach a concept classification task?

Prototype formation. First, the learner should form a prototype. You can facilitate this by presenting a prototypical example. This example should be very common and highly representative of as many examples of the concept as possible.

Discrimination. Next, the learner should learn what the members of the concept class have in common so that she or he can distinguish them from nonmembers. These commonalities are the critical characteristics, and their acquisition can be facilitated in two major ways. One way is to tell the learners what they are. This is called a generality, or definition, of the concept. The other way is to contrast an example of the class with a nonexample that is as similar as possible to that example. This is called a matched nonexample, because its variable characteristics and all but one of its critical characteristic are matched with those of an example. The example and matched nonexample are presented simultaneously to facilitate identifying the critical characteristic which makes one an example and not the other.

Generalization. The learners must also learn to generalize from the prototype to all other members of the class. That is, they must learn how examples can differ from each other and still be members of the class. This requires learning which are the variable characteristics that should be ignored. You can facilitate this learning in two ways: by presenting a generality which identifies the most common of the variable characteristics or by presenting examples that are as differentas possible from each other. These are called divergent examples. Of course, divergent practice is just as important.

It is helpful to notice that two learning processes occur in concept classification tasks. One of them is acquisition of some general representation of the concept in memory, which is probably a combination of the generality and the prototypical example. The other is learning to apply the concept representation to the classification of new examples. Acquisition of the generality is usually facilitated by presenting the generality and the prototypical example *simultaneously*. You could even make a game out of the instruction by presenting lots of examples without the generality and having the learners try to *discover*the critical characteristics (discover the generality). But this is very different from facilitating application of the generality, which requires presenting divergent examples and practice and matched nonexamples.

Therefore, there are two kinds of learner participation which can be designed into the instruction: one to facilitate acquisition of the generality, which is inductive in nature, and one to facilitate application of the generality, which is deductive in nature. Inductive participation alone is insufficient if concept classification is your objective. So what tactics should instruction have for concept classification tasks? It may be helpful to distinguish between "routine" tactics (which are routinely included in *all* instruction for concept classification) and "power" tactics (which are usually only used to strengthen the instruction for difficult concept-classification tasks. This distinction may well be useful for teaching all kinds of skill application, and perhaps even for facilitating other levels of learning.

Routine Tactics

We can group the tactics into three routine tactics: presentation, practice, and feedback:

— *Presentation*: Generality ó label, superordinate concept, critical characteristics.

Examples ó new particulars which show the critical characteristics.

— *Practice*: Practice ó new particulars which show the critical characteristics.

— *Feedback*: Feedback ó confirmation or correct answer.

Generality: The generality should only include things which help the learner to classify. When we want the learner to learn other things about the concept, a different type of learning is involvedóunderstanding. However, it is helpful to understand that some concepts are defined on the basis of critical characteristics, whereas others are defined on the basis of functions. These are called criterial definitions and functional definitions, respectively. For example, "chair" can be defined as something to sit in with back support, or it can be defined as having a seat, raised off the ground, and a back. A definition can also have bothcriterial and functional tactics. For example, a chair is something to sit in, and it has a back.

Practice: Since the learners need to be able to generalize the classification skill to examples that they have never seen before, your practice should always present new instances (ones not used in the examples), and they should be divergent from each other, including at least one "minimum critical subset" of instances.

Feedback: If learners practice the wrong responses without being corrected, those wrong responses are likely to become difficult to change. Thus, it is very important to correct wrong responses as soon as possible after they occur. This is called "informational feedback." If the learners get it right, you can confirm their response. If they get it wrong, you can give them the correct response with explanations or give them hints that help them to figure out how to correct their own responses. We have seen that the instruction should begin with prototype formation. Hence, a prototypical example should lead the instruction, usually with a simultaneous presentation of the generality.

Also, young learners tend to benefit from plentiful examples before presentation of the generality, and you may want to use a discovery approach where the generality isn't presented at all until it has been discovered. Next, it is often helpful for learners to be able to skip around among the instructional tactics. After looking at the generality and prototypical example, a learner might think she already knows the concept. She could then go directly to the more difficult practice to test herself. If she gets it wrong, she could go back and look at an example of medium difficulty, then go and try out a practice item of medium difficulty or take a look at the generality again, and so forth. All that's needed to facilitate such learner control is to clearly label the various routine tactics. This is a more practical and empowering solution to individual differences than designing different instruction for each learner.

Power Tactics

When a concept is difficult for the learners to learn to classify, additional tactics can be used to increase the power of the instruction. It is helpful to think of such instructional enhancement as existing for *each*routine tactic.

Generality: So how can the generality be srengthened? There are several ways. You can facilitate encoding by focusing the learner's attention on the important parts of it: the label and the critical characteristics. Or you can facilitate encoding by providing a variety of representations of the generality, like a diagram or a paraphrase. You can also present an algorithm, a set of steps for the learner to use in checking to see if all of the critical characteristics are present.

Examples. The most obvious way to enhance this routine tactic is to increase the number of examples. But we can also make it easier to learn from each example. Since examples are different from each other, some are likely to be harder to identify as examples of the concept. The easier examples should be presented first, followed by progressively more difficult ones. This is called an easy-to-difficult sequence. We can also use attention-focusing to relate the example to the generality by pointing out the presence or absence of critical characteristics in the example. And we can use a variety of representations for the examples, to facilitate "dual encoding" of the information.

Practice: The only ways that practice itself should be enhanced are to increase the number of practice items, to use an easy-to-difficult sequence, and to include prompting on early practice items. Otherwise, ehancements should be reserved for the feedback.

Feedback: Enhancement on the feedback should be much like on the examples. We can use attention-focusing which relates the instance to the generality by pointing out the presence or absence of critical attributes. And we can use a variety of representations for the correct-answer feedback. Of course, motivational enhancement can also be used: praise for correct answers and encouragement for wrong answers.

The following guidelines (or prescriptive principles) are likely to improve the quality of your instruction:

— Make sure prerequisites (critical characteristics) have been mastered.

— Present a prototypical example, with explanation.

— Make a generality available.

— Make additional examples available, with explanations.

— Present some of the examples with matched nonexamples.

— Make practice available.

— Provide feedback on all practice (confirmation, explanation, or hint)

— Make instances as different as possible.

— Arrange instances in an easy-to-difficult order.

— Use a variety of representations.

Common Errors Novice Designers Make

There are several errors that novice instructional designers commonly make when designing instruction on concept classification tasks. First, they often name the subordinate concepts (kinds) in examples and practice. For example, suppose you were teachinσ the concept "woodwind instrument" in music, and your only objective was for the learners to be able to classify any musical instrument as a woodwind or not a woodwind. Many novice designers would say in an example, "This is a clarinet, so it is a woodwind." Or they would say in their feedback, "No, this is an oboe, so it is a woodwind." There is nothing wrong with this if the learner already knows what a clarinet or oboe is. But if a learner doesn't, then this just adds to the amount the learner needs to try to figure outóit makes learning more difficult rather than easier.

Even when such subordinate concepts are also among your objectives, it is generally better to help them master the higher-level concept (woodwind instrument) first, and then teach its subordinate concepts. The subordinate concepts can be taught simultaneously with each other, as long as there aren't too many of them. Otherwise they can be taught in sets of 3 or 4 at a time. A second error novice designers commonly make is not indicating the criterion for mastery on the practice. This is important for both situations in which the learner will exercise full control over their progress and situations in which a teacher (or computer) will exercise such control.

Development Procedure for Designing a Concept Classification Lesson

Here is a procedure that you may find helpful for applying the above-described principles to develop your lesson.

1. Identify the critical characteristics, and write a generality that includes the label (if any), the superordinate concept, and the critical characteristics. To do this, you should observe or ask your SME about the nature of the post-instructional requirements for classifying the concept and assess the entry level of the learners with regard to the critical characteristics.

2. Identify and list all dimensions of divergence for the concept.

3. Assess the difficulty level of the concept for the target learners (on, say, a scale of 1-5).

4. Create an instance pool that contains roughly x items per dimension of divergence, where x = the difficulty level times 2.

5. Create a test, using at least one item randomly selected from each dimension of divergence. If the concept is a difficult one, increase the number of items per dimension.

6 Create practice items, using at least two items randomly selected from each dimension of divergence. If the concept is a difficult one, increase the number of items per dimension.

7. Create examples, using at least one item randomly selected from each dimension of divergence. If the concept is a difficult one, increase the number of items per dimension. Include appropriate power components, depending on the difficulty level of the concept.

8. Create the feedback for the practice items so as to be virtually identical to the enhanced examples.

9. Think about motivational needs and media selection, and modify the instruction as appropriate to each.

PROCEDURE USING

Procedural Task

You have been given an assignment that entails teaching a procedural task. A procedural task involes performing a procedure, which is a sequence of activities to achieve a goal. Synonyms include method, technique, skill, and rule (sometimes). A procedure can be either of two types:

— A physical procedure, which entails the execution of physical movements, like performing a serve in tennis.

— A mental procedure, which entails the execution of mental operations, like adding two numbers in your head.

Actually, most procedures are a combination of physical and mental activities. A case in point is the procedure for writing an essay. But usually only one of the two kinds of activities needs to be taught—the other has already been mastered. In this case, the physical activity of writing has already been mastered. Procedures are invented, but the fact that they work or don't work can be explained by principles (although the principles may not have been discovered yet). A person can learn to perform a procedure without understanding why it works. For example, one can learn how to calculate force using the formula F=Ma (Force equals Mass times acceleration) without understanding anything about force or mass or acceleration (which are all concepts) or about the causal interrelationships among them (which are principles), such as: an increase in acceleration will cause an increase in force. So procedures can be learned rotely at the application level.

Importance of Procedural Tasks Important

In almost everything we do, we do it at least partially by using a procedure (following steps), from reading, writing, and arithmetic, to flying airplanes, doing our jobs, using our cars, cooking our meals, and getting dressed. We even use procedures to classify concepts.

Principles

How is a procedural skill learned? Let's consider the procedure for adding fractions, since everyone is familiar with it. Its steps include: Procedures can be branching or linear. This is a branching procedure, because different steps are used for different problems (cases). A branching procedure always has at least one decision step, and every decision step has at least two branches.

A linear procedure has no decision steps and hence no branches. Therefore, it only has one path. Another important aspect of procedure learning is that procedures can vary tremendously in size. For example, we could identify the procedure for solving mathematical problems of any type. Such a procedural task would have many decision steps, which would direct the performer to different "branches" for each kind of problem: addition, multiplication, etc.; whole numbers, fractions, equations, etc.; and so forth. Obviously this will be a very big (long) procedure. On the opposite extreme, we could identify the procedure for subtracting single-digit numbers, which is basically just one step: recall the appropriate subtraction facts. It is interesting to note that this latter procedure would be a part of the former.

In essence, each step is itself a procedure which needs to be learned on the skill-application level. Furthermore, virtually any step can be broken down into substeps. Steps 2, 3, and 6 above would probably need to be further broken down into substeps to teach the procedure for adding fractions. The only way you can tell how far to break a procedure's steps down into simpler substeps is to first determine what your learners already know. Then you keep breaking down steps and substeps until each is expressed at the learners' current level of knowledge.

For the sake of simplicity, let's assume that the learners already know enough to be able to learn from the steps as stated above. Then how is the procedure learned? It is possible to memorize the statement of the procedure. It is also possible to memorize one particular performance of the procedure. Dave Merrill, in his "Component Display Theory," refers to these as "remember-a-generality" and "remember-an-instance", respectively. But what we really want is for the students to be able to generalize to "previously unencountered" cases. This makes the task "skill application," or what Merrill calls "use-a-generality".

The need to generalize is based on yet another important aspect of procedures: the amount of variation from one performance (or instance) to another. Not all procedures have a lot of variation. Some procedures are always performed exactly the same way. Perhaps the name which comes closest to characterizing this type of procedure is recipe. Such procedures are virtually remember-level tasks. "If you've seen one, you've seen 'em all." If you've learned one instance, you've learned them all. So it has become a memorization task, rather than an application task, even though what you are learning is a procedure. In reality, there is a continuum of procedures ranging from recipes on one extreme to very highly divergent procedures on the other extreme. This has important implications for your instruction, especially for divergence of examples and practice.

Generalizing is required whenever a procedure has divergence or variation (is done differently) from one performance to another. The ways in which the performances vary are called the variable characteristics of the procedure. So, what are the variable characteristics for a procedure? Joe Scandura has identified them as features of the inputs to the procedure.

For example, the fractions to be added are the inputs to our procedure, and they could have common denominators, or one's denominator could be a multiple of the other's, or the two denominators could have a common factor, or the denominators could be none of the above. Joseph Scandura calls each of these types of problems equivalence classes, because all problems within an equivalence class are performed using the same path (steps) in the procedure.

Conversely, the procedure will be performed differently for each different equivalence class. There may also be some variable characteristics of the inputs which don't require that the procedure be performed differently. For example, the procedure for adding 1/4 and 1/4 is the same as the procedure for adding 1/12 and 1/12; it doesn't matter that the denominator is a one-digit or two-digit number. One must learn to generalize across these differences, but it is usually not difficult to do so.

Development procedure for designing a procedure-using lesson

1. Identify all the steps, break them down to entry level, and write a generality that includes the label (if any), the goal, and the steps at entry level. To do this, you should observe or ask your SME about the nature of the post-instructional requirements for using the procedure and assess the entry level of the learners with regard to the steps.
2. Identify and list all dimensions of divergence for the procedure. Make sure the generality deals with all of them.
3. Assess the difficulty level of the procedure for the target learners (on, say, a scale of 1-5).
4. Create an instance pool that contains x items per dimension of divergence, where x is about twice the difficulty level.
5. Create a test, using at least one item randomly selected from each dimension of divergence.
6. Create practice items, using at least two items randomly selected from each dimension of divergence. If the procedure is a difficult one, increase the number of items per dimension.
7. Create examples, using at least one item randomly selected from each dimension of divergence. If the procedure is a difficult one, increase the number of items per dimension. Include appropriate power components, depending on the difficulty level of the procedure.
8. Create the feedback for the practice items so as to be virtually identical to the enhanced examples.
9. Think about motivational needs and media selection, and modify the instruction as appropriate to each.

PRINCIPLE USING

— A principle is a relationship between two or more changes, like "water expands when it freezes". There are two major kinds of principles: process and causal.

— A process principle is a sequence of natural events.

Example: "A seed grows into a seedling, which grows into a mature plant, which develops a flower, which produces seeds, and the cycle continues."

— *Contrasted with procedures*: A sequence of natural events is not a sequence of actions performed by a person, which is a procedure rather than a principle.

— *Kinds*: A process principle may be linear (with a beginning and an end) or cyclical (with no beginning or end).

— A causal principle is a cause-effect relationship between two or more changes.

Example: "An increase in the price of a good causes a decrease in the amount demanded and an increase in the amount supplied".

— *Contrasted with process principles*: In process principles you can't say that one change causes the other.

— *Kinds*: Causal principles usually have multiple causes and/or multiple effects.

Importance of Principle Using Important

A unique feature of principles is that, unlike concepts and procedures, they are discovered rather than invented. Principles are the only kind of content which represents "truth" in any significant way. Certainly, facts (which can only be learned on a memorization level) are often either true or false, but they are trivial compared to principlesóthey are particulars rather than generalities. Also, a procedure can either produce the desired outputs (the goal) or not. But procedures don't provide us with an understanding of how things work, and procedures can often be changed and still produce the desired outputs. Furthermore, there are often several different procedures for accomplishing the same goal.

In contrast, principles provide us with an understanding of the world around us, among us, and within usóan understanding of how things happen and why they happen the way they do. Therefore, principles are probably the most important kind of content for us to include in the majority of the Instruction. And it is usually helpful to learn how to apply the principles to new situations. Given the importance of principle using, it is essential that we know how to teach it well.

Principles for Learning to Use Principles

Process principles

How is a process principle learned? As with concepts and procedures, the statement of the principle could certainly be memorized. It is also possible to memorize one particular demonstration of the principle. Dave Merrill refers to these as "remember-a-generality" and "remember-an-instance", respectively. But what we really want is for the students to be able to apply the principle in new situations. This makes it skill application, or what Merrill calls "use-a-generality". But how are process principles applied? Let's look at a case in point. The life cycle of a flowering plant is a process principle.

A seed grows into a seedling, which in turn grows to become a mature plant, which then develops flowers, which produce seeds, which grow into seedlings, and the cycle continues. It is a process principle rather than a causai one because it is a sequence of changes in which one change does not cause the next, it just naturally precedes it. So how can this principle be applied? Application entails generalizing the sequence of events to new cases. So we can look at a "new" plant and describe what phase or change is going to occur next (e.g., the flower will form seeds), or we can look at it and describe what phase or change occurred immediately prior to now, or we can look at all of the various phases or changes which occurred and arrange them in the proper sequence.

Statements which are often used include "arrange the events in proper order", "predict what will happen next", and "infer what happened just prior to now". But all of these are essentially the same in that they entail describing a sequence of events as they apply in a new (previously unencountered) situation. As with concept classification, there is some evidence that there are two phases to learning a principle at the application level. Similar to the notion of prototype formation, the learner needs to comprehend the principle. We refer to this as the acquisition phase. Then the learner needs to learn to generalize it to new situations, which is called the application phase. When generalization is involved, we know that there have to be variable characteristics across which we generalize. What are those likely to be for process principles? What would they be for the life cycle of a flowering plant? Is there such a thing as "equivalence classes" for principles? Think about these issues, and discuss them with a colleague.

As with concepts and procedures, not all principles require a lot of generalization. Remember the "one-dollar bill" phenomenon for concepts and the "recipe" phenomenon for procedures. Some principles have very little variation among their instances. For example, the phases of the moon comprise a process principle. Each week brings a new phase, yet each month's phases vary little from the previous month's phases. As with concepts and procedures, such principles are virtually remember-level tasks: if you've learned one instance, you've learned them all. Again, there is a continuum ranging from such principles on one extreme to very highly divergent principles on the other extreme. This has important implications for your instruction.

Causal Principles

How is a causal principle learned? Like a process principle, it can be learned at the "remember-a-generality" level or the "remember-an-instance" level, and either of those can be rote (memorization) or meaningful (understanding). But what we really want is for the students to be able to "use the generality"óapply the principle in new (previously unencountered) situations. So how are causal principles applied? We saw that process principles are applied by describing the sequence of events in a new situation. But causal principles are much more complex. There are three very different forms of behavior by which causal principles can be applied. These three behaviors can most easily be understood by looking at the two changes which comprise a simple cause-effect principle: the cause and the effect. For example, in the law of supply and demand, an increase in price (the cause) results in a decrease in demand (the effect).

— *Prediction*: One way to apply a causal principle is when a particular *cause* is given and the learner must predict what its particular *effect* will be. For example, the learner is told that the price of gasoline will soon increase due to a gasoline tax, and is asked what effect it is likely to have. "Implication" is another term which is commonly used.

— *Explanation*: Another way a causal principle can be applied occurs when a particular effect is given, and the learner must explain what its particular cause was. For example, the learner is told that consumption of sugar in the U.S. decreased considerably in the early 1960s and is asked for a possible reason. "Inference" is another common term for this form of application.

— *Solution*: A third way a causal principle can be applied is when a particular desired *effect* is given, and the person must select and implement the necessary particular *causes* to bring it about. It is similar to procedure using, except that the appropriate procedure is unknown and must be invented or derived by the person. For example, the learner is asked to figure out how to decrease the consumption of electricity (to reduce pollution and conserve fossil fuels). "Problem solving" is the common term for this form of application.

These three forms of behavior are in addition to the one for *process* principles:

— *Description*: In a process principle, the kind of behavior that represents application of the principle is to describe what occurs in what order in a particular situation. For example, a learner is shown a marigold in flower and is asked to predict what will happen next to it. Verbs that are often used include "arrange the events in proper order", "predict which event will come next", and "infer what event occurred just prior to now". But all of these are essentially the same in that they entail *describing a sequence of events* as they apply in a new (previously unencountered) situation. They are not prediction or explanation in the sense you have with causal principles.

For each of these four kinds of behavior, we can identify a procedure (or "cognitive processing routine") which is used to apply a particular principle in that way. Hence, there are two distinct things which are learned: the principle itself and the procedure for applying it. This is quite similar to concept classification, where prototype formation preceded generalization (algorithm formation). In essence, then, there are two phases to learning a principle at the application level: acquisition and application. This has important implications for how to teach principles on an application level. Take a moment to think back now. What are the four types of behavior one could acquire in learning to apply a principle? Try to recall and define each without looking back. And what are the two phases to learning a principle at the application level?

The Complex Nature of Principles

There are some interesting features of both process and causal principles, an understanding of which can help us to teach them better. First, they may be anywhere on a continuum of certainty as to their validity, ranging from hypotheses through propositions, postulates and rules, to laws. When people talk about "fundamental concepts", they are often referring to principles, as in the "fundamental concepts of science". Second, principles vary greatly in the consistency with which a given cause has a given effect. If a principle is highly consistent, it is called "deterministic", whereas if it only sometimes has that effect, it is called "probabilistic".

Principles also exist on a broad range of levels of complexity, which vary depending on whether they are correlational or causal, directional or nondirectional, and quantitative or qualitative. Another aspect of their complexity is their level of generality. Compare:

— Light bends when it passes from one medium to another.

— When light rays pass into a denser medium, they bend toward the normal.

The greater the difference in optical density between two media, the more the light rays will bend when they pass from one medium into the other.

Another aspect of the complexity of principles is their level of inclusiveness. A principle like "Prejudice is caused by ignorance and intolerance toward others" is very inclusive, applying to very many situations; whereas the related principle, "People of one race or ethnic group become intolerant toward another because they feel their way is the only way or the only right way", applies in far fewer situations and is therefore much less inclusive. Yet another aspect of the complexity of principles is that there are usually multiple causes for any given effect and multiple effects of any given cause. For example, an increase in price will cause an increase in the amount supplied as well as a decrease in amount demanded. There are often tens of factors that can "cause" a given event (result), and tens of effects that can result from any given event (cause).

Furthermore, causes and effects usually exist in chains, whereby a cause has a certain effect, which in turn is a cause of another effect, which in turn is a cause of another effect, and so forth. Take a moment now to think about each of the ways principles can differ from each other: certainty, consistency, causality, directionality, magnitude, generality, inclusiveness, multiple causality, and chaining. Before you read on, state in your own words what each of these terms means, and think of an example of each. You will find it very helpful to understand them!

Principles for Teaching Principles

Process principle

Since there are two phases of learning a process principle on the application level.

Acquisition

We have seen that prototype formation for a concept is quite similar, and it is taught by presenting a prototypical exampleóone which is very common and highly representative of as many examples of the concept as possible. The same should be useful for teaching acquisition of a process principle. But to help the learner understand what is happening in the example, it is helpful to present a simultaneous generality which describes and usually even labels each phase in the sequence. Labeled illustrations, such as you may have seen for the water cycle, are particularly helpful for this. But what should the prototypical example be like? To be an example of a sequence of events, it should be a dynamic demonstration, if possible. By dynamic, it should entail motion, which of course requires a dynamic medium, like video or computer-based instruction, or observing the real thing.

The demonstration should show each event in the sequence, in the order in which it naturally occurs. To be prototypical, the example should be as typical and simple as possible. In the case of the life cycle of a flowering plant, we would probably pick a common flower like a dandelion, rather than a maple tree (which is more complex because it requires far more than one season to complete its cycle) or a corn plant (which is less familiar and its flower doesn't look much like a flower). And what should the simultaneous generality be like? It should usually describe and label each of the individual events or phases which make up the entire sequence, clearly indicating its beginning and end (or its continuity, if it is a cyclical process). And it should usually describe the order of those events or phases. To avoid redundancy with the demonstration, you may find it unnecessary to include the description of each event (phase) or the order of those events (phases). This would just leave you with providing a label and clear indication of the beginning and end of each event (phase) within the overall process.

Application

The prototypical example and simultaneous generality should result in the learner's acquisition of an understanding of the principle. What instructional components should you use to facilitate the application process? In the case of process principles, application entails using your understanding of the sequence of events to describe what has occurred, is occurring, or will occur in one specific instance. The major obstacle to learning is difficulty in generalizing, and it is dealt with by providing lots of divergent casesóinstances which are as different as possible from each other. These instances may be either expository (told to the learner) or inquisitory (asked of the learner).

The expository instances are examples (or demonstrations), similar to the prototypical example, except that they no longer need to be common or simple. In fact, they should be uncommon (as different as possible from each other), and should gradually increase in complexity. The inquisitory instances are practice items. They should always present new (previously unencountered) cases and should require such behaviors as

a. presenting all the events (phases) and asking the learner to arrange them in the proper order,

b. presenting one event (phase) and asking the learner to predict what will come next, or

c. presenting one event and asking the learner to explain (or infer) what came immediately before.

Naturally, there should also be immediate feedback on the practice: confirmational for correct responses and corrective for wrong responses. The feedback for wrong responses should be almost identical to the examples.

Causal principles

Again, let's start with the acquisition phase and then address application.

Acquisition

What instructional tactics should be used to facilitate the acquisition phase for causal principles? Acquisition entails gaining an understanding of the cause-effect relationship. For concept classification and process-principle application, we have seen that a generality and a prototypical example are very helpful for acquisition. So it's pretty likely that they will also be helpful for causal principles. But should the generality and example just be presented to the learner? Benjamin Bloom has identified active learner participation as very important in instruction. We usually think of active learner participation as being practiceósomething which is reserved for application. But it can also be applied to acquisition.

To get a learner to participate in acquiring a generality, we need to get her or him to discover it. This is an inductive (particular-to-general) form of active participation, as opposed to practice, which is a deductive (general-to-particular) form. We can also get the learner to participate in an example. Rather than just having the learner obsersove a dynamic presentation of the cause and its relation to an effect, allow the learner to manipulate the cause and observe how the effect varies. This is referred to as exploration of an example.

It is not the same as practice because it does not entail doing what the objective calls for. For example, to teach a learner to predict the effects of the thickness of a convex lens on the behavior of light, we can show on a computer a diagram of a convex lens with light rays passing through it, and allow the learner to manipulate the thickness of the lens with arrow keys. As the thickness of the lens changes, the path of the light rays will also change, along with the focal distance and magnification of the image.

The learner's activity does not entail making any predictions at all, so it is not practice. So the generality portion of a presentation can be of two types, depending on the amount of active learner participation: it can be an expository presentation or a discovery presentation. Similarly, the example portion of a presentation can be of two types, also depending on the amount of active learner participation: observation or exploration:

	No Participation	Participation
Observation	Expository Presentation	Discovery Presentation
Example	Observation of an Example	Exploration of an Example

But these two types of participationódiscovery and explorationóare completely independent of each other; you can have discovery without exploration and vice versa:

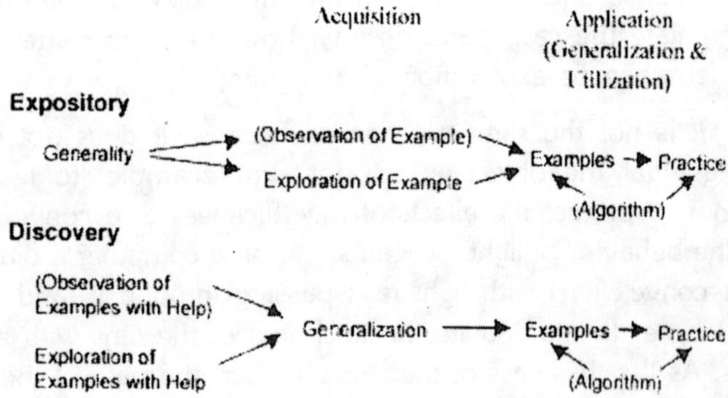

But when should each be used? It seems that exploration should always be used, unless it is too expensive. But what about discovery? It is often much more time consuming than an expository approach, depending on the amount of help provided. But if developing the learners' ability to discover is one of your goals, it will likely be worth the extra time. If not, then learner characteristics may be the most important consideration for choosing between discovery and expository approaches. Some students may get impatient with not just being told the generalityóthey may feel that discovery is a waste of their timeówhile others may prefer to figure it out on their own. On a computer system, you could provide both options and allow learners to choose. Otherwise, perhaps the best thing is to mix in some of each: use discovery for acquisition of one principle and expository for another.

Application

What instructional tactics should be used to facilitate the application phase? Application of a causal principle entails two things: generalization and utilization. Generalization is accomplished by presenting divergent instances (or cases). Those instances can be either examples or practice, which differ in that examples do not require a learner response, whereas practice does (one kind of active participation). Examples can also be designed as observation or exploration, which differ on the basis of a different kind of active learner participation, as discussed earlier. Utilization, the second aspect of application, occurs when the learner develops a performance routine which indicates when and how to use the principle for a given kind of application (prediction, explanation, or solution). This can be facilitated in several ways. You can provide an algorithm with the principle, along with examples and practice on the use of the algorithm. But often the algorithm is simple enough that it can be acquired through just the same examples and practice which are used for generalization of the causal relationship.

Routine Tactics

The following summarizes the tactics which you can use in each strategy: Keep in mind that the power of the instruction should vary depending on the difficulty of the principle for the target learners. For very easy principles, a generality alone may be sufficient. For moderately difficult principles, the generality and a prototypical example to observe would likely be good for acquisition, followed by a few practice items with feedback for application. And for very difficult principles, exploration and discovery would probably help acquisition, followed by an algorithm with examples, practice, and feedback for its use in applying the principle. Other kinds of power tactics similar to those used for concepts and procedures would also be helpful in progressively greater amounts for progressively more difficult principles.

Enrichment Tactics

Generality: As with the other skill-application tasks, there are several ways of enhancing the generality. You can: Facilitate encoding by focusing the learner's attention on the important parts of it. But the important parts are different.

— Use a mnemonic of some kind if it is difficult to remember the events.

— Use an algorithm if it will facilitate application of the principle.

Examples. As with concepts and procedures, examples can be enhanced in the following ways:

— Increase the number of examples.

— Use divergence to make the examples as different as possible from each other.

— Use an easy-to-difficult sequence of examples.

— Use attention-focusing to relate an example to the generality, either by explaining in general terms what is causing or what is resulting from what, or by highlighting the key events.

— Use an alternative representation for the example, such as a causal diagram.

— Use a reminder of the mnemonic if one was presented earlier.

— Use an algorithm if one was presented earlier.

There does not seem to be an equivalent to nonexamples or common errors.

Practice: As with concepts and procedures, the only ways that practice should be enhanced are to:

— Increase the number of practice items.

— Use divergence.

— Use an easy-to-difficult sequence.

— Include prompting on early practice items.

— Otherwise, enrichment should be reserved for the feedback.

Feedback: As with concepts and procedures, power on the feedback should be much like on the examples:

— Use attention-focusing to relate the instance to the generality by pointing out, depending on the nature of the learner's mistake, what is causing or what is resulting from what, or by highlighting the key events.

— Use a variety of representations for the correct answer feedback.

— Use a reminder of the mnemonic if one was presented earlier.

— Use a reminder of the algorithm if one was presented earlier.

— Use motivational enhancement: praise for correct answers and encouragement for wrong answers.

Development Procedure

Identify all the changes involved in the principle, and write a generality that includes the label (if any), the changes, and the relationship among the changes (causal or natural process). To do this, you should observe or ask your SME about the nature of the post-instructional requirements for using the principle.

— Identify and list all dimensions of divergence for the principle. Make sure the generality deals with all of them.

— Assess the difficulty level of the principle for the target learners (on, say, a scale of 1-5).

— Create an instance pool that contains roughly x items representing each dimension of divergence, where x = the difficulty level times 2. But note that a single item will usually represent more than one dimension of divergence.

— Create a test, using at least one item representing each dimension of divergence. If the principle is a difficult one, increase the number of items per dimension.

— Create practice items, using at least two items representing each dimension of divergence. If the principle is a difficult one, increase the number of items per dimension.

— Create examples, having at least one item representing each dimension of divergence. If the principle is a difficult one, increase the number of items per dimension. Include appropriate power components, depending on the difficulty level of the principle.

— Create the feedback for the practice items so as to be virtually identical to the enhanced examples.

— Think about motivational needs and media selection, and modify the instruction as appropriate to each. (This should be done throughout the process, not just after all else is done.)

UNDERSTANDING

Understanding is meaningful learning. It is usually contrasted with rote learning (memorization), although it is also distinct from skill application and generic skill application. So, what is the difference between applying concepts and understanding concepts? You can learn to follow steps successfully without having any understanding of why you are doing what you are doing, nor why what you are doing works. In fact, it is principles which give one that understanding. Behind every procedure there is at least one principle which explains why it works. Hence, it is not procedures which are directly understoodóthey are only understood by understanding the principles which underlie them. Let's consider a principle like the law of supply and demand.

To understand the relationship between price and the quantity of a good supplied (by producers) and demanded (by consumers) is to form a mental model which integrates it with what you already know. Each such mental model, or cluster of interrelated knowledge, is referred to as a schema. Understanding is probably the least studied and least understood type of learning within the cognitive domain. Fortunately, it is an area which is currently receiving a lot of attention by learning psychologists.

Important of Understanding

When something is meaningfully understood, it is retained much longer, can be built upon to acquire further understanding, is usually very versatile in the situations and ways it can be used, and facilitates creativity. For example, the law of supply and demand (understanding that a higher price for something will reduce the amount demanded and increase the amount supplied) is something which one is not likely to forget once it is meaningfully understood. It is important for acquiring an understanding of consumption theory. It can be applied in a broad range of ways, including deciding how much to charge for cutting someone's lawn and deciding for whom to vote. And it helps one to be creative in finding ways to maximize your income. Similarly, once you understand what an atom is, you are not likely to forget it; it is essential for understanding the chemical behavior of matter (atomic theory); it is a broadly useful concept in chemistry; and it greatly facilitates a chemist's ability to develop creative ideas and products.

Principles for Learning Meaningful Knowledge

David Ausubel, a pioneer in studying this type of learning, pointed out that two things are necessary for understanding to occur: (1) the content must be potentially meaningful, and (2) the learner must relate it in a meaningful way to his or her prior knowledge. For *potentially* meaningful knowledge to *become* meaningful knowledge to a learner, it is usually, according to Ausubel, subsumed under a broader, more inclusive piece of meaningful knowledge closely related to it. Understanding of the concept "sonnet" is enhanced when we learn that it is a kind of poem. The more distinct the new knowledge is from the relevant subsumer, the harder it is to understand.

The key to understanding, it appears, is relating it to appropriate prior knowledge. But sometimes, particularly when one's understanding is incorrect, subsumption does not come easily ó it doesn't fit right. Then there is a restructuring of knowledge Ausubel calls "integrative reconciliation". Schema theory extends Ausubel's theory of meaningful learning by identifying other types of relationships which help lend meaning to new knowledge. But the same two processes remain, only with different names: what Don Norman refers to as "accretion" (plugging new ideas into a schema) and "restructuring" (making important changes to a schema). He has also identified an intermediate process, which he calls "tuning" (making smaller changes to a schema), which shows that there is a continuum between these two extreme forms of understanding.

Assimilation occurs when you plug new knowledge into an existing schema, whereas restructuring occurs when the new knowledge results in your reconceptualizing (significantly modifying a schema) in order to understand (reconcile conflicts with your prior knowledge). Understanding is like a light bulbóit changes suddenly from darkness to lightóin contrast to the gradual process by which rote memorization and skill application occur. Small steps are taken when accretion occurs; medium steps when tuning occurs; and large steps (momentous insights) when restructuring occurs.

The issue of what is understanding is a difficult one. One view is that there are two major kinds of understanding: understanding things (concepts), and understanding how things change (principles, or causal models).

Conceptual Understanding

Concepts are understood by establishing relationships with prior knowledge. But what are the kinds of relationships which help lend meaning to new concepts? Norman identified the "isa", "hasa", "cause", "act", "iswhen", "location", and "object" relationships, among others. Therefore, it appears that meaningful learning of some kind can occur when appropriate links are made to any of a *variety* of kinds of relevant prior knowledge, including:

— Superordinate knowledge, which is broader and more inclusive. For example, for teaching the concept of erosion, you might relate it to the superordinate concept of movement of material, if the learners already learned what that is.

— Coordinate knowledge, which is on the same level of breadth and inclusiveness. For example, erosion might be related to the opposite kind of movement of material, the coordinate concept of sedimentation (the depositing of material in layers), if the learners already learned what that is.

— Subordinate knowledge, which is narrower and less inclusive. For example, erosion might be related to the subordinate concept of wind erosion, if the learners already learned what that is.

— Experiential knowledge, which is specific cases of the new knowledge. For example, erosion might be related to the little gully that was formed in the dirt outside the school in the last big rain storm, if the learners were already familiar with that.

— Analogic knowledge, which is similar but outside the content area of interest. For example, erosion might be related to sanding down some wood, if the learners were already familiar with that.

— Causal knowledge, which indicates how something influences or is influenced. For example, erosion might be related to its effects on transportation (e.g., washing out dirt roads), if the learners were already familiar with that.

— Procedural knowledge, which indicates how something is used. For example, erosion might be related to methods of contour plowing for preventing water erosion on farmland, if the learners were already familiar with that.

It is important to note that superordinate, coordinate, and subordinate knowledge can be of two types: kinds or parts. Any concept can be a kind of something or a part of something;

it and a coordinate concept are both kinds of the same superordinate concept, or parts of the same superordinate concept; and it has both kinds and parts of itself. A circulatory system is a part of an organism and a kind of body system. Its parts include a heart and arteries and veins; and its kinds include 2-chamber circulatory systems and 1-chamber systems. As can be seen from the above examples, each of these types of prior knowledge has a corresponding type of relationship which can contribute to one's understanding. It may be useful to think of these relationships as dimensions of understanding, many (but not all) of which will be important for any given idea that is to be understood. This is related to the notion of "breadth of understanding".

Causal Understanding

Principles, or interrelated sets of principles called causal models, are a very different kind of understanding. The water cycle is a causal model in which various changes (evaporation, condensation, and precipitation) occur, and a variety of other changes (events) influence them (temperature, humidity, wind, convection currents, and so forth). Causal models are understood primarily by: (1) establishing relationships between the real events that constitute a causal model and the generalities (principles or causal models) that represent them, and (2) learning about the network of causal relationships among those events (changes).

What are the obstacles to conceptual understanding?

It is helpful to think in terms of obstacles to initial *acquisition* of conceptual understanding and obstacles to *retention* of that understanding. Understanding is quite the opposite of memorization in that acquisition is what is difficult; retention is relatively easy. Since acquisition is mainly a matter of relating the new knowledge to appropriate prior knowledge, there are three major obstacles. First, the appropriate prior knowledge must indeed have been acquired already. Second, the appropriate prior knowledge must be "activated"óthat is, it must be brought to mind. And third, the proper relationship between the new knowledge and the prior knowledge must be learned. The more links which are created with relevant prior knowledge, the greater the depth and/or breadth of understanding.

Once conceptual understanding has occurred, retrieval problems are relatively rare. However, if some piece of meaningful knowledge is not used for a long time, it can undergo what David Ausubel calls "obliterative subsumption" (I love that term!). To the extent that conceptual knowledge is subsumed under a broader, more inclusive representation of it, lack of use can result in the more detailed refinement being merged back into the subsumer from which it sprang, becoming indistinguishable from it.

The more similar it is to its subsumer, the more quickly it is learned, but the more quickly it can also be forgotten. How can you tell if someone understands? It is a lot more difficult to measure (or test for) understanding than to measure rote memorization. This is because understanding cannot be directly observed. It can only be inferred from various observable behaviors. There are observable behaviors for each of the kinds of relationships. They include contextualizing, comparing and contrasting, analyzing, instantiating, analogizing. and so forth.

A development procedure

1. Pick a concept that needs to be understood (needs analysis and content analysis).
2. Pick which relationships constitute the important dimensions of understanding for that concept (needs analysis and content analysis).
3. Identify which of those relationships have not already been acquired by the learners, and list them as new relationships to be taught (learner analysis).

4. Pick the best "objects" (ideas which are related to the idea of interest by each relationship) for each new relationship (e.g. what you compare and contrast the main concept with).

5. Identify which of those objects have not already been acquired by the learners, and list them as new objects to be taught (learner analysis).

6. Design a sequence for teaching the new objects and relationships.

7. Design a strategy (or approach) for teaching the whole understanding.

8. Design the tactics (e.g. comparison/contrast, analogy) for teaching each dimension of understanding.

GENERIC SKILL

A generic skill is a skill which:

— can be applied across a variety of subject domains, and

— takes longer to acquire than domain-dependent (subject-area) skills.

It is what Gagné refers to as "cognitive strategies" and what many cognitive scientists refer to as "domain-independent knowledge." The major kinds of generic skills include thinking skills (such as problem solving techniques), learning strategies (such as creating mnemonics to help you remember things), and metacognitive skills (such as monitoring and revising your problem solving techniques or mnemonic-creating techniques). There are at least three major parts of a generic skill. The most prevalent component is a procedure—a set of steps you use to perform the skill. But you also usually need to understand and be able to apply certain principles that provide guidance as to how to perform each step, or even guidance as to when to use which procedure (approach). Third, it is often necessary to memorize the order of the steps—a memorization component.

Principles of Learning for Generic Skills

So how is a generic skill learned? Since a generic skill is made up of simpler components (primarily procedures and principles), we need to look at how those components are learned. A generic skill differs from a domain-dependent skill in that it is applied across different content domains and it takes longer to learn. Both of these differences have important influences on how a generic skill is learned. The fact that it is applied in different content domains means that it can only be learned through application to domain-dependent knowledge. Therefore, it must be integrated with domain-dependent knowledge.

In learning a generic skill like problem solving, the problems must be from at least one particular domain. Therefore, you must decide what domain-dependent content to use for teaching the generic skill at each point in your instructional sequence. Secondly, if we want the learners to be able to apply it in different content domains, they need to learn to generalize it to different content domains. This is a whole new kind of variable characteristic, or equivalence class. This has very important implications for the way you would want to design instruction on a generic skill. The fact that it takes longer to learn means that the order of learning becomes an important issue. Think about how you learned problem solving.

You didn't learn how to deal with the most complex cases all at once, did you? You probably started by learning problem-solving techniques that enabled you to solve very simple kinds of problems. You probably didn't start by learning all the discriminations and concepts relevant to the most complex problem-solving techniques, and then gradually work your way up a Gagnéan learning hierarchy to being able to integrate all those simpler component parts into a whole. Rather, you likely started by learning the few discriminations, concepts, and rules you needed to solve the very simplest kinds of problems, and you mastered that level of problem solving before you proceeded to slightly more complex techniques to deal with a slightly more complex kind of problem. This also has very important implications for the way you would want to organize instruction on a generic skill.

Principles for Teaching a Generic Skill

Given that a generic skill is made up of simpler skills and knowledge, we can use the principles for teaching each of those components. But the instructional designs must also take into account the other aspects of learning a generic skill: that it is applied across different content domains and that it takes longer to learn. Perhaps the first issue to address is how to sequence the instruction. We should figure out what the simplest kind of case is, and teach it to mastery, complete with all the procedures, principles, and other content needed to learn it.

Then we should figure out what the next simplest kind of case is, and do the same. A certain kind of task analysis is necessary to do this, and it will result in an outline of the sequence of levels of complexity of the generic skill. The next activity should be to identify the procedures and principles to be taught for each level of complexity. This requires a certain form of content analysis, and it will result in an outline of the sequence of content (skills, understandings, and information) to be taught for each level of complexity.

9

INSTRUCTIONAL OBJECTIVES

Instructional objectives may also be called performance objectives, behavioural objectives or objectives. All of these terms are used interchangeably. Objectives are specific, outcome based, measurable and describe the student's behaviour. So what does that mean? Let's take a closer look.

— *Specific*: Objectives are very specific. This means that they should describe precisely what the learner is expected to do.

— *Outcome based*: Objectives are outcome based. This means that the objective is going to state what the learner should be able to do after the instruction is complete. The process of how the instruction happens is not considered in an objective.

— *Measurable*: Objectives are measurable. This means that objectives should describe learning outcomes that can be measured; objectives should be seen or heard.

— *Describe*: Student behaviour Objectives describe student behaviours. This means that objectives should relate what the student should be able to do after the instruction.

Instructional objectives are key to effective instruction. Keep in mind that effective instruction occurs only when student behaviour is changed in desired ways. Because instructional objectives are tools for describing student outcomes, they provide a means to making the instruction effective. Let's look at what instructional objectives really do.

Serve as a guide for students Objectives alert students to what is expected of them. They eliminate the "guess work". Expectations are very clearly defined.

Serve as a basis for the selection of instructional media and materials AND instructional procedures Objectives allow the instructor to determine the media and materials that will facilitate the learning. The procedures to be used to teach the new information become clearer once the objective is defined.

Determine the appropriate ways to evaluate Evaluation should always be based on each instructional objective. Determining the objective classification will assist you in determining the appropriate methods for evaluation.

WRITING AN INSTRUCTIONAL OBJECTIVE

You should first determine the learning outcomes of the lesson. In other words, what do you want the student to be able to do when the lesson is over. Following the ABCDs of instructional objectives is a great way to make sure you have included all the necessary parts in an objective. Link to the A, B, C, and Ds of instructional objectives followed by interactive practice writing instructional objectives.

Teachers should classify objectives because the type of objective dictates the selection of instructional methods, media and evaluation used in the lesson. Objectives may be classified according to the primary learning outcomes that take place. These learning outcomes typically are classified into three domains or categories:

— cognitive,

— psychomotor and

— affective.

Now that you have prepared your course content outline, you are ready to write specific instructional objectives, know also as behavioural, terminal, and performance objectives—statements that describe what the student will be able to do upon completion of the instructional experience. You will learn how to write instructional objectives in behavioural terms because:

— Learning is commonly defined as being an observable and desired change in behaviour; that is, you can tell that learning has occurred when you observe the expected change in the learner's behaviour.

— For course syllabi and courses of study, Instructors are expected to write course objectives in behaviour terms

— Objectives stated in behavioural terms clearly communicate to students the course expectations

— Evaluative items (test questions) can then be written that are congruent with state objectives.

Instructional objectives are not the same as "instructor goals" which tell what the instructor intends to do; nor are they the same as "course goals", which are general statements telling about the course. Behavioural objectives are much more specific and are student centered. It is unfortunate if what an instructor states as goals and that which the same instructor does are two separate matters, because it creates an unwanted dichotomy that confuses students. To students, your objectives and test questions should be clear indicators of your real goals. Matching objectives to goals, then stating the objectives clearly and in behavioural terms, while measuring student learning against those objectives facilitates teaching effectiveness and student learning.

When preparing behavioural objectives you should ask yourself: "How is the student to demonstrate that the objective has been achieved?". For example, enough the following might be an appropriate course goal, it is flat a behaviourally stated objectives "The student will develop an appreciation for art." It is too ambiguous. Although "will develop an appreciation" is a student centered phrase, it does not state how the intended learning is to be demonstrated. The objective should include a behaviour that will demonstrate the intended appreciation, such as: The student will demonstrate an appreciation for an by volunteering to guide visitors at a local, an gallery." We assume that volunteering to serve as a gallery guide is indicative of the expected achievement of appreciation.

The example in the preceding paragraph represents a "responding" objective in the affective domain. For evaluation, objectives of that domain are complicated because they represent behaviours involving attitudes, values, and feelings, that are difficult to measure objectively. Examples for each domain will follow, but first let's consider the key components of a behaviourally stated objective.

A completely stated behavioural objective has four key components. Referred to as the ABCDs of writing behavioural objectives, the key components are:

— The audience (the student for whom the objective is intended).

— The terminal behaviour (the anticipated measurable performance).

— The observable conditions (the setting in which the behaviour is to be demonstrated and observed).

— The performance level (the degree of proficiency, primarily for the purpose of evaluation, and frequently omitted). For exercises that follow you may ignore this ingredient, as we assume a mastery (100 percent) performance level expectation.

Audience: Behavioural objectives are usually written with a beginning phrase such as "The student will be able to ...". In order to eliminate repetitious writing we suggest that when preparing objectives for inclusion in your course syllabus and course of study, you introduce all of the objectives with the following sentence written once: "Upon completion (of this course) you will be able to ..,'" then proceed to list each behavioural objective by its anticipated measurable performance, thus eliminating repetition of the phrase "You will be able to..." (YWABT). An alternative is to begin each objective with the abbreviation "YWBAT," followed by the anticipated performance. Also, especially for the course syllabus, we prefer the personalization provided by the use of "you will be able to . . .," rather than student will be able to.. .

Anticipated Measurable Performance: Success with writing behavioural objectives depends on the selection of performance words that are measurable, i.e., action verbs. The primary ingredient of a well-stated objective is the anticipated measurable performance. There are verbs to avoid—verbs that are too vague, ambiguous, and that are not clearly measurable.

With Exercise 1, try your skill with recognizing Instructional Objectives that are measurable. While other components, not yet discussed, may be absent, with Exercise 1 our concern is the question "is the objective student-centered and measurable?"

Conditions: Another component is the condition, or setting, in which the performance is to be demonstrated and observed. Returning to the earlier example, about the student demonstrating an appreciation for art, to include the condition, we write as follow: "From a list of options, the student will demonstrate an appreciation of art by volunteering to serve as a gallery guide". The condition is the "list of options", one of which is assumed by the instructor to best indicate achievement of that objective.

Performance Level: The fourth and final component of a completely state behavioural objective is the degree or level of expedited performance. For one or reason, this ingredient is frequently omitted. In the previous example, because the expected performance is Mastery1, the level is omitted (because it is understood).

Using another example, in another domain, suppose a mathematics instructor's goal is to teach students to solve quadratic equations. For this goad, a behavioural objective could read as: "When give ten quadratic equations (the condition), the student will solve them (the Measurable behaviour performance), with 80 percent accuracy (the performance level).

Performance level is used to evaluate student achievement; sometimes it is used to evaluate instructor effectiveness. Student grades might be based on performance levels; evaluation of instructor effectiveness might be based on student performance levels. As colleges move ever closer to competency base (know also as outcome-based or performance-based) instruction, instructors' knowledge of how to write behavioural objectives becomes significantly important.

Objectives written by college instructors usually fall within the cognitive domain, but when you look at the instructional goals of those same instructors, there also is interest in psychomotor and in affective learning. Perhaps instructor anention is too trequently directed to the cognitive while only assuming that the psychomotor and affective will take care of themselves. Some argue the reverse, that is, when the affective is directly anended, the psychomotor and cognitive will develop. Leaving the argument to the learning theorists, we shall say simply that instructors should direct their planning so that students are guided from the lowest to highest levels of operation, and that attention is given to student development within all three domains.

Undoubtedly, from your own formal education you can recall classes where instructor expectations went no further than the lowest cognitive level—the simple recall of isolated facts. Effective learning extends beyond mere memorization ot facts. Indeed, to develop student skills in reasoning and in critical thinking, such must be the case. Competent college instructors provide instructional objectives and experiences designed to raise the level of student thinking and behaving. Later exercises are designed to help you learn how to do that. Now, your attention is directed to the hierarchies of levels of operation within each of the three domains. Operation at each level requires the ability to perform at each preceding level.

View the Cognitive Domain Hierarchies: Whereas identification and ciassiflcation within the cognitive domain is generally agreed upon, classifications of the psychomotor and affective domains demonstrate less consistency, and for those domains, other authors may illustrate variations from the classifications shown here. For a college instructor, it is less impoflant that an objective be absolutely classified than ills for the instructor to be cognizant of hierarchies of levels of thinking and to understand the importance of attending to student development from low to higher levels of operation in all three domains.

The following illustrate classification schemes for the Psychomotor and for the Affective domains.

— View the Psychomotor Domain Hierarchies

— View the Affective Domain Hierarchies

Once again let us make it clear that it is expected that you will plan well and specifically that which you intend to teach that you will convey your specific expectations to your students, and that you will evaluate student learning against that specificity. But there is a danger inherent in such performance-based teaching, and that is, because it is highly objective. It could become over-objective, and over-objectivity can have negative consequences.

The danger is when students are treated as objects, when the relationship between instructor and learner is impersonal and counter-productive to real learning. Highly specific and impersonal teaching can discourage serendipity creativity and an excitement for real discovery. With performance-based instruction, the source for student motivation is largely extrinsic: instructor expectations, grades, society and peer pressures are examples of extrinsic, sources. To be an effective college instructor, your challenge Is to use performance-based criteria, but simuftaneously with a teaching style that encourages the development of intrinsic sources of student motivation and that allows for, that provides for, and that encourages, learning beyond what might be considered as immediately measurable and that is beyond your minimal expectations.

TAXONOMY OF EDUCATIONAL OBJECTIVES

This is a revised version of Benjamin Bloom's work with the addition of the Psychomotor Domain as developed by Anita Harrow. Dr. Bloom's intent was to develop a classification framework for writing educational objectives. The questions and examples were added by Tom Allen to make the Taxonomy more useful for beginning teachers as a tool to facilitate appropriate questioning.

Cognitive Domain

Knowledge: recognize or recall information.

- Q: What is the capital of Maine? Who wrote "Hamlet?"
    - Words typically used: define, recall, recognize, remember, who, what, where, when.
    - Comprehension: demonstrate that the student has sufficient understanding to organize and arrange material mentally.
- Q: What do you think Hamlet meant when he said, "to be or not to be, that is the question?" (Rosenshine, among others, would argue that one of the best ways to teach is to teach pupils how to ask their own questions about the topic under consideration.)
    - Words typically used: describe, compare, contrast, rephrase, put in your own words, explain the main idea.

— *Application*: a question that asks a student to apply previously learned information to reach an answer. Solving math word problems is an example.

— Q: According to our definition of socialism, which of the following nations would be considered to be socialist?

— Words typically used: apply, classify, use, choose, employ, write and example, solve, how many, which, what is.

Analysis: higher order questions that require students to think critically and in depth. Unless students can be brought to the higher levels of analysis, synthesis, and evaluation, it is unlikely that transfer will take place, i.e., this is stuff we can use rather than this is just more dumb school stuff that we can forget after we take the test. If teachers don't ask higher level questions, it is unlikely that most students will transfer school work to real life. They may not even be able to apply it to school situations other than the one in which it was "learned." In analysis questions, students are asked to engage in three kinds of cognitive processes:

— identify the motives, reasons, and/or causes for aspecific occurrence (Q: Why was Israel selected as the site for the Jewish nation?),

— consider and analyze available information to reach a conclusion, inference, or generalization based on this information (Q: After studying the French, American, and Russian revolutions, what can you conclude about the causes of a revolution?), or

— Words typically used: identify motives/causes, draw conclusions, determine evidence, support, analyze, why.

Synthesis: higher order question that asks the student to perform original and creative thinking. Synthesis questions ask students to:

— produce original communications. (Q: What's a good name for this invention? Write a letter to the editor on a social issue of concern to you. Make a collage of pictures and words that represents your beliefs and feelings about the issue.)

— make predictions. (Q: How would the U.S.A. be different if the South had won the Civil War? What would happen if school attendance was made optional? What is the next likely development in popular music?)

— solve problems—although analysis questions may also ask students to solve problems, synthesis questions differ because they don't require a single correct answer but, instead allow a variety of creative answers. (How could we determine the number of pennies in a jar without counting them? How can we raise money for our ecology project?

Words typically used in synthesis questions: predict, produce, write, design, develop, synthesize, construct, how can we improve, what would happen if, can you devise, how can we solve.

Evaluation: a higher level question that does not have a single correct answer. It requires the student to judge the merit of an idea, a solution to a problem, or an aesthetic work. The student may also be asked to offer an opinion on an issue. (Q: Do you think schools are too easy? Is busing an appropriate remedy for desegregating schools? Do you think it is true that "Americans never had it so good?" Which U.S. senator is the most effective?)To answer evaluation questions objective criteria or personal values must be applied.

Some standard must be used differing standards are quite acceptable and they naturally result in different answers. This type of question frequently is used to surface values or to cause students to realize that not everyone sees things the same way. It can be used to start a class discussion. It can also precede a follow-up analysis or synthesis question like, "Why?"

The cognitive domain involves knowledge and the development of intellectual skills. This includes the recall or recognition of specific facts, procedural patterns, and concepts that serve in the development of intellectual abilities and skills. There are six major categories, which are listed in order below, starting from the simplest behaviour to the most complex. The categories can be thought of as degrees of difficulties. That is, the first one must be mastered before the next one can take place.

Knowledge: Recall of data.	Examples: Recite a policy. Quote prices from memory to a customer. Knows the safety rules. Key Words: defines, describes, identifies, knows, labels, lists, matches, names, outlines, recalls, recognizes, reproduces, selects, states.
Comprehension: Understand the meaning, translation, interpolation, and interpretation of instructions and problems. State a problem in one's own words.	Examples: Rewrites the principles of test writing. Explain in one's own words the steps for performing a complex task. Translates an equation into a computer spreadsheet. Key words: comprehends, converts, defends, distinguishes, estimates, explains, extends, generalizes, gives examples, infers, interprets, paraphrases, predicts, rewrites, summarizes, translates.
Application: Use a concept in a new situation or unprompted use of an abstraction. Applies what was learned in the classroom into novel situationsin the workplace.	Examples: Use a manual to calculate an employee's vacation time. Apply laws of statistics to evaluate the reliability of a written test. Key Words: applies, changes,

computes, constructs, demonstrates, discovers, manipulates, modifies, operates, predicts, prepares, produces, relates, shows, solves, uses.

Analysis: Separates material or concepts into component parts so that its organizational structure may be understood. Distinguishes between facts and inferences.

Examples: Troubleshoot a piece of equipment by using logical deduction. Recognize logical fallacies in reasoning. Gathers information from a department and selects the required tasks for training.

Keywords: analyzes, breaks down, compares, contrasts, diagrams, deconstructs, differentiates, discriminates, distinguishes, identifies, illustrates, infers, outlines, relates, selects, separates.

Synthesis: Builds a structure or pattern from diverse elements. Put parts together to form a whole, with emphasis on creating a new meaning or structure.

Examples: Write a company operations or process manual. Design a machine to perform a specific task. Integrates training from several sources to solve a problem. Revises and process to improve the outcome.

Keywords: categorizes, combines, compiles, composes, creates, devises, designs, explains, generates, modifies, organizes, plans, rearranges, reconstructs, relates, reorganizes, revises, rewrites, summarizes, tells, writes.

Evaluation: Make judgments about the value of ideas or materials.

Examples: Select the most effective solution. Hire the most qualified candidate. Explain and justify a new budget.

Keywords: appraises, compares, concludes, contrasts, criticizes, critiques, defends, describes, discriminates, evaluates, explains, interprets, justifies, relates, summarizes, supports.

Affective Domain

The Affective Domain addresses interests, attitudes, opinions, appreciations, values, and emotional sets. The original purpose of the Taxonomy of Educational Objectives was to provide a tool for classifying instructional objectives. The Taxonomy is hierarchical (levels increase in difficulty/sophistication) and cumulative (each level builds on and subsumes the ones below). The levels, in addition to clarifying instructional objectives, may be used to provide a basis for questioning that ensures that students progress to the highest level of understanding. If the teaching purpose is to change attitudes/behaviour rather than to transmit/process information, then the instruction should be structured to progress through the levels of the Affective Domain:

— *Receiving*. The student passively attends to particular phenomena or stimuli [classroom activities, textbook, music, etc. The teacher's concern is that the student's attention is focused. Intended outcomes include the pupil's awareness that a thing exists. Sample objectives: listens attentively, shows sensitivity to social problems. Behavioural terms: asks, chooses, identifies, locates, points to, sits erect, etc.

— *Responding*. The student actively participates. The pupil not only attends to the stimulus but reacts in some way. Objectives: completes homework, obeys rules, participates in class discussion, shows interest in subject, enjoys helping others, etc. Terms: answers, assists, complies, discusses, helps, performs, practices, presents, reads, reports, writes, etc.

— *Valuing*. The worth a student attaches to a particular object, phenomenon, or behaviour. Ranges from acceptance to commitment (e.g., assumes responsibility for the functioning of a group). Attitudes and appreciation. Objectives: demonstrates belief in democratic processes, appreciates the role of science in daily life, shows concern for others' welfare, demonstrates a problem-solving approach, etc. Terms: differentiates, explains, initiates, justifies, proposes, shares, etc.

— *Organization*. Bringing together different values, resolving conflicts among them, and starting to build an internally consistent value system—comparing, relating and synthesizing values and developing a philosophy of life. Objectives: recognizes the need for balance between freedom and responsibility in a democracy, understands the role of systematic planning in solving problems, accepts responsibility for own behaviour, etc. Terms: Arranges, combines, compares, generalizes, integrates, modifies, organizes, synthesizes, etc.

— *Characterization by a Value or Value Complex*. At this level, the person has held a value system that has controlled his behaviour for a sufficiently long time that acharacteristic "life style" has been developed. Behaviour is pervasive, consistent and predictable. Objectives are concerned with personal, social, and emotional adjustment: displays self reliance in working independently, cooperates in group activities, maintains good health habits, etc.

Affective domain includes the manner in which we deal with things emotionally, such as feelings, values, appreciation, enthusiasms, motivations, and attitudes. The five major categories listed in order are:

Receiving phenomena: Awareness, willingness to hear, selected attention.	Examples: Listen to others with respect. Listen for and remember the name of newly introduced people.

	Keywords: asks, chooses, describes, follows, gives, holds, identifies, locates, names, points to, selects, sits, erects, replies, uses.
Responding to phenomena: Active participation on the part of the learners. Attends and reacts to a particular phenomenon. Learning outcomes may emphasize compliance in responding, willingness to respond, or satisfaction in responding (motivation).	Examples: Participates in class discussions. Gives a presentation. Questions new ideals, concepts, models, etc. in order to fully understand them. Know the safety rules and practices them. Keywords: answers, assists, aids, complies, conforms, discusses, greets, helps, labels, performs, practices, presents, reads, recites, reports, selects, tells, writes.
Valuing: The worth or value a person attaches to a particular object, phenomenon, or behaviour. This ranges from simple acceptance to the more complex state of commitment. Valuing is based on the internalization of a set of specified values, while clues to these values are expressed in the learner's overt behaviour and are often identifiable.	Examples: Demonstrates belief in the democratic process. Is sensitive towards individual and cultural differences (value diversity). Shows the ability to solve problems. Proposes a plan to social improvement and follows through with commitment. Informs management on matters that one feels strongly about. Keywords: completes, demonstrates, differentiates, explains, follows, forms, initiates, invites, joins, justifies, proposes, reads, reports, selects, shares, studies, works
Organization: Organizes values into priorities by contrasting different values, resolving conflicts between them, and creating an unique value system. The emphasis is on	Examples: Recognizes the need for balance between freedom and responsible behaviour. Accepts responsibility for one's behaviour. Explains the role of systematic planning in solving problems.

comparing, relating, and synthesizing values.	Accepts professional ethical standards. Creates a life plan in harmony with abilities, interests, and beliefs. Prioritizes time effectively to meet the needs of the organization, family, and self. Keywords: adheres, alters, arranges, combines, compares, completes, defends, explains, formulates, generalizes, identifies, integrates, modifies, orders, organizes, prepares, relates, synthesizes.
Internalizing values (characterization): Has a value system that controls their behaviour. The behaviour is pervasive, consistent, predictable and most importantly, characteristic of the learner. Instructional objectives are concerned with the student's general patterns of adjustment (personal, social, emotional).	Examples: Shows self-reliance when working independently. Cooperates in group activities (displays teamwork). Uses an objective approach in problem solving. Displays a professional commitment to ethical practice on a daily basis. Revises judgments and changes behaviour in light of new evidence. Values people for what they are, not how they look. Keywords: acts, discriminates, displays, influences, listens, modifies, performs, practices, proposes, qualifies, questions, revises, serves, solves, verifies.

Psychomotor Domain

Instructional objectives and derived questions/tasks typically have cognitive/affective elements, but the focus is on motorskill development. The suggested areas for use are speech development, reading readiness, handwriting, and physical education. Other areas include manipulative skills required in business training [e.g., keyboarding], industrial technology, and performance areas in science, art and music. American education has tended to emphasize cognitive development at the expense of affective and psychomotor development. The well rounded and fully functioning person needs development in all three domains. In the psychomotor domain, performance may take the place of questioning strategies in many cases.

— *Reflex movements*. Segmental, inter segmental, and supra segmental reflexes.

— *Basic-fundamental movements*. Locomotor movements, nonlocomotor movements, manipulative movements.

— *Perceptual abilities*. Kinesthetic, visual, auditory and tactile discrimination and coordinated abilities.

— *Physical abilities*. Endurance, strength, flexibility, and agility.

— *Skilled movements*. Simple, compound, and complex adaptive skills.

— *Nondiscursive communication*. Expressive and interpretive movement.

Sample general objectives: writes smoothly and legibly; accurately reproduces a picture, map, etc.; operates a [machine] skillfully; plays the piano skillfully; demonstrates correct swimming form; drives an automobile skillfully; creates a new way of performing [creative dance]; etc.

Behavioural terms: assembles, builds, composes, fastens, grips, hammers, makes, manipulates, paints, sharpens, sketches, uses, etc.

The psychomotor domain includes physical movement, coordination, and use of the motor-skill areas. Development of these skills requires practice and is measured in terms of speed, precision, distance, procedures, or techniques in execution. The seven major categories listed in order are:

Perception: The ability to use sensory cues to guide motor activity. This ranges from sensory stimulation, through cue selection, to translation.	Examples: Detects non-verbal communication cues. Estimate where a ball will land after it is thrown and then moving to the correct location to catch the ball. Adjusts heat of stove to correct temperature by smell and taste of food. Adjusts the height of the forks on a forklift by comparing where the forks are in relation to the pallet. Keywords: chooses, describes, detects, differentiates, distinguishes, identifies, isolates, relates, selects.
Set: Readiness to act. It includes mental, physical, and emotional sets. These three sets are dispositions that predetermine a person's response to different situations (sometimes called mindsets).	Examples: Knows and acts upon a sequence of steps in a manufacturing process. Recognize one's abilities and limitations. Shows desire to learn a new process (motivation). NOTE: This subdivision of Psychomotor is closely related with the "Responding to phenomena" subdivision of the Affective domain. Keywords: begins, displays, explains, moves, proceeds, reacts, shows, states, volunteers.
Guided response: The early stages in learning a complex skill that includes imitation and trial and error. Adequacy of performance is achieved by practicing.	Examples: Performs a mathematical equation as demonstrated. Follows instructions to build a model. Responds hand-signals of instructor while learning to operate a forklift. Keywords: copies, traces, follows, react, reproduce, responds
Mechanism: This is the intermediate stage in learning a complex skill. Learned responses have become habitual and the movements can be	Examples: Use a personal computer. Repair a leaking faucet. Drive a car. Keywords: assembles, calibrates, constructs, dismantles, displays,

performed with some confidence and proficiency.	fastens, fixes, grinds, heats, manipulates, measures, mends, mixes, organizes, sketches.
Complex Overt Response: The skillful performance of motor acts that involve complex movement patterns. Proficiency is indicated by a quick, accurate, and highly coordinated performance, requiring a minimum of energy. This category includes performing without hesitation, and automatic performance. For example, players are often utter sounds of satisfaction or expletives as soon as they hit a tennis ball or throw a football, because they can tell by the feel of the act what the result will produce.	Examples: Maneuvers a car into a tight parallel parking spot. Operates a computer quickly and accurately. Displays competence while playing the piano. Keywords: assembles, builds, calibrates, constructs, dismantles, displays, fastens, fixes, grinds, heats, manipulates, measures, mends, mixes, organizes, sketches. NOTE: The key words are the same as Mechanism, but will have adverbs or adjectives that indicate that the performance is quicker, better, more accurate, etc.
Adaptation: Skills are well developed and the individual can modify movement patterns to fit special requirements.	Examples: Responds effectively to unexpected experiences. Modifies instruction to meet the needs of the learners. Perform a task with a machine that it was not originally intended to do (machine is not damaged and there is no danger in performing the new task). Keywords: adapts, alters, changes, rearranges, reorganizes, revises, varies.
Origination: Creating new movement patterns to fit a particular situation or specific problem. Learning outcomes emphasize creativity based upon highly developed skills.	Examples: Constructs a new theory. Develops a new and comprehensive training programming. Creates a new gymnastic routine. Keywords: arranges, builds, combines, composes, constructs, creates, designs, initiate, makes, originates.

10

System Approach

Besides Instructional System Design (ISD), there are several traditional systematic approaches to training such as Performance-Based Training (PBT) and Criterion Referenced Instruction (CRI). These approaches have some common elements: Competency Based (Job Related): The learners are required to master a Skill, Knowledge, or Attitude (SKA). The training focuses on the job by having the learners achieve the criteria or standards necessary for proper task performance.

— *Sequential*: Lessons are logically and sequentially integrated.

— *Tracked*: A tracking system is established that allows changes and updates to the training materials to be performed efficiently.

— *Evaluated*: Evaluation and corrective action allows continuous improvement and maintenance of training information that reflects current status and conditions.

So, why ISD? Simply stated, this process provides a means for sound decision making to determine the who, what, when, where, why, and how of training. The concept of a system approach to training is based on obtaining an overall view of the training process. It is characterized by an orderly process for gathering and analyzing collective and individual performance requirements, and by the ability to respond to identified training needs. The application of a systems approach to training insures that training programs and the required support materials are continually developed in an effective and efficient manner to match the variety of needs in an ever rapidly changing environment. ISD is often called SAT (System Approach to Training) or ADDIE (Analysis, Design, Development, Implement, Evaluate).

SYSTEMS AND PROCESSES

A system is defined as a set of concepts or parts that must work together to perform a particular function. An organization is a system or a collection of systems. Every job in an organization is used by a system to produce a product or service. The product or service is the means by which a organization supports itself. There are four inputs necessary in every system to produce a product or service:

— *People*: The workers making up a group and linked by a common activity.

— *Material*: The raw products which go into the system.

— *Technology*: The technique for achieving a practical purpose or goal.

— *Time*: The measured period during which an action or process begins and ends.

Every system must also have at least one output in order to survive. The output can be a material product, such as a television or computer software; or a service, such as a protection agency or an insurance policy. The output of a particular system in an organization may be the final product, a service sold to its customers, or a product or service to aid or enhance the organization in its goal to produce a marketable product or service.

An example of a system might be a production team (people) who transform electronic components, cases, parts, etc. (materials) into computers by working on an production line (technology), and completing each production run within a given deadline (time). The final products (output) are then used in the organization to sell to its customers. Someone developed this system by:

— Analyzing what was required by the organization.

— Designing the system to meet the needs of the organization.

— Developing the system using the outputs of the analysis and design phase.

— Implementing it.

— Evaluating the project throughout its creation and implementation.

This process could have been an haphazard creation, which generally waste time and money; a planned action; or a combination of both. A Systems Approach to Training is a planned creation of a training program. It is a development program that uses step-by-step processes to solve problems. A large company may have several systems, which are generally broken down into departments or groups, while a small company may only have one system. All of these systems have three basic functions:

— *Input*: Something must be going into the system, otherwise, it is a mysterious sphere where products or services mystically radiate from it. The basic inputs of a system are material, people, technology, and time. Training is mostly concerned where people and technology meet.

— *Process*: Some type of work must be accomplished in the system. This work is the technology performed that changes the material input into the systems output. Look for the means to help workers master and apply the unique technology governing their tasks.

— *Output*: A desired service or product must be produced. If there is no output, then it is a black hole where things go in, but nothing emerges. The goal in training is to allow the workers to use the available technology efficiently and effectively to produce the desired product or service.

Processes

A process is a planned series of actions that advances a material or procedure from one stage of completion to the next within a system. A system generally has several processes in it. Like a system, it also has an input and an output. In the system example given above, a couple of processes within the computer production system might be: The circuit-board assembly team (people) who solders electronic parts (materials) onto circuit boards by working on a specialized production line (technology), and completing each production run within a given deadline (time). The final products (output) are then used by other members of the production team in the assembly of a computer.

An inspection team (people) who test each computer (materials) by using specialized test equipment and software (technology), and completing each production run within a given deadline (time). The computers are then passed on to the packing team who boxes and palletizes them. Notice that in these examples there is always a customer and a supplier. These can either be internal or external. Parts are received from vendors and then moved from various stages throughout the production line. The final process would be the completed computers going from the warehouse or showroom to outside customers (the sales process). Lets look at a training department, which can also be viewed as a system:

— *Input*: People who need to acquire skills.

— *Process*: Learning takes place within the system

— *Output*: Trained people.

Some of the process which take place in a training department would include:

— *Registration*: people who want to learn -> registration forms completed -> people who are now registered for class.

— *Development*: training need -> develop courseware -> a training program.

— Computer Training Class -> students who need to learn MS Word -> learning program -> trained employees.

Being able to break an organization into systems and process will help you in your training development. By identify a process within a system, you will be able to concentrate on a small chunk of a very large piece. For example, when you are analyzing a job, you break it into duties, tasks, and steps to make your task more manageable.

Training Defined

Before trying to understand system type training, we must first understand what training is. We need to clarify the definition of training and then do the same for human resource development. Training is defined as learning that is provided in order to improve performance on the present job. A person's performance is improved by showing her how to master a new or established technology. The technology may be a piece of heavy machinery, a computer, a procedure for creating a product, or a method of providing a service.

Notice that the last part of the definition states that training is provided for the present job. This includes training new personnel to perform their job, introducing a new technology, or bringing an employee up to standards. Earlier it was stated that there are four inputs to a system: people, material, technology, and time. Training is mainly concerned with the meeting of two of these inputs -- people and technology. That is, having people learn to master a given technology.

Human Resource Development Defined

Training is part of Human Resource Development (HRD). Do not confuse HRD with the term "human resource department." A human resource department is concerned with all aspects of the employees, such as pay, benefits, equal opportunity, and of course training. HRD is concerned with training, development, and education. HRD has been defined as an organized learning experience, conducted in a definite time period, to increase the possibility of improving job performance and growth. Organized means that it is conducted in a systematic way. Although learning can be incidental, training is concerned with the worker learning clear and concise standards of performance or objectives.

Having an objective is important. Without an objective, you could end up someplace else...and not even know it. Objectives are the tools for guiding managers, learners, and trainers. Managers need objectives so that they know what kind of return they are receiving from their training investment. Learners need them so that they know exactly what is expected of them. And trainers need them to plan and conduct the learning environment so that they may achieve the desired results. The second part of the definition, conducted in a definite time period, means that the amount of time the learner will be away from work must be determined and specified at the onset of the training program.

The last part of the statement, to increase the possibility of improving job performance and growth, is basically the definition of training. By possibility, it means that although a organization can provide tools to help the learner succeed, such as education and training specialists, counselors, coaches, and state-of-the-art training materials, the ultimate responsibility for success belongs to the learner.

— Training for the present,

— Educating for the future,

— Developing to lead.

Training, Development, and Education

HRD programs are divided into three main categories: Training, Development, and Education. Although some organizations lump all learning under "Training" or "Training and

Development," dividing it into three distinct categories makes the desired goals and objects more meaningful and precise.

Training is the acquisition of technology which permits employees to perform their present job to standards. It improves human performance on the job the employee is presently doing or is being hired to do. Also, it is given when new technology in introduced into the workplace. Education is training people to do a different job. It is often given to people who have been identified as being promotable, being considered for a new job either lateral or upwards, or to increase their potential. Unlike training, which can be fully evaluated immediately upon the learners returning to work, education can only be completely evaluated when the learners move on to their future jobs or tasks. We can test them on what they learned while in training, but we cannot be fully satisfied with the evaluation until we see how well they perform their new jobs.

Development is training people to acquire new horizons, technologies, or viewpoints. It enables leaders to guide their organizations onto new expectations by being proactive rather than reactive. It enables workers to create better products, faster services, and more competitive organizations. It is learning for growth of the individual, but not related to a specific present or future job. Unlike training and education, which can be completely evaluated, development cannot always be fully evaluated. This does not mean that we should abandon development programs, as helping people to grow and develop is what keeps an organization in the cutting edge of competitive environments. Development can be considered the forefront of what many now call the Learning Organization.

Development involves changes in an organism that are systematic, organized, and successive and are thought to serve an adaptive function. Training could be compared this metaphor — if I miss one meal in a day, then I will not be able to work as effectively due to a lack of nutrition. While development would be compared to this metaphor — if I do not eat, then I will starve to death. The survival of the organization requires development throughout the ranks in order to survive, while training makes the organization more effective and efficient in its day-to-day operations. Also, do not confuse development with change. Change refers to alterations that occur over time in the learners' internal cogitative or affective characteristics. This change may be quantitative or qualitative and it implies no directionality, encompassing both regression and progression.

Development is always progressive. Using a systems approach to design training, education, and development programs ensure that an organization gets the most from its resources. The goal of instruction is to overcome a deficiency in a skill, knowledge, or attitude. The designer must understand the instructional goals so that the courseware's content, layout, strategies, and activities may be built to maximize the learning experience.

The Training System

When some people see or hear the word system, they think of mega-methodologies that require several bookcases and intense training to use. A System Approach to Training is not that difficult or complicated. The Instructional System Development (ISD) Model was designed to solve training problems. Figure 2 shows the ISD model. It was first established by the Department of Defense, but can now be found in almost any type of organization. It grew out of the "systems analysis" concepts that became popular after World War II. It is probably the most extensively used instructional design model in use today. ISD is concerned with the identification of training requirements based on the analysis of job performance requirements data obtained from experts in the job to be performed.

Training objectives are formulated as a result of the job analysis process and tests are developed to be used to assess the learner's progress toward meeting the training objectives. ISD or SAT also attempts to bring structure to the instructional design process when determining the optimal instructional strategies, instructional sequencing, and instructional delivery media for the types of training objectives involved. Although there are minor difference, most development systems follow an approach similar to this: Analyze the system in order to completely understand it, and then describe the goals you wish to achieve in order to correct any shortcomings or faults within the system.

— Design a method or model to achieve your goals.

— Develop the model into a product.

— Implement the courseware.

Evaluate the courseware and audit-trail throughout the four phases and in the field to ensure it is heading in the right direction and achieving the desired results. The ISD model is a tool for solving many types of performance problems. But, designers must step step back to see where they are going, otherwise the tool will control them, instead of them controlling the tool. Evaluations must be performed throughout the entire ISD cycle. Designers often blame the model because they think it is wrong or a waste of time to start over.

The ISD Model

There are a variety of ISD models that have been developed since the initial military ISD model. Most ISD models have the same basic five phases although the terminology differs somewhat. The real differences are the specific steps within these five phases of the basic ISD model.

Basic ISD Model

Figure 1

The ISD model had five basic phases:

— *Analysis*: assessing needs, determining the causes of the needs, establishing requirements for outcomes

— *Design*: identifying the necessary content, establishing objectives and tests, examining the learners

— *Development*: - planning the instructional strategies, creating the instruction

— *Implementation*: operating the education or training program

— *Evaluation*: determining effectiveness, revising until mastery is achieved

Hannum's ISD Model

There are several specific steps within the overall ISD model. Note that the top level contains the basic five phases in the generic ISD model. The specific steps that are required to accomplish each phase are shown under each of the general phases. The steps within each phase are followed primarily in a sequential order. However the steps are only somewhat sequential as people revisit previous steps when actually developing educational systems.

Dynamics of the ISD model

Although the above models shows the processes, it does not really show the dynamics of the ISD model. For that purpose, Figure 3 is used. This figure highlights the importance of evaluation and feedback throughout the entire training program. It also stresses the importance of gathering and distributing information in each of the five phases and shows the training process is NOT a static (waterfall) model, but a iterative flow of activities (dynamic or spiral). The five phases are ongoing activities that continue throughout the life of a training program.

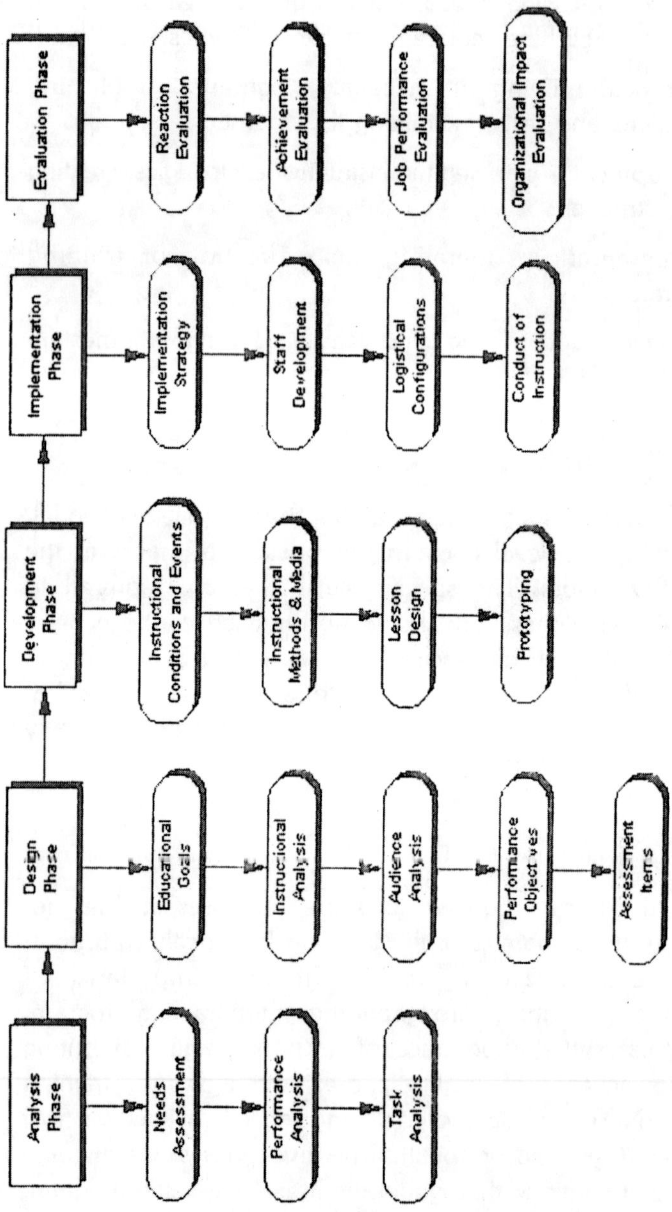
Analysis Phase
Needs Assessment
Performance Analysis
Task Analysis
Design Phase
Educational Goals
Instructional Analysis
Audience Analysis
Performance Objectives
Assessment Items
Development Phase
Instructional Conditions and Events
Instructional Methods & Media
Lesson Design
Prototyping
Implementation Phase
Implementation Strategy
Staff Development
Logistical Configurations
Conduct of Instruction
Evaluation Phase
Reaction Evaluation
Achievement Evaluation
Job Performance Evaluation
Organizational Impact Evaluation

Figure 2

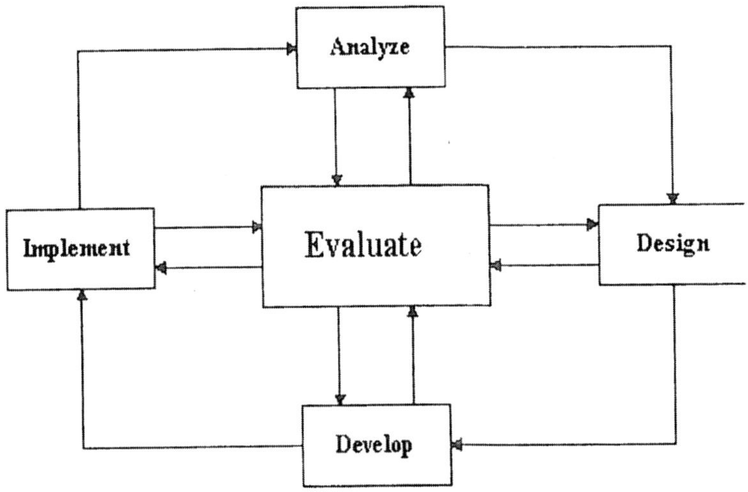

Figure 3. ISD Model Flowchart

After building a training program, the other phases do not end once the training program is implemented. The five phases are continually repeated on a regular basis to see if further improvements can be made.

A brief description of the ISD process:

— Analyze Analyze system (department, job, etc.) to gain a complete understanding of it.

— Compile a task inventory of all tasks associated with each job (if needed).

— Select tasks that need to be trained (needs analysis).

— Build performance measures for the tasks to be trained.

— Choose instructional setting for the tasks to be trained, e.g. classroom, on-the-job, self study, etc.

— Estimate what is going to cost to train the tasks.

— Design Develop the learning objectives for each task; to include both terminal and enabling objectives.

— Identify and list the learning steps required to perform the task.

— Develop the performance tests to show mastery of the tasks to be trained, e.g. written, hands on, etc.

— List the entry behaviors that the learner must demonstrate prior to training.

— Sequence and structure the learning objectives, e.g. easy tasks first.

— Develop List activities that will help the students learn the task.

— Select the delivery method such as tapes, handouts, etc.

— Review existing material so that you do not reinvent the wheel.

— Develop the instructional courseware.

— Synthesize the courseware into a viable training program.

— Validate the instruction to ensure it accomplishes all goals and objectives.

— Implement Create a management plan for conducting the training.

— Conduct the training.

— Evaluate Review and evaluate each phase (analyze, design, develop, implement) to ensure it is accomplishing what it is supposed to.

— Perform external evaluations, e.g. observe that the tasks that were trained can actually be performed by the learner on the job.

— Revise training system to make it better.

Making The System Effective

One important point must be made. The ISD model is a system to aid in the design and development of a training program. It is a valuable toolbox that provides a proven method of building a viable training program. But, the people in the organization must control the training system, the system should not control the people. Immediate problems often arise that require rapid solutions. Don't get hung up in the system model by refusing to bypass a step, switch steps, modify a step, or include steps of your own. Managers and supervisors often need quick and ingenious solutions, not another bureaucracy.

In other words, the training department's motto should be: "We provide training solutions!" Not, "We follow the ISD model." The steps in each phase should not be thought of as concrete in nature. That is, one step does not have to be completed before the next one is started. For example, some training designers will have to complete part of the work in the design phase before they can complete the estimate step in the analysis phase. In the development phase, the first three steps, list learner activity, select delivery system, and review existing material, might be combined into one step by many developers. Every training project will develop its own rhythm.

The developers must find the natural flow of the steps required to produce a successful training program. Although the SAT process is a formal one, in that the five phases should be performed as shown in the flowchart, it requires both art and science in its implementation. Also, in many instances, steps may be bypassed. For example, if a manager comes to you with a training problem, the task identification steps will be skipped, since you know which task needs trained. If you have developed a similar course before, then many steps, such as reviewing existing material and selecting the instructional setting, will only be briefly visited as you have gone through similar processes before and probably have a good ideal of where you are going.

The less you know about a subject or the more technical the material is, then the closer you need to follow the model. At work, the potter sits before a lump of clay on the wheel. Her mind is on the clay, but she is also aware of sitting between her past experiences and her future prospects. She knows exactly what has and has not worked for her in the past. She has an intimate knowledge of her work, her capabilities, and her markets. As a craftsman, she senses rather than analyzes these things; her knowledge is 'tacit.' All these things are working in her mind as her hands are working the clay. The product that emerges on the wheel is likely to be in the tradition of her past work, but she may break away and embark on a new direction. Even so, the past is no less present, projecting itself into the future.

To make a training program usable, the following activities must take place in its development: An early focus on the clients must be maintained. This is done by direct contact with the clients through interviews, observations, surveys, and participatory design and development methods. You must ensure that the clients are made owners of the training program throughout the entire SAT process. If they feel the program is being shoved down their throats or their turf is being invaded, the program will fail. The five phases - analysis, design, development, implementation, and evaluation should be under one management team to ensure that a symmetrical program is constructed.

The design must be an empirical one. This requires observation, measurement of behavior, careful evaluation of feedback, and a strong motivation to make design changes when needed. The process of implementation, testing, feedback, evaluation, and change must be repeated throughout the training system's life to improve upon it. Do NOT fall into the old adage, "If it ain't broke don't fix it." Make it better before your competitors do! Records must be maintained. The audit trail should contain the data gathered in the analysis, the reasons for developing a piece of courseware, and documents that explain why certain decisions were made. This information could prove invaluable in the future when changes are needed or when a similar program must be built.

A lot of learning theory is part of the descriptive sciences, which describe the way things function in the natural world; while ISD is part of the design sciences, which offer ways to perform certain human-defined tasks. Descriptive sciences can be considered the law, while design sciences are roadmaps, and there is always more than one way to get from point A to point B.

Critiques of the System Approach To Training

Some of the benefits of a system approach are characteristic of all systematic approaches. The ISD model is a management tool that makes courseware production more efficient. Effective training programs are more likely because the ISD model increases the probability that the courseware will match the objectives and not veer off in a different direction. The approach is scientific as it is empirical and can be replicated. The courseware can be improved and strengthened through data collection and analysis.

On the other hand, the ISD model has been criticized because it is frequently presented in flowchart form, as shown in figure 2, leaving the impression that it is mechanistic and liner in its approach. It is this heuristic design that has been criticized by others because it tells training designers what to do, but not how to it. This argument is not valid because there is a considerable body of educational, learning, and training literature that tells how to implement the various steps in the ISD model. A frequent criticism is that it is too time-consuming to be practical in the real world. Yet, not knowing the basic procedures for building a learning program leads many novices down the wrong path which wastes more resources. Once designers are comfortable then many of the steps can be skimmed over.

Some say that systematic models take a "top-down" behaviorist and subject-matter-expert approach to learning instead of championing a constructivist approach. But, training has traditionally been task driven by discovering how experts performs their jobs and then mirroring this performance in the learning environment. Also, nothing says a constructivist method cannot be used for learning the task.

Prototyping and the ISD model are both directly linked. But many developers have the wrong picture of ISD. The traditional ISD model, which advocates evaluation throughout its entire life cycle, has often been thought of as a linear process (step-by-step, static, or waterfall), when in reality, it is more iterative (dynamic or spiral) due to the constant updating. No single model is the silver bullet of instructional design, including ADDIE. Each model has its advantages and disadvantages. But many developers will come closer to that silver bullet by using the key advantages of each system, depending upon the training project they are working on.

Comparing ISD With Other Models

It often helps to understand a model better by looking at other models:

Evolutionary model

An evolutionary approach includes both deterministic and incremental systems, in contrast to the systems approach, which is entirely deterministic. This means that in an evolutionary approach, tentative or short term goals may be specified. This approach is particularly appropriate for situations where there is limited past experience from which to draw guidance. A major benefit is that it enables a designer to test new ideas without making a long term commitment. A major disadvantage is that it lacks a defined set of steps. Also, it is difficult to specify in advance the amount of time and money that will be needed to complete significant events and it is logically impossible to specify the outcome of an evolutionary process.

In the 1960's, the PLATO system for Computer Assisted Instruction (CAI) was developed. A systems approach was implemented at the time. In 1972, the National Science Foundation funded the University of Illinois to implement a new version of the PLATO system and to develop courseware for schools and colleges. An evolutionary approach was used to design the courseware. The evolutionary approach was apparent in all facets of the new PLATO system and its accompanying courseware. Although many outstanding lessons were made using this approach, when time for production was limited due to constraining resources, such as time or money, quality lessons could not be produced unless the authors took a systematic approach. Courseware authors either failed to complete lessons on time or produced lessons that made full use of graphics and other computer features, but were instructionally ineffective. Although the SAT method may look large and expensive, it has proven itself to be reliable and inexpensive in the long run.

Rapid Prototyping Design (RPD)

Rapid Prototyping Design (RPD) uses a more formative model that is based on usability testing of prototypes. Results of usability tests on the prototypes is used to modify and improve the product. This model shares many attributes in common with the ISD model, and stresses the importance of iterative analysis and evaluation.

A comparison of the two models would look something like this:

Step	RPD	ISD
1.	Assess Needs and Analyze	Analysis
2.	Set Objectives	Design
3.	Build skeletal (prototype) system	Develop

4.	User evaluation	Evaluate
5.	Concept refinement	Develop
6.	Implementation of refined requirements	Evaluate
7.	Concept refinement	Development
8.	Implementation of refined requirements	Evaluate
9.	etc., etc., in a continuous cycle	etc., etc., in a continuous cycle
10.	Install and Maintain System	Implementation and Evaluate

So, when are you using RPD and when are you using ISD? If you know the subject, how learners best learn that subject, or have build similar training programs, then you will perform less prototyping, thus your development will fall more into the what is pictured as the traditional (dynamic) ISD method. When the subject is new, controversial, etc., then more prototypes are going to be built, hence you are more into RPD. If you know exactly what you are doing and exactly what needs to be built, then you are using the ISD (static or waterfall) method (however, this rarely happens in the real training world).

ROBERT GAGNÉ'S INSTRUCTIONAL DESIGN APPROACH

When Robert Gagné initially published his influential book, *The Conditions of Learning*, his instructional design theories were heavily rooted in the behaviorist psychology paradigm. However, in later editions of The Conditions of Learning, Gagné's theories evolved to incorporate cognitivist psychology theories, specifically the information-processing model of cognition. According to Gagné, "This model posits a number of internal processes that are subject to the influence of a variety of external events. The arrangement of external events to activate and support the internal processes of learning constitutes what is called instruction".

A Seminal Model

Gagné's approach to instructional design is considered a seminal model that has influenced many other design approaches and particularly the Dick & Carey systems approach. Gagné proposed that events of learning and categories of learning outcomes together provide a framework for an account of learning conditions. The diagram below, from the third edition of The Conditions of Learning, illustrates his vision of how the events of learning impact the conditions learning, which ultimately result in the learning outcomes, or learning capabilities.

In The Conditions of Learning, Gagné acknowledges that he was considering the question "What factors really can make a difference to instruction?" when developing his learning and instructional design theories. His model proposed that the conditions of learning—some internal and some external to the learner—that affect the process of learning make up the events of learning. When deliberately planned, those events constitute instruction. "Thus it is reasonable to define instruction as being made up of events external to the learner which are designed to promote learning".

Gagné's model proposed nine events of learning or instruction. These events are specific functions of communication behaviors that he identified as components of instruction. Gagné divided these nine events into two groups: the first five represent communication behaviors that occur before the acquisition of information. The last four occur after acquisition has developed. The nine instructional events are outlined below and applications for group, tutorial, and individual delivery are provided. According to Gagné, the events of instruction are labels that "serve to relate the internal processes to the external events that constitute instruction; that is they provide names for the total set of events (internal and external) that must be considered to take place during each phase of learning".

Conditions of Learning

In addition to the nine events of instruction, Gagné's instructional design theory proposed eight different conditions or types of learning. As an instructional psychologist, Gagné perceived learning conditions as building blocks for designing instruction. By categorizing each type of learning, the instructional designer is aware that each type of learning can potentially require a different event of instruction to optimize learning. The following chart outlines the eight conditions learning.

Learning Condition Definition

— *Signal Learning*: The learner associates an already available response with a new stimulus or signal

— *Stimulus-Response Learning*: The learner responds precisely to a discriminated stimulus

— *Chaining*: The learner acquires a connection to a set of individual stimulus-responses in a sequence (two or more stimulus response connections equals a chain)

— *Verbal Association*: The learning acquires a connection to a set verbal chains

— *Discrimination Learning*: The learner makes different identifying responses to many different and seemingly similar stimulus

— *Concept Learning*: The learner becomes capable of making a common response to a class of stimuli

— *Rule Learning*: The learner recognizes a chain of two or more concepts

— *Problem Solving*: The learner recalls and connects a combination of previously learned rules which can be applied to achieve a solution for a novel situation

Learning Outcomes

Gagné classified learning outcomes into five categories or taxonomies. These represent the variety of capabilities or outcomes that are possible as a result of the learning process. According to Gagné, "One way to make sense of the enormous variety of outcomes learning produces is to consider them as performance categories." The different learning outcomes—or performance categories—"not only differ in the human performances they make possible, they also differ in the conditions most favorable for their learning".

Systems Approach to Instructional Design

Gagné's learning theories have had a positive influence on the evolution of the systems approach to designing instruction. The continued process of evaluation and revision that Gagné has subjected his instructional design model to has been the key to its ongoing acceptance and success. Dick & Carey's instructional design model stresses and incorporates much of Gagné's model. Their systems approach to instructional design especially relies on Gagné's domains of learning or learning outcomes. According to Dick & Carey, "The first step in conducting a goal analysis is to categorize the goal into one of Gagné's domains of learning. Each goal should be classified into one of the domains because of the implications for the goal analysis and to identify the appropriate subordinate skills analysis techniques".

In adopting Gagné's learning theories, Dick & Carey chose, however, to omit the fifth domain of learning—cognitive strategies—from their model. They felt that "From the instructional design perspective these can be treated like intellectual skills and taught as such". Dick & Carey also adopted Gagné's hierarchical approach to analyzing goals. "The hierarchical analysis technique suggested by Gagné consists of asking the question "What must the student already know so that, with a minimal amount of instruction, this task can be learned? By asking this question, the designer can identify one or more critical subordinate skills that will be required of the learner prior to attempting instruction on the step itself...This hierarchy of skills is helpful to the designer because it can be used to suggest the type of specific subordinate skills that will be required to support any step in the goal".

INDEX